You Ought To Write All That Down

A Guide to Organizing and Writing Genealogical Narrative

~ PAUL DRAKE, J.D. ~

HERITAGE BOOKS, INC.

Published 1996 by

HERITAGE BOOKS, INC.
1540E Pointer Ridge Place
Bowie, Maryland 20716
1-800-398-7709

ISBN 0-7884-0445-8

A Complete Catalog Listing Hundreds of Titles
On History, Genealogy, and Americana
Available Free Upon Request

Dedication

To Brittany, Bethany, Evan, Diane, Allison, and those
now unknown who are sure to follow, from Grandpaw

Acknowledgments

As in all literary efforts, I am indebted to many. Among those; for the opportunity to do the work, my gratitude goes out to Karen Ackermann and Laird Towle; for the inspiration and many of the ideas, I thank James Houston, Jo White Linn, Paul R. Drake, Diane Drake Haskins, and Dr. Cheryl Drake Bater; for the generous assistance given by Ms. Susan Acree, Staff Genealogist, National Society of Sons of the American Revolution; for the patience and assistance with the manuscript over many months, during some of which it was intellectually and physically very difficult to continue, I am very much indebted to Roxanne Carlson; for the chores done that otherwise would have been mine, I thank dear Marty; and finally, for the need, I thank you, the readers.

Paul Drake

Crossville, Tennessee, 1996

CONTENTS

CHAPTER III: EVIDENCE AND PROOF

CHAPTER IV, PART 1: GLEANING WHAT WE MISSED;
Courthouse, Family, and Non-Genealogical Sources

CHAPTER IV, PART 2: GLEANING WHAT WE MISSED;
Libraries, Archives, and Archival Type Sources

CHAPTER V: PREPARING FOR AND WRITING NARRATIVE

Preface

"In all matters, before beginning, a diligent preparation should be made."
Cicero (106-43 B.C.)

In almost every family there will be found one or two people who, because of their genealogical study, have been asked by other family members to write the family history; the suggestion that "You sure ought to write a book" is familiar to all of us. In addition to that encouragement, all of us hope that at least some of the tremendous effort we have expended will be saved for those of our families who will, one day, be interested.

Despite the encouragement from others and the desire from within ourselves to do so, most of us do not ever write that book, or if we do, from the thousands of facts gathered over the many years, we end up writing but a few pages of our own recollections and a handful of what we think are interesting tales told to us by our parents and cousins.

That failure to write our history in a meaningful way usually arises simply from 1) a lack of knowing how to organize the materials, and 2) not knowing where and how to start. This book seeks to help with both those problems.

Introduction

"Writing is learned and accomplished by the doing of it, and not by wishing, thinking, planning, promising, or talking about it."

(Anonymous)

It is a long time from now to the end of your book. It may take many weeks, or months, or even longer, depending upon how much of each day or week you dedicate to the work. How long it takes is not very important; when you start and how well you do it are.

The great writers of history—Bruce, Churchill, Comager, Foote, etc.—all started with a handful of thoughts, turned those thoughts into sentences, and when the sentences were several in number, converted them into paragraphs and the paragraphs into chapters. As they worked, they learned, and thought, and reviewed, and reconsidered, and changed their mind about this or that; none had all the facts at the beginning of the task.

They did still one more thing: no matter how long it seemed that the work would take, they started. And their writings all began with the first word of the first sentence of the first page. So will yours. The best advice you can have is: No matter where you start, start NOW, not some day, NOW.

As has every one of us, you have made a lot of mistakes: you put off interviewing people who now are dead, notes have been lost, sources of needed information were not written down, and facts that you thought you would never need or want were ignored or passed over. Never mind; you can do nothing about those lost opportunities.

What you can do is firmly resolve that from this moment forward you will no longer procrastinate about interviews, and every time you learn a new fact, without using abbreviations or shorthand, you will enter that information and the source into your records fully, completely, and in sentence form. Then too, from now on write every source—citation—of every bit of information in one of the accepted forms (of which we shall speak) in order that they may be copied into your book without further effort. If you do this, with every new discovery you will have commenced a sentence or paragraph about that person or place, which writings will fit within one of your yet unwritten chapters. In short, no morre abbreviations, ever.

One of the nice things about writing family history is that a large portion of the organization is already done for us, since we almost always think in chronological order when considering our families. When speaking of our ancestors, we usually start at their birth, work through their lives, and then tell of their deaths. Likewise with whole family lines; we either start now and move backwards through time and generations, or we start with some early ancestors and move forward. Whichever direction we go, once we have the people in their proper places, we usually have most of the organization done.

No matter how much advantage we have, organizing your materials so that they conform to your thoughts and become a book is still necessary. To do that you must have knowledge of the basic elements of books, where these elements are placed, and what they contain. Those matters are dealt with in Chapter 1, *Basic Elements and Order of a Book.*

Following that, Chapter 2, *Planning Format*, discusses available genealogical tools, and how to select and use those tools based upon the nature and quantity of your materials.

Chapter 3, *Evidence and Proof* considers what evidence and proof are all about, how to apply those standards to your materials, and how to write about such things.

Next in order are *Gleaning What We Missed*. In these—Chapters 4, Part 1 and 4, Part 2—you will revisit old sources and seek out new ones, all the while gathering every last little bit of information that is to be found there.

Chapter 5 is *Preparing For and Writing Narrative*, and it speaks about the writing itself; of context and historical background, themes and directions, flow and transition, closure and equity in treatment of your people, of removing yourself from the scene, of sentence structure, and of the sorting and planning of illustrations.

Finally, Chapter 6, *Copyright Considerations, Publishing, and Marketing*, considers copyrights, and the protection there available to you (and those you might want to quote), and speaks of some of the methods and avenues of publication open to you, and some of the economics involved.

So, all the while remembering that a family history is little more than a collection of many short biographies set forth in a flowing and organized form along a common theme, with illustrations and historical facts woven in, you are ready to commence the learning and the doing of it.

Chapter I: The Basic Elements and Order of a Book

"Books are well written or badly written. That is all."
Wilde, *The Picture of Dorian Gray*

Through the centuries, the great writers (and those who were not so great, as well) have established an order in which books and similar writings usually are written. Those customs have come about mostly through trial and error, but also as a result of sincere efforts by many to make the task of the readers as easy and convenient as might be.

While no law requires you to abide by these traditions, your readers will expect you to do so, and in no small measure it is they who are to be pleased. Similarly, any manuscript submitted to a publisher for serious consideration should be arranged in a logical and traditionally accepted manner. So it is that we suggest you follow the conventional methods, not only because they are the easiest, but also because your readers will understand them. If you choose to do otherwise—re-invent the wheel— then, at the very least, be certain to state and fully explain your methods in the *preface* to your writing.

In this chapter, we offer some general guidelines to arranging your book, and we discuss the functions and purposes of each section. As to conventional format, if you need assistance in matters of vocabulary, punctuation, and grammar, simply visit your local library or bookstore and inquire as to texts or reference works that are timely. For assistance in style and publishing guidelines, ask for a reference work such as *The Chicago Manual of Style*, published by the University of Chicago Press.

Three General Divisions

Most writers speak of books as consisting of "front matter," the "body," and "end matter." The "body" is the main narrative part of your book, that is, the chapters, or the "meat." Front and end matter are simply those parts that come before and after the body. Front matter typically includes the title page, copyright page, table of contents, and such; while end matter is made up of additional material such as appendices, the bibliography, and the index. We will discuss each of these parts.

Pagination

Look at any well written and scholarly book in your library. You will find that almost every section or chapter starts on the right-hand (*recto*) page with an odd number. (Left-hand, or *verso* [think "reverse"] pages, are always even-numbered.) So, suppose you find yourself at the end of the first chapter, and the page on which the last sentence appears is an odd page (and as often as not, you will). It makes no difference; the next chapter (or section) still starts on the next odd page, and that blank even page between the two is a fine place for illustrations. You could, of course, fill up that blank page by going back into the body of that chapter and there placing an illustration, thus moving the narrative forward.

As to the numbering itself, typically, you will employ two kinds of pagination; Roman numerals and Arabic numbers. Their use is easy to remember and simple to apply. All "front matter" (anything that precedes the first chapter) should be numbered in Roman numerals, beginning with the title page as page i. Continue numbering the pages in Roman numerals throughout the front matter, arranging it in the order shown on the following page. Then, begin the first chapter with Arabic numeral 1.

And now for a few more words about "front matter." While all books should contain a title page, copyright page, table of contents, and preface, the rest of the front matter is optional and should only be added if it enhances the reader's understanding of your book.

Here's a tip: This may sound rather "backwards," but it is easiest to put together your front matter *after* you are finished writing the main part—the body—of your book. This is because you likely will decide to rearrange the chapters or illustrations several times before you are done or you may want to add a dedication, or ask someone to write a preface. Then too, you may want to rewrite your preface or introduction due to some new information uncovered during the production of the book. Any of those changes would mean that you would have to re-do your front matter, perhaps even several times.

Such changes also could result in an increase or decrease in the number of pages in the front matter. This is one of the main reasons to use Roman numerals for the front matter and Arabic numerals for the rest of the book: if, while writing your book, you decide to add or subtract some pages in the front matter, it would change the pagination of the whole book, and you would have to re-number all of the rest of the pages. But as long as Chapter One begins on Arabic page 1, you may add or subtract pages from the front matter with no effect on the pagination of the rest of the book. (Imagine the mess, if you had already indexed that book!)

Here is a list showing the order in which front matter should appear. Notice, as we said, that each new section begins on an odd-numbered page (except the copyright page, which always appears on the reverse of the title page); and blanks are inserted when necessary. You may choose not to include all of these sections in your book, and some sections may be several pages long, but they should always appear in this order:

i	title page
ii	copyright page
iii	dedication
iv	blank
v	table of contents
vi	blank
vii	list of illustrations
viii	blank
ix	foreword
x	blank
xi	preface
xii	blank
xiii	acknowledgments
xiv	blank
xv	introduction
xvi	blank
xvii	list of abbreviations

As mentioned, the first chapter begins with Arabic numerals, starting on a right-hand (*recto*) page numbered "1." The pagination in Arabic numbers (2, 3, 4, etc.) continues through the rest of the book: all the chapters, the conclusion, the appendices, the use of the index and the index, the glossary of terms, the bibliography, and suggestions for further research.

Now let us examine the functions, purposes, and accepted style of the different parts of your book.

Title Page and Copyright Page

The book should begin with page i, the *title page*. As are the first pages of all other sections and chapters, the title page is on the right sheet. The *copyright page*, page ii, is on the reverse side of the title page, and is the second printed page of the book. Notice that, for the sake of appearance, the page numbers usually do not appear on the title and copyright pages.

Notice also that the title page bears the complete title; under that the name or names of the author or authors; beneath that or those, sometimes, the word "Illustrated" (if illustrations are included); then sometimes the same drawing or illustration that appears on the outside front cover, and beneath that the name and usually the city of the publisher.

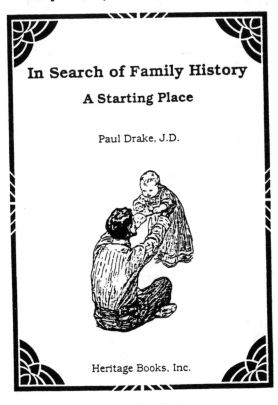

Sample title page

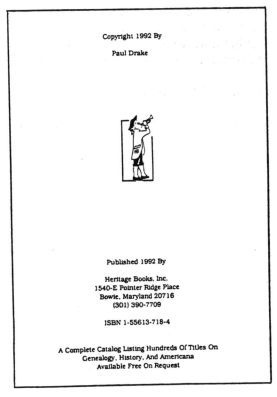

Sample copyright page

Finally, as shown, the overleaf—the copyright page—contains, first the statement, "Copyright [year]" or "© [year]" declaring copyright protection, followed beneath by the author's name. Beneath those are shown the publisher's "logo," the year of publication, and the name and address (or abbreviated address) of the publisher. The ISBN (International Standard Book Number), and the Library of Congress Catalog Number [LCCN] (if there is one) come next. The ISBN and the logo will be supplied by your publisher.

If you wish to register your copyright or obtain a Library of Congress Catalog Number, you must submit the proper forms and fees (about $20.00). Call the Library of Congress, (202) 479-0700, to find out how to obtain these forms. As we shall see later in Chapter VI when we discuss copyrights, you may use the words, "Copyright 1996 by Joe Author" without actually *registering* your copyright, but for maximum legal protection, you should do so.

Dedication

The *dedication*, an optional feature of your book, follows the copyright page. Ideally it should be kept short: "To my father." However, if you feel that several persons deserve mention by reason of your feelings for them or for their encouragement or common interest in your research, do not hesitate to spell out wherein they are dear to you. The book is a product of your intellect, and you are at liberty here to publicly display sentiment and tender feelings. Still though, be always aware that being solicitous, patronizing, gushy, or fawning is never becoming to a writer and serves only to detract from your long efforts. Do not confuse the *dedication* with the *acknowledgments* (see page 7).

Many writers of genealogical works have dedicated their efforts to friends, parents, children, or descendants. Many others have chosen someone who is loved, highly respected, or who served as a source of inspiration, and many have chosen to make no dedication whatever. There is no rule; no right or wrong. Dedicate your effort to whomever you choose, or to no one, but if you do, let it be with dignity and honesty.

Table of Contents

Immediately following the *dedication* section is the *table of contents*. This very important section of your book is almost an outline of your work.

Tables of contents set forth the order, number, and title of each chapter and, in a few words, tell something of the contents of each chapter or section. Just as those titles are descriptive of content (as discussed below), if it is to be helpful, the table must expand upon or explain those titles.

Some tables of contents are extensive, and thereby provide the reader who has limited research time with a convenient means by which to select specific portions to read or to ignore. If, for example, you have a chapter dedicated to the marriage and descendants of Terry and Olga Bosca Connor, that chapter may be of particular value to a future Connor researcher, even though no other portion of your book may be of any interest whatever to that researcher at that time, and unless the Connor chapter is described in the table its presence may not be apparent to such a researcher. So, but for a simple sentence or so of description you have lost a reader, a researcher, and perhaps a cousin. While each member of that Connor family unit also would appear in the index under the name of that member, the fact that a chapter or section was dedicated to those individuals and their family may be more readily determined through the table of contents.

If you have dedicated a chapter to the lifestyles of folks of the early nineteenth century and have used anecdotes, charts, forms, and facts concerning, as an example, your Martin and Carner families as being typical of those aspects of life during that period, the title of the chapter might be "Daily Lives of Some Martin and Carner Ancestors, 1800 to 1850," and in the table of contents that title might be set forth as

> **Chapter 9: Daily Lives of Some Martin and Carner Ancestors, 1800 to 1850**; the Pennsylvania families of John Carner and Henry Martin, including anecdotes and historical facts concerning their marriages, church activities, home life, 'Dutch' food, furniture, and funerals.

Notice that even though the Carner and Martin lines will be discussed there at some length, since their daily activities and pursuits, more so than their lineage, are to be the thrust and purpose of that chapter, it should not have a title such as "The Families of John Carner and Henry Martin, 1800-1850." The reason is that while it would be easy for you to set forth their names in the index, to reveal to a reader your discussion of the social aspects of their lives would require entries carrying their names under index headings, "churches," "food," "'Dutch' food," "funerals," "home lives," "marriages," and "furniture," and still several others.

On the other hand, if that chapter is, for the most part, dedicated to a discussion of the ancestors, families, kin, and descendants of that line of Martins and Carners, and only incidentally discusses lifestyle, marriages, etc., then the title to the same chapter might better be and appear in the table of contents as:

> **Chapter 9: Some Ancestry, Kin, and Descendants of the Families of John Carner and Henry Martin**; ascendant and descendant kin of John Carner and his wife, Magdalena _?_, and of Henry Martin and his wife, Mary Bush, and some discussion of their daily activities and institutions, 1800-1850.

In both titles the thrust or direction of the chapter is revealed, and the reader is able to select and move quickly to those matters that are of interest to him or her, and ignore those chapters that are not.

Then too, if written carefully the table of contents will reveal much about how you have organized the discussion of family lines. Since your readers may view the matter of the family in some quite different lights, the table will help those persons to organize their thoughts and prepare to absorb what you have to say. As an example, suppose, for the most part, that you have viewed your Martin family as New Englanders because you, your parents, and your grandparents lived there. It is easier for a future reader, who equally considers the Martin family to have been Southern by reason of his roots there, to understand why you have commenced the story in Connecticut if, through titles and explanations, the table reveals that later chapters also treat Southern branches of the family.

Finally, regarding tables of contents: to enable your readers to find the chapter or heading they seek, be sure that you list each chapter title in your table of contents exactly the same way that the title appears in the heading on the first page of each chapter. For example, do not list the above chapter titled, **"Daily Lives of Some Martin and Carner Ancestors, 1800 to 1850,"** as, **"Anecdotes and Historical Facts."** Magazines often break this basic rule. How many times have you searched in the table of contents for the cover story, only to find it under some completely unrelated topic? Don't treat *your* readers in such a rude manner.

So, the table of contents is very important, requires careful thought, and provides the readers with explanations and directions that are not easily related in an index.

Lists of Illustrations and Maps

This important section of your book follows the table of contents, is listed therein, and reveals to the reader where you have placed the photos, clippings, copies, diagrams, and maps that are important to the enjoyment and understanding of your narrative. The *list of illustrations* is in order of the pages upon which the illustrations appear, and generally reveals little more than a descriptive name or title of the illustration. Notice however, if you intend to include numerous maps, it will be helpful to your reader to have, in addition to the list of illustrations, a separate *list of maps*.

If an illustration or map bears a formal title, that wording should be copied into the list of illustrations or list of maps, accompanied by any further few words needed to describe it. As examples, you might list entries as: "*Certificate of Discharge*, Civil War, Oscar W. Midlam;" or perhaps "*Report Card*, Maggie Carner Midlam, 1884;" or "*Property Owners Map*, 1853, Marion County, OH."

Where an illustration has no title, or where that title is not revealing of the importance of the content, then a very few words of description should be set out, e.g., a photo of a dog might be "*Bruno*, a pet of the Midlam children, c. 1902;" a drawing labeled only as a seventeenth-century house might be "A seventeenth-century house, typical of the period of Richard and Judith Huntt Parker;" and a township map might be shown as "*Map, Madison Twnshp., Pickaway Co., OH, 1847*, showing lands of Lewis Fridley." As with all aspects of your work, give serious thought to the illustrations to be included and to the words that identify them in the list of illustrations. If you want readers to look at illustrations, write descriptions that reveal their content.

Notice too, the illustrations themselves should be so placed within the book so as to complement and explain the text or narrative that is located near them. If the size of the illustration prohibits its placement with the text to which it speaks, the illustration is better placed immediately after the text than before it. Recall your own experiences; if you come upon a map and have not yet read any discussion about that area, the map is almost meaningless, however, if the same map follows very shortly after that narrative, it will be familiar when it is encountered.

Perhaps most important, be sure to enlarge or reduce the size of all illustrations to achieve a size which will clearly reveal the matter you desire to illustrate, yet does not waste space. As examples, a photo of a husband and wife need not be so large as to reveal the texture of her dress or of his shoes, yet must be of a size sufficient to render those folks readily recognizable. Similarly, if a map is so small as to make it difficult or impossible to identify specific sites, roads, or other features discussed in the narrative, there is no point in including it. So, insert all illustrations in a size that will make it easy for your readers to understand and appreciate their significance.

A word here about photographs: the quality of the reproduction of your photographs and illustrations will only be as good as the quality of the copy that you provide to your printer or publisher. For best results, have prints made of your original pictures— **never** send **originals** to a printer or publisher! Do not waste your money on "glossy" photos; they do not work well and probably will not be accepted.

Ask a reliable photo lab to develop the prints as "positive half-tones." This is a process that produces a picture made up of tiny dots, as in newspaper photos. The density of the dots can be specified, so ask your printer or publisher what they prefer. The process costs about $8.00 per photo, so select your photos carefully. The result will be a nice, clear photo in your finished book.

If you are providing "camera-ready" copy to your printer/publisher, you will be expected to provide the half-tones, or else you will be charged for having the prints processed. Computer-scanning is a less expensive process than making half-tones, but the final result is less predictable and may be very dark. In some cases, the printer or publisher *may* agree to process your prints at no cost to you. Line drawings photocopy nicely and there is no need to make them into half-tones. Just be sure not to send in glossy photographs of line drawings. Notice too, that photocopies ("xerox" copies) of photographs reproduce poorly. The best advice: Once you have found a prospective printer or publisher, ask them how to proceed with your photos and illustrations.

Foreword

This is a *word* that comes be*fore* the rest of your book. Please spell it correctly: it is not Forward, Forword, or Foreward.

The foreword is intended to be a statement by someone *other* than the author. This person is usually selected by the author because of their experience or knowledge of the subject matter of the book, and because of the credibility their reputation lends to the work. The author's own statement about his work should appear in the preface or introduction, which follows the foreword.

Preface

The *preface* usually appears immediately after the *foreword* and just before the *acknowledgments*. The preface tells the reader what motivated the writer to undertake the effort, what effort was expended and resources considered and, equally, what sources and topics were not included, what the parameters of the effort were, and what if any constraints or restrictions were felt by the writer. Any shortcomings in your research or limitations imposed upon you, voluntarily or otherwise, should be set forth here as a guide to the contents of your work, but not as an apology for it. If you have to apologize for your work, why should anyone bother to read it?

For example, if you have decided that your knowledge of your family before the year 1700 was so sparse that, except for some pedigree and family unit charts, you should exclude from the narrative what little you do have and leave that search to the future, that decision should be stated in the preface. Similarly, if you have run into a blank wall and so, despite your best effort, have no information concerning some family line before a certain person, year, or event, that lack of data also would be revealed here. Then too, if, because you had no means by which to visit distant courthouses and there study records not yet abstracted by other writers, your research was limited to only those sources and materials available through local libraries and facilities, that limitation also would be stated. Likewise, if personal reasons or distance prohibited interviews with certain persons or classes of persons, such as an estranged or distant branch of the family, that absence of discussion would be made known.

In short, the preface speaks, not of kin, but of why you undertook the effort, what you have done and, particularly, what you have not done, and appropriately advises and cautions the reader about whatever is incomplete or unfinished and therefore is left to future researchers. Upon concluding the preface, your readers should know what your goals and limitations were, and something of why that was the case.

Acknowledgments

The *acknowledgments*, if you choose to include them, should follow the preface, and precede the introduction. Here is where you name, acknowledge and demonstrate your appreciation for those who have assisted you in the writing, editing, and publication of the work.

Many books acknowledge those who gave suggestions or advised the writer in technique and method, those who typed the manuscript or otherwise helped with the editing (and you quite likely will need such a person), those who supplied research time or effort, those who supplied or loaned photos or located maps or other illustrations and thereby saved time for the writer, any publishers or members of their staffs who went beyond the call of duty in assisting or being helpful, and often the spouse, children, or other family members who were deprived of time and companionship by the long effort. Even pets that provided quiet companionship at the typewriter or computer keyboard occasionally are remembered in the acknowledgment section. As with dedications, who, if anybody, deserves to be remembered is entirely up to you, and there is no right or wrong in the matter.

Introduction

The *introduction* provides the historical and family setting and, as the word suggests, introduces the reader to the subject and the first matters to be considered: it is the steps that lead down to the pool that is the body of your work.

As does the *table of contents*, it also reveals to the reader the broad and general order that you have selected for the discussions that are to follow. All too many authors write introductions with abandon, thereby losing the reader's interest. The introduction should be used as a device to pique the curiosity of your reader, often sufficiently to see him through many of the moments of tedium and waves of meaningless names and dates that surely lie ahead in even the best of genealogical writing.

Suppose, for example, that you have chosen to commence the narrative in Chapter 1 with a discussion of the life of your very first immigrant ancestor, a Thomas Sherwood who, with his wife and children, came to New England in the year 1638, and first lived a few miles from Salem, Massachusetts. Your introduction might explain that he and his family will be the starting place for the story, and that you will proceed to discuss his life, then the lives of his children, their spouses, and their lives insofar as known, then move to his son, Thomas, Jr., who was your direct ancestor.

You then would go on to explain that in the second chapter you will discuss the spouse of Thomas, Sr., and her ancestry and kin, and, following that, chapter by chapter, you will move through the succeeding generations, each containing a discussion of the families and spouses of all the members of that generation, so far as they are known.

Then too, in order to provide a measure of context and historical setting, your introduction might relate some facts concerning the area to which that immigrant family came. You might mention that within a generation of their arrival, many of the colonists in Massachusetts, especially in Salem, were caught up in a frenzy of fears, accusations, and trials concerning the practice of witchcraft, culminating in late 1692 with the hanging of a number of witches; that even in the far off Virginia Colony, where another of your ancestors was about to land, witches also were being "discovered," all to the consternation of the citizenry; that threats from coastal American Indians were by then more imagined than real; and that religion played a dominant role in every aspect of the lives of the people of those early communities. By setting forth such historical background, even though briefly (and such historical facts are readily obtainable in every library), the backdrop has been provided for the great play of history that is the heritage of you and all of your family.

So, while the preface tells of the nature and limits of your sources and search, what you did and did not do and consider, where you began and where you stopped, and what presumptions you made in writing the narrative, the introduction leaves you, your efforts, and your sentiments behind, sets the stage for the play that is about to begin, and forewarns and forearms the reader as to what the order of things will be. It is very important; construct the introduction very carefully.

List of Abbreviations

In the body of your work—where you will be writing narrative—abbreviations should not be used at all; they give an appearance of laziness. You may, however, need abbreviations in appendices and notes, especially where you have abstracted dates and events from newspapers or vital records such as marriages or tax rolls, and to that extent you should explain and define the words to be abbreviated. Such words might be listed as "b." = born, "bapt." = baptised, "enl." = enlisted, "m." = married, "lvd." = lived, "svd." = served, "d"= died, "bu." = buried.

Further, if you intend to cite other sources or authors frequently you probably will want to abbreviate their names or book titles, eespecially where the titles are long (and many are) or where an author has written several books. If, as examples, you several times used Maurice B. Gordon's *Aesculapius Comes to the Colonies* and Philip Bruce's *Institutional History of Virginia in the Seventeenth Century*, the writing of those long titles over and over is both tedious and unnecessary. So, since your reader is not likely to confuse that work with any other, when citing Gordon, as an example, you might write it as *Gordon, p. 33-34*, or *Aesculapius, pp. 33-34*, and when citing Bruce, since you used two of his books, you would need only use the abbreviation *Institutional History, pp. 80-85*, or *Economic History, p. 21*.

Chapters and Chapter Titles

As seen in the discussion of the table of contents, the *titles* to chapters are very important. After the title given to the book itself, and the information set forth in the table of contents (which, unfortunately, too often goes unread), chapter titles are the next opportunity you have to arouse interest in your readers, to partially inform them again of what to expect, and to coax them to continue on. If you will but dedicate some thought to creating interesting and descriptive titles, your effort will be repaid many times over in the numbers of folks who read through, remember, and comment upon your work.

Suppose you intend that your next chapter tell of the lives of your Haskins relatives, more particularly of a Todd Evan and Diane Allison Haskins (he, a merchant), who made their home in Salem, Massachusetts, during the last quarter of the seventeenth-century. Recall, as mentioned, that it was during those years that the Salem witchcraft trials were held, the same resulting in executions then, and study of the matter even to now. What might be a good title?

Notice that if we title that chapter, "Todd Evan (1659-1709) and Diane Allison (1660-1725) Haskins" we have said nothing that will arouse the interest of the readers. If the decision to be made by some late evening reader is to read further or go to bed, it is a safe bet that sleep is not far off. If we label it, "Witch Trials of Old Massachusetts," not only have we been inaccurate—indeed, even deceptive—in providing clues as to what will be found there, we also have lost the attention of those who have no interest in that subject matter. Even if they are genealogists and students of the Haskins line, with such a title, once again, bed time is not far off.

But suppose that we title that chapter, "Some Haskins Ancestors During the Period of the Witch Trials." We now have the attention of all who are studying the early Massachusetts Haskins lines, of those who are interested in the martyrs of the period, witchcraft generally, and its effects on ordinary people, of those who are interested in the laws and judicial actions having to do with that subject, and of those who wonder if the Haskins families were involved, directly or indirectly, in that very interesting period. All that from a ten-word title to the chapter.

So, as you write, give much consideration to chapter titles, and do not be in a hurry to compose them. The final decisions as to such matters as chapter titles may be (and usually are) put off until the final manuscript.

Body of the Work: the Narrative

Here is where you will set out the large percentage of the total effort. The body of your book contains the discussion of virtually every one of those matters that you feel deserve attention and study. Conversely, with the exception of occasional charts or numbering systems and footnotes or endnotes, the body of the text does not include matters that, though interesting, are remote from your objective of setting forth the births, lives, families, activities, moments of joy, travails, accomplishments and failings, and deaths of your ancestors and kin.

In considering what rightly should be 1) included in the body of your text, 2) included by way of brief foot- or endnotes or in a more lengthy appendix, or 3) be totally excluded, consider the Welshman, Owen Griffith. Shortly after 1658 Owen came to Virginia as an indentured servant. Because those facts place him in a precise historical setting, they should be included in the body of the narrative and at the beginning of any discussion having to do with him and his family. At some point in the narrative you might also include the name of the ship upon which he came, its master, and the date of its departure from Bristol, England. By so doing, he becomes a real person undertaking a new life in what then was a very new world.

The additional fact that his "headright" (contrary to the spirit of the law) was used by others to gain land no less than three times, the last such use having taken place even after his death, very properly should appear in a footnote (or endnote) appended to the discussion of his passage and servant life here. But, any further discussion of the many legal rights and duties growing out of such passages, headrights, or master and servant relationships, if thought to be of interest to any reader sufficient to justify inclusion at all, should appear in an appendix and not in the narrative or notes. Such matters are simply too far afield from any discussion of his life and family, and so are not the stuff of the narrative.

To take the matter a step further, notice that discussions of topics such as attitudes toward servants and headrights in neighboring colonies, or of the legislation that created and perpetuated such rights, while doubtless interesting to many researchers with servant ancestors, belong in another book, and not even in the appendices to Owen's family history. If, instead of genealogical narrative, the intention is to write of servitude and the society affected by it, then family history should be set aside for the time being, and servitude taken up.

Notice here, by careful consideration as to extent and placement of the Owen Griffith servitude information—whether to set it out in the narrative, in the notes to the narrative, or in the appendices—the reader has been given the choice 1) of reading nothing further about the subject by simply ignoring the notes and continuing with the narrative, 2) of learning a bit more by taking the time to read those notes, or 3) of gaining considerably more information having to do with that matter through a study of the appendix. By reason of that careful selection of position, the reader has not been forced to wade the quagmire of law and servitude unless he or she so chooses. Thereby, that reader's interest in the main theme of that chapter—Owen's immigration, life, and family—has been maintained, which was the purpose anyhow.

Conclusion of the Narrative

As the name says, the *conclusion* is the end of the body of your work. In genealogical writings, it often serves as a short review, reveals the author's view as to where in the great scheme and chronology of things the family has been shown to fit, speaks of family members of whom all may be proud (or not so), serves as a reminder to the readers of what they have learned, discusses where the writer left off and what research or study is yet to be accomplished, and frequently challenges the readers to continue in the effort.

Perhaps more than at any other place in your book, conclusions also provide an opportunity to display a measure of pride. After a summary of poignant moments in the history of the family, and a review of individual accomplishments by and noteworthy hardships that befell certain ancestors, one recent work concludes with a quote from Churchill: "We have not journeyed all this way across the centuries—across the oceans, across the mountains, across the prairies—because we are made of sugar candy." [1] (Notice too, the construction of this footnote.)

Conclusions should not be lengthy, should be carefully planned and set forth, should leave the reader with a sense of satisfaction and a feeling that, even though much remains to be done, the author's purposes and goals have been met, and, especially where deep sentiment is expressed, should be written with dignity and sincerity. In short, the writer should tie up the loose ends, remind the reader of his place in the history of the family, and, offering a challenge, leave softly and gently.

End Matter: Arrangement

After the body of the book comes the end matter. We will discuss the different kinds of end matter, several of which may not be relevant or necessary in your book. They should be arranged in the following order:

---

1. Paul Drake, *In Search of Family History: A Starting Place* (hereafter referred to as Drake, *In Search of*) (Heritage Books, Bowie, MD, 1992), p. 95, quoting Winston S. Churchill, speech to Canadian Commons, December, 1940.

     appendices
     endnotes (if used instead of footnotes)
     glossary
     bibliography
     suggestions for further research
     how to use the index
     index

Appendices

Appendices (or *appendixes*), **if needed**, are placed following the the *conclusion*, and preceding other "end matter" such as a glossary, bibliography, or index. As noted in the prior discussions of notes and citations, the appendices provide information that, while often afield from the main thrust or theme of any of the chapters or of the book itself, is desirable as a supplement to or enlargement upon some matter mentioned or discussed in the narrative.

Using Appendices to Achieve Balance

Appendices also are used to achieve balance or equality of treatment among your characters. Most of us know a great deal about one or two of our ancestors; enough, perhaps to occupy a full chapter, and far more than we know of most others. Were we to use the narrative to tell all we know about those people, extremely interesting though the facts may be, the narrative would be quite out of balance.

So, while trying in the main body of your work to dedicate equal space and time to all folks of the same generation, we often achieve balance by utilizing an appendix. Just as we avoided drifting afield with the subject of indentured servitude, so too may we use an appendix to extend the coverage of a person or family.

Suppose you have an ancestor—a great-grandfather named George Drake, for example—about whom you know details concerning his birth, baptism, marriage, children, residences, final illness and death, and have several newspaper clippings, photos, and mementos; more than any other great-grandparent. Suppose you also know that during the Civil War he enlisted in the 43rd North Carolina Infantry, was on the Confederate left while serving in Ewell's Corps at Gettysburg, participated in the Valley Campaign under General "Jube" Early, was in the thick of it at Spotsylvania Courthouse, and participated in many other battles and skirmishes, about which you have many details. After the war, he returned to Edgecombe County, where he lived, farmed, and died in 1880.

The military facts stated are too much. They bring a measure of detail that not only creates imbalance, but also may not be interesting to many of your readers. Still, those details should be preserved and provided somewhere, and the place is an appendix, not in the narrative. If a reader appreciates a discussion of war, you will have supplied it.

In this context, as with the law and customs surrounding servitude, further facts having to do with the life of Confederate infantrymen in general, their pay and food, their letters home, their commanding generals, even the 1864 activities of Early's command about Washington that were designed to bring anxiety and fear to Washingtonians, etc., while perhaps of great interest to some readers, are not good genealogy, and belong in some other book, not even in an appendix. Do not drift off to another subject.

Revealing the Presence of Appendices

The presence of appendices and some minimal remarks as to content must be revealed to the reader. In addition to listing and identifying them in the table of contents, a footnote and occasionally a parenthetical comment may be placed within or immediately following the sentence or paragraph where the subject is introduced.

So, in speaking of the soldier, George Drake and his life, the paragraph revealing the presence of the appendix might read:

> George G. Drake...participated in and later proudly told of many battles and skirmishes of that great war[2]...and after the war returned to Edgecombe County...." or:

> George Drake...participated in and later proudly told of many battles and skirmishes of that great war (See *Appendix #10*, infra)...and after the war returned to Edgecombe County...." or, finally:

> George Drake...participated in and later proudly told of many battles and skirmishes of that great war...and after the war returned to Edgecombe County....(See *Appendix #10* for a discussion of his military activities while in the 43rd North Carolina Infantry.)

Notice again, where you supply a footnote or notation revealing the presence of an appendix having to do with a particular subject, your readers have an idea of what to expect in that appendix, and, as with the notes, may choose to read on rather than be diverted to that additional material. You have made your readers more comfortable by giving them a choice.

Since they also appear in the table of contents, as with chapter titles, titles to appendices must be carefully considered, and so composed as to reveal something of their content. The appendix mentioned above having to do with Confederate George Drake's military activities might be entitled:

> Appendix #10: Some 1863, 1864, and 1865 Civil War Activities of the 43rd North Carolina Volunteer Infantry.

Other Matters and Writings in Appendices

Finally, an appendix is a fine and proper place for poignant letters, extended newspaper articles or obituaries, written recollections—memoirs—of a cousin or other relative, and for family unit charts, numbered pedigrees, or "trees" of remote or collateral branches of the family. Here again, be sure to make the titles reflective of the contents, such as:

> Appendix 13: **Recollections** of Zora Drake, sister of George G. Drake, 1902
> Appendix 14: **Obituary** of Confederate veteran, George Gustus Drake, 1880.

Notes and Citations

Now, everyone knows that if you were not there at the time that some event occurred, you had to learn of it from witnesses who were there or from the writings of

---

2. See Appendix #10 hereof for his wartime activities.

other people; there is no other way you could know. *Notes* and *citations* reveal where you gained that information. Accordingly, while casual readers (and most of your relatives will be of that category) sometimes require no such notes, read solely for the pride to be gained and enjoyment to be had by sharing in your intellectual experiences concerning common ancestry, and likely will never double-check what you have written, no serious genealogist, now or in the future, will quote what you have written unless such sources are revealed. To that latter category of folks, without citations your conclusions are but unsubstantiated guesses.

So, what are citations and notes? A citation is simply a reference to another source or person, and a note is a <u>short</u> explanation of some matter appearing in the body or text. Suppose you have established a Drake marriage date by an entry in the family Bible which lists that date as May 18, 1888. A note (footnote or endnote) might read:

> 1) The author is in possession (1994) of the Bible owned by Dr. William K. Drake (1824-1882), in which he made numerous entries, including that under "Marriages" which revealed May 18, 1888, as the date of the marriage of Bethany Drake to Evan Haskins.

A citation for that same matter of proof, on the other hand, might read simply,

> 1) Drake Family Bible, at "Marriages."

Notice, as often, the above lengthy note also contains the citation; it both explains and gives the source. The short citation, however, though quite adequate when no explanation is needed, does very little more than reveal from where the information was gained.

Whether notes are placed at the end of each chapter (and then called "endnotes") or are placed at the bottom of each page (and therefore known as "footnotes"), is a choice you need not make until the body of the text—the narrative—is finished. At that time, it will be easier to make the decision, since you will know 1) how many notes there were, 2) how lengthy or abbreviated most were, and 3) whether or not they piqued interest or contributed substantially to the narrative, hence should be at the bottom of each page for easy reference, or, instead, served primarily to prove your contentions and provide the reader with a mechanism by which he or she later could examine your original sources, and so should be placed at the end of each chapter. The decision as to where to place them is left largely to your preference, and that choice need not be made now.

Wherever you put the notes, one of their purposes is to reveal why you are sure of what you have written. The other purpose of notes is to provide a place where explanations or clarifications may be given, or where related matters may be stated (any of which also might be accompanied by or contain a citation of authority). Again though, remember, for more elaborate explanations your reader should look to the appendices (discussed previously), and for knowledge as to where still further discussions of some topic may be found, that reader should seek out your bibliography, which will be discussed later.

Suppose you have written that, "Thomas Drake owned land in Virginia before 1740." You should prove that statement, and if Isle of Wight County, Virginia, was the location of a recorded deed revealing such ownership, the footnote might read:

> 1. Isle of Wight County, VA, *Deed Book 2*, pp. 111-113.

If Thomas was a grantee in that old deed (meaning that he purchased or otherwise gained the land), the matter is proven, and no further explanation is needed in the note. He owned the land as of the execution of that deed, and that is the fact you have stated.

Suppose that you went on to relate that "Thomas Drake and Anne Griffith were married before 1703." Once again, citation of authority is required as proof of that marriage, and your footnote might read as follows:

> 2. Isle of Wight County, VA, *Deed Book 3*, p. 9, wherein, on March 27, 1703, the wife of Thomas Drake signed her name, "Anne Drake;" and Isle of Wight, *Great Book, 1675-1705*, part 2, pp. 45-47, the "Will of Owen Griffith," 1698, where Owen bequeathed a cow to his "daughter Anne" and stated that one of his sons-in-law was Thomas Drake."

Standing alone, the deed was not proof of the date of the marriage, nor of Anne's maiden name. An additional reference was needed, and it came in the form of Owen's will which established that in 1698 Owen had a daughter named Anne, and a son-in-law named Thomas Drake. Both references were needed to complete the proof.

Finally, sometimes multiple sources are needed in establishing proof, and yet again no additional explanation is needed from you. As an example, suppose you wrote "John Martin was living on his 140-acre farm in Blair County, when he died on December 17, 1870." If you based that statement on the facts that 1) the tax records of that county show that John paid taxes on 140 acres of land in that year (1870), 2) that the 1870 census stated his occupation as "Farmer," and 3) his son wrote a letter stating that his father had died on the "only land he had ever owned," your foot- or endnote might read:

> 14. Blair County *Real Estate Tax Rolls, 1857-1878*, p. 14; *Decennial Census, 1870*, PA, Roll M593-1309, p. 249; and *Letter of January 8, 1872*, John Martin, Jr. to Prudence Drake, Accession #1217, Ohio State Historical Society Library, Cols., OH. [3]

So, while you must carefully set forth whatever number of sources and other background information you relied upon to arrive at your conclusion, you need not think for your readers.

It is of the greatest importance that you enter the notes at their proper places in the narrative as you write, beginning with the first draft. To later return to each sentence or paragraph and then attempt to enter the references would be an enormous undertaking, and will require that the notes you have pored over in composing the text again be located, handled, considered, summarized, and entered. So always, always enter the notes in place as you compose and write.

Notes, whether as footnotes at the bottom of each page or as endnotes at the end of each chapter, should commence with the number 1 in every chapter, and continue numerically until the end of that chapter. So, while Chapter 10 might have footnotes #1 through #12, another chapter might have notes from #1 through #35.

---

3. All three sources are needed, since the tax records do not prove that John lived on the land upon which he paid taxes, the census records do not prove that he farmed his own land, and the letter does not prove that the land he died on was a farm.

Your sole purpose in composing notes is to explain and to provide that information needed by future readers, should they want to return to the precise place in the materials used by you as your proof. Insofar as your methods permit that measure of precision, they will suffice.

Nevertheless, some methods, more than others, are convenient and easily read. As an example of one such easily understood format, a footnote might read:

> 59. Paul R. Drake II, editor, *The Daybook of Dr. W. K. Drake, 1841-1856* (Hotel 1880 Press, Columbia, SC, 1944); p. 48.

Another method easy of comprehension is that prescribed by the American Society of Genealogists.[4] If using this format, a citation might read:

> 26. Mary Lindsey Thornton; *A Bibliography of North Carolina, 1589-1956* (University of North Carolina Press, 1958), pp. 41-56.

Notice above that we have supplied a footnote (#4) revealing the source for this suggested method. Should you wish to review the discussion by the Society to that effect, you may (and should) consult the footnote at the bottom of this page, and observe its form, as well.

Even if your authorities for facts stated were, variously, your grandmother, an old letter, and a family Bible, you still must reveal those sources in the notes, lest you be thought to have hypothesized—dreamed up—a "fact" stated. As examples, your footnotes #17, #61, and #66 might read:

> 17. Tape-recorded interview with Mrs. Ida C. Roberts Drake, December, 17, 1948, she then aged 82, tapes now in the collection of of Dr. Cheryl Drake Bater of Columbus, OH.

> 61. Excerpt from *Letter* dated Feb. 2, 1832, T. B. Worrell to Prudence Williams, the same preserved in the family archives of John Worrell of Norfolk.

> 66. Midlam family *Bible*, at "Births," the same in the charge (1994) of Allison Drake Haskins of Birmingham.

So, in order that your work may be reviewed or further considered by those who follow you, we advise that whenever possible your statements should be backed by a citation of authority.

Glossary of Terms

The purpose of a glossary is to make it easier for your reader to understand some of the no-longer-used words of ancestors, and some of your own as well.

Suppose you have spent some considerable effort setting forth and discussing items of early inventories, military activities or units, associations, unusual cooking utensils or furniture, horses and farm animals, vehicles and carriages, trains, callings and occupations, firearms and game animals, or ships and boats. Such items as a "Belgian horse" or a "diamond stack woodburner," an ancestor's "birdgun," her "chaise," "buck

---

4. Am. Soc. of Genealogists; *Genealogical Research Methods and Sources*, 2 vols. (by the Society, Washington, 1960), vol. 1, p. 223.

wagon," or "holographic will," a "planter's desk," a "crane," or a reference to an ancestor as a "cooper," "sawyer" or "joiner" all might appear in the glossary.

While any good unabridged dictionary quite likely would serve the purpose of providing definitions, by defining such once common but now obsolete or seldom seen terms, you have once again assisted your readers in finding enjoyment in your work; you have made the book "user friendly," as we now say, and much easier to comprehend.

While any unusual or early words or expressions might be of interest to some readers, explanations or definitions of military activities, occupations, foods, and furniture seem to be particularly desirable reading material. If, as examples, an ancestor served in the 55th Ohio or the 8th Air Force, many descendants—especially veterans—will find a definition of those units to be interesting; if a great grandfather was a wagonmaker, a cabinetmaker, a pewterer, or a gunsmith, explanations of the work and training of men of those callings are interesting to many. If an ancestress was known for the way she prepared a particular food, e.g., poke sallet, scrapple, bratwurst, lobster pie, a definition of those terms would be particularly interesting to those who enjoy cooking (or eating); or if you have a plank bottom chair of a fourth-great grandmother, a definition of that term might make possible a visual image of the chair.

Remember, too, while compiling the glossary, that words common today or recently—even such as "xerox," "carbon paper," "hi-fi," "typewriter," and "push-mower"—very soon will be obsolete, hence might also be included. As always, you should view the glossary as one more opportunity to assist and continue the interest of your readers.

Bibliography

After the glossary is found the *bibliography*. It is a listing of other books and writings that may be necessary or desirable in further research by your readers. Many researchers will advance and expand their own efforts through the use of your referrals to other writings and sources. If a reader is researching lines of Hunt, and learns through your bibliography that some Hunt families appear in a volume previously unknown to that reader, you have assisted that person greatly. You have saved time for that reader, time that will gain him or her knowledge.

Our Owen Griffith indentured servitude discussion above provides an example of the value of bibliographies. Numerous articles and studies have been written and done concerning this unique tool of early transport (indentured servitude), which, even though much too far afield for any genealogical narrative or even the appendices to such, surely are deserving of a place in a bibliography of any study of Griffith's life, activities, and lineage. So, remember that a bibliography provides the reader with knowledge of additional reading materials concerning topics touched upon within the text, which, while interesting, were so lengthy and far afield from the genealogical discussion as to not warrant inclusion.

As you write, you will put aside many sources and materials as being too remote from your efforts. As you make the decision to exclude those writings, make a note, just as you would make a foot- or endnote, relating the author, title, publisher, and date or edition, e.g., Philip A. Bruce, *An Institutional History of Virginia in the Seventeenth Century*, 2 vols. (G. B. Putnam's Sons, Knickerbocker Press, New York, 1910). By so doing, without again searching you will have that title at hand for inclusion later in the bibliography. Once again, your writing will have been rendered more convenient to use.

Suggestions for Further Research

Following the bibliography in many genealogical writings is what has come to be called *suggestions for further research*. Here is the place where you refresh the readers' memories as to where you stopped in various ancestral lines, and make suggestions as to geographical areas, records, and names that may be starting places for additional efforts. Such suggestions should be brief and follow the order of the chapterage; your purpose here is to inform, not to rehash what you said back in the narrative.

One example will suffice. If the earliest information you have concerning your Carner line was the enlistment of John Carner in the Revolutionary Army, then you might write:

> ....In searching further concerning John Carner and his family, the researcher of the future should note that we took up his life with his enlistment at Reading, Pennsylvania, in 1777. That town likely was not more than a day or two of travel—20 to 30 miles—from his home. Then too, we know that after discharge he was found in the records of White Deer Township of what is now Union County, Pennsylvania.

Thereby, your readers have a place to commence the search for John before the Revolution, and a location where he may have left records after that conflict. Following that paragraph, similar directions should be written as to other lines, all designed solely to assist a future student of the family.

Index: How to Use

You may not need to include a "How to Use This Index" section if your index is simple and self-explanatory. Usually it is sufficient to give it a heading, such as "Index of Names and Places" so that the reader knows what to expect. Still though, if the index is complicated and requires explanation, then, by all means, do so.

Index: How to Construct

One of the very most important, yet perhaps the most tedious and least pleasurable of your efforts, will be the construction of an index. This phase will not begin, of course, until your manuscript is completely paginated and finalized, otherwise, if changes are made, you will have to amend your index.

Indexes (or indices) vary in quality from those that list only surnames that appear in the narrative to those that are complete in every way. Yours will likely fall somewhere in between, and, as so many times, the choice is entirely yours.

The most desirable of the indexes, and that which is recommended, sets forth every appearance of all individuals named anywhere in the writing, including in the introduction, the preface, the body, the conclusion, and the appendices, and reveals every illustration, memento mentioned, subject or topic discussed, disease and cause of death, county, city, town, township, ward and precinct, named pet and wild animal, war, battle, and notable event (such as blizzards, fires, earthquakes, and floods) and all specifically identified ships, trains, planes, rivers, streams, swamps, and other waterways. In short, and difficult though it may be, in an index of this quality your readers will be provided access to every person, object, place, or subject that could in any way lead to further research sources, and they won't have to read the whole book to find them.

The next most acceptable indexes for genealogical writings are those that list every surname and given name, as well as the name of every place, including counties, cities, towns, battles, rivers and streams, and cemeteries. Notice that an index containing this degree of detail still provides the genealogist with all of the people and with most of those places which might provide or lead to other genealogical records.

Now consider those indexes that contain only surnames with accompanying given names. While such indexes allow a researcher to continue searching for names already known, unless that worker expends the time to read the entire narrative concerning those named people, he or she has no further clues to other sources.

As examples, if I find that Thomas Drake is in the name-only index to your book, I must read about him to whatever extent is necessary to learn that he owned land in Virginia's Albemarle Parish, or was a communicant of Nottoway Chapel, or traded at Cotton's Landing, etc. Further, if I want to learn more from you about that parish, or that chapel, or that landing, short of reading the whole book, I am simply out of luck.

Similarly, if I look up Daniel Carner in your index, turn to that page, and there learn that he was in the Battle of Gettysburg, I am at a loss to learn more about that battle or who else of your ancestry was there, unless, again, I read the entire narrative. Had your index also listed places, including Gettysburg, I would have been able to read as much more as I chose to, and I would be much more pleased with your work.

Compare those alternatives with a "surname only" index. These are, at best, tedious to use and, at worst, next to useless for serious researchers. Perhaps nothing more deters a busy researcher from examining your writings than to find that you have created an index with nothing but surnames. If one is serious about ancestry—particularly where some lines bear common surnames—he or she simply does not have time enough in life to look up every incidence of that surname in every book.

If you are searching a line of Smiths (and most of us do at one time or another), you know that there were hundreds of thousands—even millions—of people with that surname. The task is monstrous enough where the given names are known, and is next to impossible where an index sets forth only the occurrences of that last name. So, you must set forth given names and initials whenever known. There are no acceptable reasons for doing otherwise.

Most importantly, time-consuming as it is, you must also index wives by both their maiden name and their married name (including initials), or combine those names in the index entry. Suppose you are doing a study of the descendants of John Carner, and you are unable to learn what became of one of his daughters known as Betsy, who is thought to have married a man named Bush. A completely and properly indexed Bush genealogy would list her as, "Bush, Elizabeth (Betsy) Carner" and "Carner, Elizabeth (Betsy) (Bush)."

Notice that even though Betsy may be the only name you ever knew her by, another researcher who learned only her full name may not know her by that nickname, and vice versa. So, if you know the nickname, as well as the full given name, list both, the nickname in parentheses or with quote ("") marks around it. By so doing you may very much help someone who does not know both names.

Notice, had the Bush index entry above not further identified Elizabeth as a Carner, or had not indexed Betsy under her maiden name, Carner, only as a last resort would you have undertaken to examine all the variations of the very common names Elizabeth and Bush.

The need to thoroughly index the names of women is perhaps no better illustrated than in this example where Cheryl Drake married Mark Bater, and had issue, among others, Cheryl J. Bater. Those index entries should be: 1) "Bater, Cheryl Drake," thereby alerting all Bater searchers to her presence and of her maiden name, Drake; 2) "Drake, Cheryl (Bater)," thereby revealing to Drake researchers that there was a Cheryl Drake who married a Bater; and 3) "Bater, Cheryl J.," thereby revealing—since there was but one maiden surname included—that there was a Bater child or woman who was unmarried [or whose married name was not known], at least at the time of the making of that record.

So, index women who have been married completely and thoroughly. It will make your work eminently more usable (and salable) as a research tool for others.

Summary of This Chapter

Even though divided into sections, your book is one complete effort, and represents the sum total of all you know that is significant about that which you wrote. Always remember that each section has the same duty; to move the reader toward the end and then to further research with the least unnecessary diversion.

It is to that purpose that the *dedication* is your tribute and statement of the importance of some person or persons for or in memory of whom, in part, you have written the book; the *acknowledgments* do just that—give credit where it is due; the *table of contents* provides an outline and convenient way for your reader to know of the plan and organization of the book; the *list of illustrations* and *list of maps* directs the reader to the visual aspects of the work; the *preface* tells what your motivations, limitations, if any, and parameters were; and the *introduction* sets the stage and provides the backdrop for the story that is about to unfold.

Following the introduction is the *body* or *narrative*, then the *conclusion* sums it all up and allows you to display pride and perhaps poignancy. The *appendices* set forth detail found interesting, yet more expansive or afield from the principle story and its characters. The *footnotes* (or *endnotes*) come next, revealing the nature of and place from which came the proof of the statements made; the *glossary* explains the words now often as distant as your players; the *bibliography* allows your readers to move on and in greater depth in those materials from which you drew many of your own ideas, and the *suggestions for further research* allows future family historians to take up where you left off. Finally, the *explanation of the index* and the *index* provide access to all topics, places, and people of whom you spoke. The index permits your reader to freely move about in the body of the narrative.

In addition to providing data and facts concerning people, times and places, tales and traditions, inspiration, and reading pleasure for all your kinfolk, your writing should be a repository of historical information and sources from which additional research may arise. It should be an invaluable genealogical tool to be carried along by its readers as they further study the family. To turn your efforts into such a tool, a diligent effort must go into every part of the book.

Chapter II: Planning Format

"Those who depend on the merits of their ancestors may be said to search in the roots of the tree for those fruits which the branches ought to produce."

Isaac Barrow (1630-1677)

Some Preliminary Thoughts

Many ideas concerning methods and techniques for relating genealogical facts and proof have been used over the years. Your choice of method should be based upon what you hope to accomplish and how much material you have. No one can tell you how to organize and say what you have to say, and there are but few rights and wrongs.

Leaving Some Decisions for Later

While you can now formulate ideas concerning the placement of particular individuals and the illustrations and photos having to do with them, and also determine many matters having to do with layout, appendices, bibliographies, and indexes, it is almost certain that the final product will only slightly resemble what you now have planned.

Not to worry. Almost without effort you will come to know what form your work should and will take; the materials will make the decisions for you. Just as sculptors speak of a statue emerging from the marble as they work, as you progress the grand spectacle of your family will appear from the myriad raw notes and disconnected mementos that now fill your mind and files or hard drive.

Uses of Pedigree Charts

Remember that pedigree charts, family unit charts, illustrations, maps, and numbering systems are not the body of your work. They are tools—only tools—to be used for illustration, description, explanation, and as supplements to your story. That thought is important, and you will be reminded of it from time to time as we proceed.

In some of your family lines, especially in very early ones, you will have a number of facts, dates, and places concerning distant cousins and descendants of those cousins, while in other families you will have next to none. Then too, in some of those lines you will have facts that are so remote from your interests and theme that you will not want to include them in the narrative, and so lacking in detail that appendices, footnotes, or endnotes (discussed later) also are not appropriate. These are the places where pedigree charts may work well.

Family "trees" or pedigree charts are widely known and used, and as we all know, such charts show lineage and relations in the form of an easy-to-read drawing. Each generation is represented by a level or section of that drawing, with each name written in with a minimum of abbreviated data, e.g., on line 8 of such a chart you may have written "John Drake, b. Jan. 6, 1759 VA, md. Oct. 26, 1780, d. April 3, 1824 VA" and immediately below John, and concerning his wife, you may have placed the words "Martha Diane Alexander, b. Jan. 6, 1759, d. Oct. 26, 1860."

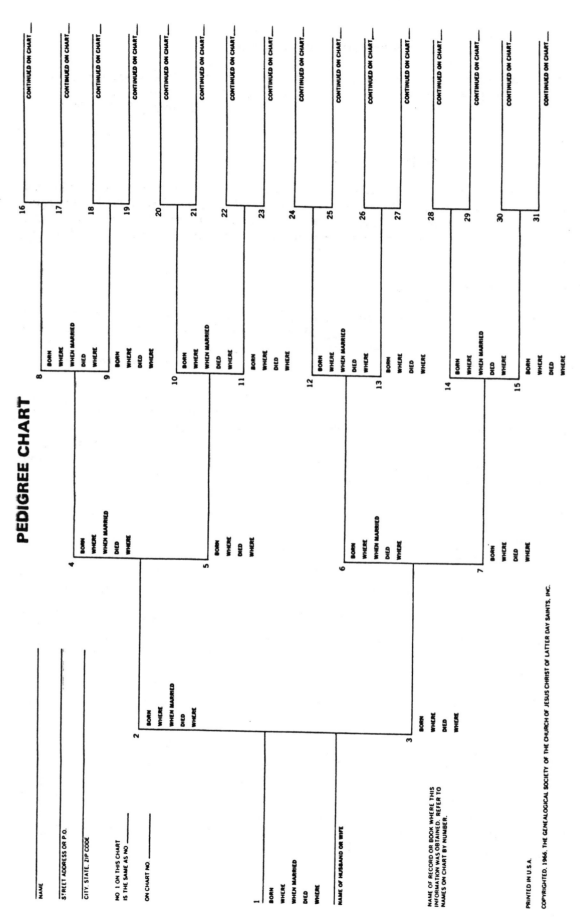

PEDIGREE CHART

NAME _____

STREET ADDRESS OR P.O. _____

CITY, STATE, ZIP CODE _____

NO 1 ON THIS CHART
IS THE SAME AS NO _____

ON CHART NO _____

1 _____
BORN
WHERE
WHEN MARRIED
DIED
WHERE

NAME OF HUSBAND OR WIFE _____

NAME OF RECORD OR BOOK WHERE THIS
INFORMATION WAS OBTAINED. REFER TO
NAMES ON CHART BY NUMBER.

PRINTED IN U.S.A.

COPYRIGHTED, 1966, THE GENEALOGICAL SOCIETY OF THE CHURCH OF JESUS CHRIST OF LATTER DAY SAINTS, INC.

2
BORN
WHERE
WHEN MARRIED
DIED
WHERE

3
BORN
WHERE
DIED
WHERE

4
BORN
WHERE
WHEN MARRIED
DIED
WHERE

5
BORN
WHERE
DIED
WHERE

6
BORN
WHERE
WHEN MARRIED
DIED
WHERE

7
BORN
WHERE
DIED
WHERE

8
BORN
WHERE
WHEN MARRIED
DIED
WHERE

9
BORN
WHERE
DIED
WHERE

10
BORN
WHERE
WHEN MARRIED
DIED
WHERE

11
BORN
WHERE
DIED
WHERE

12
BORN
WHERE
WHEN MARRIED
DIED
WHERE

13
BORN
WHERE
DIED
WHERE

14
BORN
WHERE
WHEN MARRIED
DIED
WHERE

15
BORN
WHERE
DIED
WHERE

16 _____ CONTINUED ON CHART ____
17 _____ CONTINUED ON CHART ____
18 _____ CONTINUED ON CHART ____
19 _____ CONTINUED ON CHART ____
20 _____ CONTINUED ON CHART ____
21 _____ CONTINUED ON CHART ____
22 _____ CONTINUED ON CHART ____
23 _____ CONTINUED ON CHART ____
24 _____ CONTINUED ON CHART ____
25 _____ CONTINUED ON CHART ____
26 _____ CONTINUED ON CHART ____
27 _____ CONTINUED ON CHART ____
28 _____ CONTINUED ON CHART ____
29 _____ CONTINUED ON CHART ____
30 _____ CONTINUED ON CHART ____
31 _____ CONTINUED ON CHART ____

To your relatives and descendants, no matter how neatly drawn, colored, and embellished with coat armor and fleur-de-lis, genealogy—lineage—shown in that fashion will serve mostly as a decoration for some seldom noticed wall and, except at a first reading by strangers, will be about as interesting as bugs running across the porch. Nevertheless, such charts may supplement or take the place of narrative (where, as said, early collateral lines are present of which nothing else is known), and also serve to render visible, make easier to comprehend, and to demonstrate the sometimes tedious and detailed narrative that you are about to write.

So, it is well to supplement your narrative by placing such three-, four-, or five-generation charts concerning the persons about whom that chapter or section is written, either at the beginning (preferably) or at the end of that chapter or section. That is especially true, where there is an ongoing repetition of given names. By so doing, your readers will be able to quickly place in perspective those persons of whom you write.

Such charts should be reduced to a size that does not take up any more space than is necessary, yet is big enough to be easily read. Notice that this decision as to the size of charts (and all other illustrations, maps, etc.) must be put off until later when you decide what the page-size of your book will be. If you use a publisher or printer, they will advise you of the maximum allowable dimensions they can accomodate.

In that regard, notice that a small (slightly larger than an average paperback) book is more economical to produce and to purchase; it also fits easier in the hand and on a bookshelf than the bulkier 8.5" x 11" size. Then too, special features such as fold-out maps and charts are costly to produce. Even if a publisher bears the entire cost of production, you don't want your book to be too expensive for anyone to afford!

Uses of Family Unit Charts

In addition to pedigree charts, we all have an attaché case full of "family unit charts" ("family group sheets"). These too will serve you well, where you feel the need to supplement or demonstrate the narrative, or where detail—more than that found in your pedigree charts—is needed, yet you do not intend to write at length concerning the persons and families named in these charts.

Just as you will use pedigrees at the beginning or end of each chapter or section, by also including unit charts where that marriage and family group are discussed, your readers will be introduced to the new players in the drama, and will find it easier to mentally place those family units where they belong among the many others. As with pedigree charts, when used as supplements such visual images are worth many words.

Uses of Writings of Others

In addition to pedigrees and unit charts, we all have used and read short narratives written by other members of our families; some distantly related, others more closely so. Some of such writings are well done, but unfortunately, most are dismally unprofessional, equally poorly written, carry few or no citations or references, and are usually autobiographical or consist of little more than a few unorganized anecdotes or family stories. After all, it too often is said, if Aunt Jane told us, it surely must be true. Except for the span of ten or so minutes required to read such materials, they are about as interesting as were the pedigree charts.

FAMILY UNIT CHART

X = Direct Ancestr
√ = LDS Temple Ord. Compl.

PREPARED BY _____

DATE _____

HUSBAND

	DATE -- DAY, MONTH, YEAR	CITY	OCCUPATION / COUNTY	STATE or COUNTRY	ANCESTRAL CHART #	FAMILY UNIT #
Born						
Christened						
Married						
Died						
Buried						
FATHER						
MOTHER						

OTHER WIVES:

WIFE maiden name

Born			
Christened			
Died			
Buried			
FATHER			
MOTHER			

OTHER HUSBANDS:

X √	SEX M/F	CHILDREN Living, Adopted, Dead—In Order of Birth	BIRTH Day	Month	Year	BIRTHPLACE City	County	St./Cty.	DATE OF FIRST MARRIAGE Name of Spouse	DATE OF DEATH City	County	State/Country
1												
2												
3												
4												
5												
6												
7												
8												
9												
10												
11												
12												
13												
14												

Remember though, even when poorly done, most such writings contain information that will serve as a starting place for some of your further efforts or may contain passages that are interesting and desirable for inclusion in your own more extensive writing. Indeed, if such materials were carefully done, and tell of hardships, pleasures, lifestyles, and the events of some distant time, they often add greatly to a larger work. So, all the while remembering that data without citations at best is untrustworthy, plan to add to your work (perhaps in an appendix) all reliable writings of significance.

Notice that while the unsubstantiated writings of others may not be dependable or trustworthy enough for you to cite as proof of this or that, they may be great time savers. Since that other writer apparently had some basis for believing the facts about which he or she wrote, you have an advantage in searching out proof of the information.

Suppose that without any authority or proof the suspect writing reveals to you that one of your great-grandfathers was born in New York, served in the Civil War, and died in Ohio in 1899. Your first inquiry should be an NATF-80 (see Appendix) sent to the National Archives, asking for a record of his military service. If he did serve, that record likely will be found and probably will tell you where he was born, how old he was when he was discharged and, if he drew a pension, where the pension checks were sent.

If his checks were sent to, say, Hamilton County, Ohio, from 1878 until his death, you now have a census (1880) to seek out to gain other information about him, especially the names and occupations of him, his wife and their children, and the place of birth of all. Next you might examine the county tax, deed, and mortgage records to learn of his assets and residences, local church records to seek out his religious affiliations, cemetery records of that county for the year 1899 to find his grave, and G.A.R. records to learn whether or not he was a member of that organization. If that census reveals that he was born in New York, by virtue of his age there given you have an approximate birth year and place, leading you to New York censuses and records of births, church affiliations, and marriages.

Unlike that other writer, you will have proved those facts stated and many more. So, no matter how poorly written some of your information may be, follow it up, find and make careful notes of the sources uncovered, and then write about it all. In setting forth those facts and the proof or sources, you may wish to acknowledge the effort of that less experienced researcher, thereby giving credit where it is due and perhaps creating a bond or friendship with that person. After all, but for the clues in that simple sentence, you might well have spent months gaining the same information and, indeed, may never have learned of it.

Uses of Numbering Systems

Few, if any, of us, including future readers of your writings, are able to remember the names of and important dates concerning the many ancestors of whom we have knowledge. Moreover, when met by a barrage of such dates and names, your readers will be even less able to gain an overall picture of your family.

So it is that numbering systems have been devised, providing an abbreviated view of ancestors and their relationships, one to the other. Most family histories incorporate one of these systems, to help the reader more easily understand it all. But caution; reading page after page of paragraphs filled with reference and generation numbers is not only tedious, it is as boring as a book full of family unit and pedigree charts printed out by some computer.

Children: 9 (Meacham):—

327. i. Sarah[6], b. abt. 1777; bap. Oct. 28, 1781; d. Jan. 21, 1865; said to have mar. Amos Shaw.

328. ii. Betsey[6], bap. Oct. 28, 1781; mar. —— Mosher.

329. iii. Azubah[6], bap. Oct. 23, 1781; mar. May 23, 1819, at Petersham, to Seth Hathaway.

330. iv. Benjamin[6], b. Jan. 25, 1784 at New Salem; d. Sept. 18, 1838, aged 57, at Athol; mar. Oct. 22, 1810, at Athol, Esther Blanchard, d. Apr. 7, 1849 at New Salem. Their children were: Benjamin[7], b. March 23, 1820; d. Nov. 13, 1896, at Worcester, Mass.; Hiram[7], b. Oct. 28, 1816; d. March 16, 1885; James[7], b. Oct. 24, 1813, at New Salem; mar. Nancy Hale; Clarissa[7], b. Nov. 19, 1825; mar. Nov. 18, 1846, at Athol, James Rice; Elvira[7], b. Jan. 6, 1811; mar. March 30, 1828, at New Salem, Royal Smith. Benjamin[7] (above) mar. Nov. 3, 1840, Catharine C. Walker of Petersham and was then a resident of New Salem.

331. v. Virsie (Vercey or Vira)[6], b. Oct. 7, 1794, at New Salem; mar. Jan. 4, 1816, at Petersham, Elias H. Hill; d. March 18, 1847; reported to have had 6 children. (Gravestone reads "Lucy.")

332. vi. Mary[6], ——; mar. Oct. 19, 1817, Joel Chamberlain of Dana.

333. vii. William[6], b. Dec. 27, 1789, at New Salem; mar. Sept. 11, 1811, Polly Stratton of Athol, who died Dec. 1, 1833, aged 41. William is reported to have taken a second wife, Mary Ann Stevens. He died Aug. 8, 1845, aged 55, at Athol.

334. viii. Hannah[6], b. ——, 1787, at New Salem; m. Ebenezer Stowell, d. 1862, at Ashford, N. Y.

335. ix. Rebecca[6], b. ——, New Salem; d. ——, Petersham, Mass.

134. WILLIAM[5] MEACHAM and his brother

135. JONATHAN[5] MEACHAM (William[4], John[3], Jeremiah[2], [1]), b. ab. Oct. 1730, according to his gravestone, which is probably incorrect, as his parents were married in Aug., 1731.

There is no record of the births of either of these brothers, nor of their sister Elizabeth, who were so closely associated with their cousins of New Salem, the children of Jeremiah[4] of that place. William and James Meacham are several times described as cousins of James (No. 122 ante) by Prof. Arthur Latham Perry in his *Origins in Williamstown.*

Jonathan Meacham was one of those who were interested with Capt. Ephraim Williams as promoters of the new town of West Hoosac, or Adams, in Dec. 1753 and remained in that locality for several years. In the spring of 1755 he and his brother William enlisted under Col. Ephraim Williams and were in the battle of Lake George on Sept. 8th, 1755. And in that same year William Meacham subscribed £3 and Jonathan Meacham £2, for the erection of a fort at West Hoosac. In the following year they were both engaged in service at Fort Massachusetts when, on June 7, 1756, William Meacham with his companion, Benjamin King, was shot down by a party of seven or eight Indians about 1/2 mile from the Fort while returning from a scouting trip.

Here, from the New York Genealogical and Biographical Record, Vol. 66, No. 1, 1935, pp. 34, 35 are some illustrations of narrative combined with a number system not unlike the NGS method. Notice that under #135, Meacham's activities are described and the source of that information is included within the text without the use of footnotes; in this case a

Chapter II: Planning Format

Soon afterwards, in the fall of 1779, Jonathan and his cousin John Meacham from Williamstown appeared as pioneer settlers in Fair Haven, Vt. (Hemenway, Vol. 3, p. 406) and in 1781 he was one of the first settlers of Benson, Vt. where he devoted his attention to agricultural pursuits and was prominent in civil and military affairs. He is also said to have had a family of seven sons and seven daughters with his wife THANKFUL RUGG (Carleton, Genealogical and Family History of Vt.). But Hemenway, Vol. 3, p. 407, states that Jonathan Meacham came to Benson in the spring of 1783 and settled there in the fall. He appears in the U. S. Census of 1790 as a resident of Benson with six males over 16 and five females. His sons William P. and Isaac Meacham also appear as residents of Benson in 1790, seemingly with five children each. Jonathan d. March 16, 1813, aged 83. Thankful d. Oct. 1, 1820, aged 86, "Old Cemetery," Benson, Vt.

Children: 16 (Meacham) (I.M.S.):—

336.   i. William H.[6], b. July 14, 1757, at Williamstown; d. Sept. 11, 1813, near St. Louis, Mo.; m. Eunice Olmstead.
337.   ii. Hawkins[6], b. ——; d. in infancy.
338.   iii. Lydia[6], b. 1760; d. 1773.
339.   iv. Jerusha[6], b. May 3, 1762; d. Aug. 1845; m. Feb. 9, 1780, Williamstown, Mass., to Stephen Olmstead.
340.   v. Oliver[6], b. Apr. 1763.
341.   vi. David[6], b. Oct. 6, 1764, Benson, Vt.; d. Aug. 6, 1846, Benson; m. Rhoda Parkhill.
342.   vii. Isaac[6], b. April 3, 1766, Williamstown; d. May 16, 1845, Brandon, Vt.; m. to Phebe Thompson and had family for which see Carleton Gen. and Fam. Hist. of Vt.
343.   viii. Joseph[6], b. Oct. 7, 1767, Benson; m. Katherine ——.
344.   ix. Ruth[6], b. Oct. 11, 1769, Benson; d. 1865, Prospect Park, Ill.; m. July 9, 1788 to Lemuel Standish.
345.   x. Matthew[6], b. Oct. 1771, Benson.
346.   xi. Diadama[6], b. Mar. 3, 1773, Benson; d. May 8, 1838, Benson; unmarried.
347.   xii. Peleg[6] (twin to Diadama), b. Mar. 3, 1773, Benson; d. May 18, 1814; m. (1) Anna Sherwood; m. (2) Eliza Stephens.
348.   xiii. Lydia[6], b. abt. 1777, Benson; d. Aug. 9, 1860, Benson; m. July 3, 1796, Benson, to Bishop Cramer.
349.   xiv. Thankful[6], b. 1784, Benson; d. Nov. 4, 1834, Benson; unmarried.
350.   xv. Rebecca[6], b. ——, Benson; m. to Stephen Sherwood.
351.   xvi. James[6], b. ——; d ——.

137.   ISAAC[5] MEACHAM (Isaac[4], John[3], Jeremiah[2],[1]) is the only child of Isaac[4] and Lydia (Layton) Meacham of Salem of whom there is any official record. He was born at Salem on April 27, 1726, and was married Oct. 29, 1751, at Salem by the Rev. Mr. Henchman to Ruth Dunnell, daughter of David and Keziah (Ramsdell) Dunnell, who was born in 1732. Lynn records show that Isaac died Nov. 6, 1794, aged 68 and that his widow died Dec. 15, 1814, aged 84 years.

satisfactory method of revealing the source of the information given. Notice also that the male line before Jonathan (#135) is shown in descending numbers, e.g., "William[4], John[3], Jeremiah[2], [1]" Notice too that the author of the article chose not to write concerning #136.

So, one of such numbering methods may be used where there are many names and dates, yet by reason of the lack of detail or interest, narrative is not intended. Notice, too, that just as numbering systems are not a substitute for good narrative history, pedigrees and family unit charts will not serve in the place of numbered lineage, since the charts are incapable of conveying more than a narrow range of information. So, whatever your reasons, use numbering systems, never instead of text, but as an addition to it, or as appendices.

Numbering systems assign numbers and letters to each person in each succeeding or preceding generation—1, 2, 3, 4, i, ii, iii, iv, A, B, a, b, etc. Such numbering usually is commenced with the number "1" being assigned to the earliest person of whom you intend to write (even though you may know the names of some members of earlier generations), or it may begin by assigning a letter or the number "1" to the very earliest person known in that line, whether or not you intend to write about him or her.

Let us consider a simple example: Suppose that you are tracing your Keiter lines, and the earliest member known is Heiner Keiter who was born, lived, and died in his native Germany. Next, suppose that the only son of Heiner was Johannes Keiter, who arrived at New York in 1675 with his son, Peter; that between 1700 and 1705 Peter had two sons, Johannes (II) and Harman; that Johannes and Harman, in their turns, had children, each naming a son, Peter, after the grandfather, immigrant Peter.

Suppose further that while you know but little about the others you have interesting facts concerning and narrative to write about the Peter born to Harman Keiter, he—Peter—being the fifth generation of that known line (1. Heiner, 2. Johannes, 3. Peter, 4. Johannes and his brother 4. Harman, and 5. Peter). Already the names are confusing, and if your reader is to untangle and remember these people, then the Peter born to Harman must somehow be distinguished from all other men named Peter, no matter to whom born.

Numbering Systems; Two Methods Explained (The First)

So, you are writing about the Keiters just mentioned, and intend to start with Peter, the son of Harman. You can reveal that starting point and relationship in either of two ways, 1) with numbers that <u>descend</u> to that Peter (5, 4, 3, etc.), or 2) with numbers that <u>ascend</u> to him (1, 2, 3, etc.).

If using descending numbers, you might write as follows:

> "Peter Keiter[1] (Heiner **A**, Johannes **4**, Peter **3**, Harman **2**, **1**) was born in early Pennsylvania, married there, died in the summer of 1804, and was buried on his farm at Skippack, Pennsylvania."

or:

> "Peter Keiter[1] (Heiner **A**, Johannes **4**, Peter **3**, Harman **2**, **1**) was born in early Pennsylvania, married there, died in the summer of 1804, and was buried on his farm at Skippack, Pennsylvania"

(the only difference being the superscription and font size assigned to the ancestors).

Look carefully at those numbers and letters: Peter was assigned #1 BECAUSE he is the first of whom you will write narrative, and his ancestors were assigned descending numbers from the most remote down to him.

That sequence also reveals that, even though you do not intend to write of him, the earliest Keiter known to you was Heiner, and since he did not come to the Americas he was assigned the letter "**A**." Had you known who his father and grandfather were, and if they also had not come to the American colonies, that father would have appeared just before Heiner Keiter[A] and might have been Heinrich Keiter[B], and the grandfather would have been Claudius Keiter[C].

Next, notice that Johannes was assigned the number "**4**", thereby revealing to the reader that he is the earliest Keiter known to have lived in the American colonies. Next comes Peter "**3**", by his number revealed to have been a son of Johannes and Harman's father. After Peter[3] comes Harman[2], the father of Peter[1], of whom you are about to write.

So, the letters and numbers—"Peter Keiter [1] (Heiner A, Johannes 4, Peter 3, Harman 2, 1)"—reveal the given names of the ancestors in Peter's direct Keiter line, and the number "1" standing by itself after "Harman 2" refers back to Peter—"Peter Keiter[1]"—and tells the reader that the discussion immediately following has to do with the family and activities of that person, Peter[1]. If, at this point, you do not fully understand, please reread these paragraphs until you do.

Suppose, instead of writing of Peter, the son of Harman, that you intend first to write of Peter, the son of Johannes. That could be written:

> "Our ancestor, Peter Keiter[1] (Heiner **A**, Johannes **4**, Peter **3**, Johannes **2**, 1) was born in early Pennsylvania, married there, died in about 1800, and was buried on his farm in Dauphin County."

or:

> "Our ancestor, Peter Keiter[1] (Heiner **A**, Johannes **4**, Peter **3**, Johannes **2**, 1) was born in Pennsylvania, married there, died in about 1800, and was buried on his farm in Dauphin County."

By so numbering these people, this Peter is clearly revealed to also be of the fifth generation in the line, and he is clearly shown to be a son of Johannes[2], a grandson of Peter[3], a great-grandson of Johannes[4], and a great-great-grandson of Heiner[A]. Once again, the ancestor of whom you are about to speak is assigned the number "1." As before, if you do not understand, reread the paragraph until you do.

Numbering Systems; Two Methods Explained (The Second)

While in the above examples of the first method the two fifth-generation Keiters named Peter who were to be your focus, and about whom your narrative was then to speak, were assigned the number 1, those same ancestors could just as readily have been given the number "4", with Heiner still being "A" and the next earliest known in those lines being assigned the number "1", as follows:

> "Peter Keiter[4] (Heiner **A**, Johannes **1**, Peter **2**, **Harman 3**, 4)"

or:

> "Peter Keiter[4] (Heiner **A**, Johannes **1**, Peter **2**, **Johannes 3**, 4)"

Observe in these two examples that your subjects, both Peter, even though they were in the fifth generation of Keiters named, became number "4", and not number "5". By so assigning the numbers, once again you have shown that Heiner[A] never came here, and you also have informed your readers that both Peters were of the fourth generation to live in the Americas. As before, Heiner's father, had you known him, would have been "B". Again, make sure you understand these examples or read this section over again; they are very important.

While the first method (where the numbers *descend* to the person of whom you are about to write) is preferred by some, others—including this writer—use the second method—*ascending* numbers—with the earliest American ancestor always being assigned the number "1." It is preferred because, through use of the ascending numbers method the reader always has an ongoing reference—a *generation number*—revealing the number of generations from the subject back to the earliest known American ancestor in that line.

If ascending numbers are used, as suggested, awkward as it would be, an 11th generation descendant of that first Heiner (A) might write his lineage as follows:

John Keiter[10] (Heiner A, Johannes 1, Peter 2, Harman 3, John 4, Henry 5, John 6, James 7, Peter 8, Peter 9, 10) or

John Keiter[10] (Heiner A, Johannes 1, Peter 2, Harman 3, John 4, Henry 5, John 6, James 7, Peter 8, Peter 9, 10) or

John Keiter[10] (Heiner[A], Johannes[1], Peter[2], Harman[3], John[4], Henry[5], John[6], James[7], Peter[8], Peter[9], 10).

Notice, having once set forth that clumsy sequence, thereafter (if writing of John[10], for example) the writer need only say, "John Keiter[10] (Peter 8, Peter 9, 10)", and the reader will be almost certain of John's identity.

Having selected one or the other methods—ascending generation numbers or descending numbers—you must tell your readers of that choice. The preface is a good place to do that, since some readers will not read chapters other than those dedicated to their own lines, and so may miss your explanation if it is placed somewhere other than in the preface.

So, if the first of a Bater line known to you is John[1], born New York, 1803, and his descendants were Henry, then John, then Martin, then John again (born 1908, and of whom you intend to write), your readers should be advised that you have set forth 1803 American born John as number "1" by reason of the absence of information concerning any earlier ancestors in that line. Somewhere in or following that explanation that Bater line might be written of as,

"Our John Bater[5] (John 1, Henry 2, John 3, Martin 4, 5) was born in 1898, lived in the Mohawk Valley, fought in World War I in the 8th Division, A.E.F., and died in 1964", or

"Our John Bater[5] (John 1, Henry 2, John 3, Martin 4, 5) was born in 1898, lived in the Mohawk Valley, fought in World War I in the 8th Division, A.E.F., and died in 1964."

Numbering Spouses in Direct Lines

Where you also wish to set forth a lineage of one or more spouses of people in an ascending sequence, yet again, by reason of lack of information or otherwise, you do not intend to write narrative about that marriage or spouse, or if you do, you do not intend to write it at that place in your book, a spouse's lineage is most conveniently set forth in a *descending* order. So, where Martin Bater^4 married Jane Smith, and her ancestors are known for three generations before her, the Bater sequence might be written as follows:

"Martin^4 (John 1, Henry 2, John 3, 4) married Jane Smith (John Smith 4, Henry 3, James 2)", and they had four children, (etc.)." or

"Martin^4 (John 1, Henry 2, John 3, 4) married Jane Smith (John Smith 4, Henry 3, James 2)", and they had four children, (etc.)."

By relating the wife's lineage in that fashion, your readers will know that Martin Bater^4 married Jane, whose ancestors known to you were John Smith, the earliest (John 4), then Henry (Henry 3) who followed, and then James (James 2), he James, the most recent and the father of Jane Smith Bater. Notice that it was not necessary to assign the number "1" to Jane, since it is apparent who she is. (Observe too; since none of the Smiths bear a superscripted letter, such as "A", after their name, you also know that they all lived in this country.)

It is very important that you remember here that Jane thereafter will be considered to be of the same generation as her husband, if the Bater line is that being traced. A discussion of how she would be numbered, were her Smith line being traced instead, will be found below.

A problem is also presented where we number through several marriages. Return for a moment to Peter Keiter^4 (the son of Johannes^3). Suppose that this Peter^4 had a daughter, Ruth, who married John Davis, and the Davises, in their turn, had a daughter, Betsy, who married Jim Houston. The Houstons then had you, Jane Houston. You would be an eigth-generation descendant of old Heiner Keiter^A, and a seventh-generation American in that direct line. In order that your readers understand that lineage and your place in it, somewhere at the beginning of the narrative concerning the keiters you might write:

The author, Jane Houston^7 (Heiner Keiter^A, Johannes^1, Peter^2, Johannes^3, Peter^4, **Ruth 5 Davis, Betsy 6 Houston**), married John Haskins, and had...(etc.)"

That numbered lineage for you—Jane Houston—reveals that your relationship to Heiner Keiter traces through Keiter males down to Peter^4, however, after him you trace through the female lines, namely, Peter^4's daughter, Ruth^5, who married a Davis, and the Davis daughter, Betsy^6, your mother, who married a Houston.

Be very careful to note here that the generation numbers of your grandmother, Ruth Keiter Davis, and your mother, Betsy Davis Houston, were placed BETWEEN their given names and their surnames—**Ruth 5 Davis** and **Betsy 6 Houston**, or **Ruth^5 Davis** and **Betsy^6 Houston**—thereby revealing that their generation numbers were assigned as a result of their Keiter ancestry (from Heiner down), and not as a result of their marriages to men named Davis and Houston. As always, if you do not understand any of these methods, it is advised that you reread this section.

National Genealogical Society (NGS) Method[1]

The above simple numbering methods serve nicely if the need is to state a single line of descent over several generations. However, it is easy to imagine that if such numbered lineage is extensive and continues over servral generations in several different lines, the reader will be required to undertake a tedious examination and comparison of those numbers and names, especially the common ones. That never ending problem has been addressed by many writers, and several systems have been devised.

Those systems, including what is konwn as the NGS (National Genealogical Society) method, are discussed in detail in a fine article by Ms. Joan Ferris Curran, C.G. [2] For our purposed here —to assist the writer of genealogical narrative—we suggest that the NGS system is the most easily understood and applied.

Simply stated, the NGS method directs that we assign numbers and letters to individuals in the order that they appear—come upon the scene, those numbers serving to identify discussions about that person that may appear elsewhere in the writing. So, if your mother is given number *81*, whenever that number appears in the narrative all will know that it is she who is being discussed. Likewise, when we come upon her in the writing, we can look up her number back in the big chart and see where she fits in the entire family.

Understanding The NGS System

To demonstrate the NGS method of numbering, suppose that the next marriage to be discussed in your book is "**Chapter 8: John and Cheryl Drake Bater;**" that John[5] being a son of Martin[4] and Jane. Now, if John[5] and his new wife, Cheryl, had six (6) children, and those about whom you intend to write are the daughter, Cheryl J., her marriage and some of her children, and the son, Hunter, and his marriage, those three (3) generations might be set forth at the beginning of the chapter or at that section of the narrative concerning those people as follows:

```
#60* John Bater5 md. #61* Cheryl Drake and had issue (6)
    #62  i   Prudence6, b. Feb. 2, 1932, md. Pablo _?_
    #63* ii  Hunter6, bapt. Sept. 25, 1934, md. #64* Elma Midlam; issue
#65    Evan Bater7
#66    Hunter, Jr.7
    #67  iii Anne6, b. Oct. 26, 1934, md. 1) #68 Ian Smith, 2) #180 Todd Haskins IV
    #69  iv  Mary Jane6, d. 1964 d.s.p.
    #70  v   infant6, d. Jan. 1, 1937
    #71* vi  Cheryl J.6, b. April 3, 1938, md. #72* William Cody, and had
#73*   Diane F. 7 Cody
```

First off, above notice the non-superscripted, bold-faced number "**(6)**" in parentheses at the end of the first line in the chart - "...and had issue **(6)**". Since that "**6**" is NOT superscripted and IS in parentheses we know that it represents the number of children born to the marriage of John and Cheryl.

---

1. This method is favored by most writers.
2. It is suggested that you read it; Joan Ferris Curran, *National Genealogical Society Quarterly*, Vol. 70, Number 3, September 1991, p. 183, et seq., "Numbering Your Genealogy: Sound and Simple Systems."

Then notice that each of those six children of John and Cheryl also has been assigned a number "6"; however because those ARE superscripted numbers - **6** - you know that they are "generation numbers," and they reveal the generation in that line to which those children belong (remember, John, their father, was generation 5 - $John^5$). So, where a number is superscripted AND immediately follows a name, it is a generation number, and if it is not superscripted and is in parentheses it reveals the number of children born to that person or marriage.

Next below, and within the same chart, in addition to 1) the superscripted generation numbers, 2) the non-superscripted number that reveals the number of children of the marriage, you will find 3) the Roman numerals "i" through "vi." Those numerals show the order of the birth of the six children of that marriage.

#60* John Bater^5 md. #61* Cheryl Drake and had issue (6)
    #62   i   Prudence^6, b. Feb. 2, 1932, md. Pablo _?_
    #63*   ii   Hunter^6, bapt. Sept. 25, 1934, md. #64* Elma Midlam; issue
  #65   Evan Bater^7
  #66   Hunter, Jr.^{7}
    #67   iii   Anne^6, b. Oct. 26, 1934, md. 1) #68 Ian Smith, 2) #180 Todd Haskins IV
    #69   iv   Mary Jane^6, d. 1964 d.s.p.
    #70   v   infant^6, d. Jan. 1, 1937
    #71*   vi   Cheryl J.^{6}, b. April 3, 1938, md. #72* William Cody, and had
  #73*   Diane F. 7 Cody

If, however, as often is the case, you do not know the order of birth, simply say so:

#60* John Bater^5 md. #61* Cheryl Drake and had issue (6)
(order of birth uncertain)
    #62   Prudence^6, b. Feb. 2, 1932, md. Pablo _?_
    #63*   Hunter^6, bapt. Sept. 25, 1934, md. #64* Elma Midlam; issue
  #65   Evan Bater^7
  #66   Hunter, Jr.^{7}
    #67   Anne^6, b. Oct. 26, 1934, md. 1) #68 Ian Smith, 2) #180 Todd Haskins IV
    #69   Mary Jane^6, d. 1964 d.s.p.
    #70   infant^6, d. Jan. 1, 1937
    #71*   Cheryl J.^{6}, b. April 3, 1938, md. #72* William Cody, and had
  #73*   Diane F. 7 Cody

But, back to where we were: Notice below that Arabic numbers **#60** through **#73**, **#7**, and **#180** appear just before the names of the people.

#60* John Bater^5 md. **#61*** Cheryl Drake and had issue (6)
    #62 i   Prudence^6, b. Feb. 2, 1932, md. Pablo _?_
    #63* ii   Hunter^6, bapt. Sept. 25, 1934, md. **#64*** Elma Midlam; issue
  #65   Evan Bater^7
  #66   Hunter, Jr.^{7}
    #67 iii   Anne^6, b. Oct. 26, 1934, md. 1) #68 Ian Smith, 2) **#180** Todd Haskins IV
    #69 iv   Mary Jane^6, d. 1964 d.s.p.
    #70 v   infant^6, d. Jan. 1, 1937
    #71* vi   Cheryl J.^{6}, b. April 3, 1938, md. **#72*** William Cody, and had
  #73*   Diane F. **#7** Cody

These Arabic numbers are the "individual reference numbers." They are assigned permanently to those named people, and serve to distinguish those people from everybody else in the book. These numbers are assigned as the individuals are encountered, and provide a handy and easy way to number and later identify paragraphs or sections that speak about those people.

Also notice above that **#73 Diane F. #7 Cody** carries that #7 in the middle of her name. That tells you that she appears elsewhere in association with another person - perhaps her husband, but almost certainly someone numbered #6 or #8. Then too, **#180 Todd Haskins IV** is not in order. As with Diane, you now know that he too will appear elsewhere in the book, most probably in association with #179 or #181.

Finally, notice the asterisks above - ***** - that follow the individual reference numbers assigned to numbers 60, 61, 63, 64, 71, 72, and 73. Those asterisks (or you could choose some other symbol such as "+", "^", "<", etc.) reveal to the readers that somewhere in the book you have written narrative or detail about those marked individuals. By ear-marking these reference numbers assigned to those about whom you have further written, once again your reader will have an easier task and will understand why some named people do not appear in the narrative. They will know that you intentionally left those people out, and did not just forget them (see the discussion of "closure" later in this chapter).

Applying the NGS and Other Systems

Application of the NGS method is easy. When you arrive at that point in the chapter where Cheryl J. Bater[6] and her family are to be discussed, you might commence that chapter or section with a paragraph using the NGS method, followed by the beginning sentences of the narrative, as below (notice that we have called the example paragraph that incorporates the NGS numbering a *Summary*):

> "Summary: #71 "Dr. Cheryl J. Bater[6] (John 5, 6) and her brother (#63), Hunter Bater[6] (John 5, 6), an architect of renown, were both graduated from Ohio State University in 1956. In 1958, #71 Cheryl J. married #72 William Cody[4] (Pierce 1, Virgil 2, Leonard 3, 4), he, previously a resident of South Petherton, Somerset, England, and had issue, in Columbus, Ohio, #73 *Diane F. Cody*[7] (b.1965). In 1960 Hunter married #64 Elma F. Midlam, of Marion, Ohio, and thereby had Evan·[7] (b.1962) and Hunter, Jr.·[7] (b.1964).
>
> Cheryl J. Bater, a daughter (probably the third) of World War I veteran John and Cheryl Drake Bater, was born at the General Hospital in Marion, Ohio, at about 1:00 A.M. on July 31, 1938. She first attended school at...etc."

Notice that in the Summary paragraph, since you were speaking of Bater lines and of descendants of Baters, Diane, daughter of Cheryl J.[6], became a "7"—*Diane F.*[7] *Cody*—and so too did Evan and Hunter Jr. gain the number 7—*Evan Bater*[7] and *Hunter Bater, Jr.*[7].

Yet look what happens if you are writing of the Codys and intended to continue on with that line: Diane F. now would be assigned the next number after her father,— William Cody[4]—and would be generation number 5, as follows:

> Summary: #71 "Dr. Cheryl J. Bater[6] (John 5, 6) and her brother (#63), Hunter Bater[6] (John 5, 6), an architect of renown, were both graduated from Ohio State University in 1956. In 1958, #71 Cheryl J. married #72 William Cody[4] (Pierce 1, Virgil 2, Leonard 3, 4), previously a resident of South Petherton, Somerset, England, and had issue, in Columbus, Ohio, (#73) **Diane F. Cody**[5] (b.1965).

Diane Cody, was born on September 25, 1965 in Fort Wayne, Indiana...etc., etc."

So, if discussing the Codys, when Cheryl J. married William[4], she assumed his generation number and become simply Cheryl J. Cody. Yet, if the Baters were the topic of the narrative at that point, she would be given the next number above that of her parent in the Bater line and be "Cheryl J.[6]" or "Cheryl J.[6] Cody", or "Cheryl J. (Bater[6]) Cody."

Finally, if Diane F. Cody[5] married a Thomas and had a daughter, Margaret, that child would be *Margaret [6] Thomas* of the Cody line and *Margaret [8] Thomas* in the Bater lineage. While tracing Diane in the Codys, we might write:

> #72 William Cody[4] (Pierce 1, Virgil 2, Leonard 3, 4) married #71 Cheryl J. Bater
> (John 6, Henry 5, John 4 Martin 3, John 2), and had issue #73 Diane F. Cody[5].
> Diane, in her turn married John Thomas, and had issue Margaret Thomas [6].

or, all the while speaking of the same family, yet writing of the Baters, we would write,

> #71 Cheryl J. Bater[6] (John 1, Henry 2, John 3, Martin 4, John 5) married #72
> William Cody[4] (Pierce 1, Virgil 2, Leonard 3, 4), and had issue #73 Diane F.[7] Cody.
> Diane, in her turn married #74 John Thomas, and had issue #75 Margaret
> Thomas [8]."

In all of the above, the readers are made aware that of the Bater line traced, Cheryl was the sixth generation known and her daughter, Diane, was the seventh, while, of the Codys, Cheryl was the wife of a man of the fourth Cody generation known, and had children of the fifth Cody generation.

Notice too, since Diane's child, Margaret Thomas, had not yet married, her generation number was one integer above that of the parent through whom the lineage was being traced. So, while Margaret was number 6 because her mother, Diane, was number 5 in the Cody line, that same Margaret became number 8 when it was the Bater line being stated because her mother, Diane, there was number 7.

Numbering Previously Unknown Folks

If you did not assign reference numbers to everybody, or if you did and then new discoveries are made, marriages occur, or children are born, what do you do? You must either somehow modify the numbers assigned, or renumber the entire work, which you cannot do without an incredible effort. As an example, suppose you arrive at the end of your final draft concerning all the known Bater and related lines and you have 460 numbered folks, and have not assigned numbers to any persons who died *d.s.p.*, including (iv) Mary Jane. Under those circumstances, the above Bater chart would have read:

> #60 John Bater[5] md. #61 Cheryl Drake and had issue (6)
> #62 i Prudence[6], b. Feb. 2, 1932, md. Pablo _?_
> #63* ii Hunter[6], bapt. Sept. 25, 1934, md. #64* Elma Midlam; issue
> #65 Evan Bater[7]
> #66 Hunter, Jr.[7]
> #67 iii Anne[6], b. Oct. 26, 1934, md. 1) #68 Ian Smith, 2) #180 Todd Haskins IV
> **iv Mary Jane[6], d. 1964 d.s.p.**
> #69 v infant [6], d. Jan. 1, 1937
> #71* vi Cheryl J.[6], b. April 3, 1938, md. #72* William Cody, and had
> #73* Diane F. 7 Cody

Now you learn that Mary Jane did not die young, and was a most interesting Korean War nurse about whom you surely want to write, even if only in an appendix. There is now no reference number that you can assign to her without adding some measure of confusion for the reader. Still, confusion or no, since she must be assigned some reference combination, it is suggested that you use her father's number, and add a lower case "a" to her name. In that instance, Mary Jane would become "#60a."

Similarly, suppose you had already numbered all persons in your work up to number 460, and you then learned that numbers #40 Charles B. Carner and #41 Daisy Bush had children, of whom you previously had known nothing. Your choice again is 1) exclude the children, and thereby publish a less than complete work, or 2) select some new combination number.

As with Mary Jane, that can be achieved by adding a letter and a Roman numeral to the number of the father, e.g., if that #40 Charles B. Carner and his wife, #41 Daisy Bush, had Maggie B. Carner and Edward C. Carner, Maggie could be designated, "#40a(i)" and Edward could be assigned "#40a(ii)." You would have thereby revealed their relationship to the Carners by assigning them their father's number plus "a"; and their order of birth to that couple through the use of Roman numerals (i) and (ii).

How to Include Marriages of Cousins in Numbering Systems

Finally in the matter of numbering, as frequently happens, you will encounter the problem of numbering folks who have married their cousins, distant and otherwise. The problem is easily solved. When you reach that point in the narrative where that marriage is revealed for the first time, simply tell the readers of that kinship.

So, again, if you are tracing Baters and find that our #180 Todd Haskins IV, the husband of #67 Anne Bater, was a great-great-great grandson of Henry Bater[2], hence was Anne's 3rd cousin, once removed, first add asterisks (*) to both their numbers to show that you have written of them at another place in the book, and then you might write:

#60 John Bater[5] md. #61 Cheryl Drake and had issue (6)
               (order of birth unknown)
   #62 Prudence[6], md. Pablo _?_
   #63* Hunter[6], bapt. Sept. 25, 1934, md. #64* Elma Midlam; issue
        #65 Evan Bater[7]
        #66 Hunter, Jr.[7]
   #67* **Anne**[6], b. Oct., 1934, md. 1) #68 Ian Smith,
                   2) **#180* Todd Haskins IV** [7]
   #69 Mary Jane[6], d. 1964 d.s.p.
   #70 infant [6], d. Jan. 1, 1937
   #71* Cheryl J.[6], born April 3, 1938, md. #72* William Cody, and had
        #73*Diane F.[7] Cody

Thereafter, to avoid confusion, even though they both are of the Bater line, you should use the husband's generation number (7) when you further trace that family. Notice that the confusion does not arise when tracing lines other than the Baters.

Following that chart, you should detail that marriage (and the generation difference), or, at that point, tell your readers that the story of that union will be discussed somewhere else. The summary paragraphs appearing at the first mention of those two cousins might be very elaborate, or might read simply:

Summary: #67 Anne Bater[6] married #180 Todd Haskins IV [7], her third cousin, once removed, a discussion of which lines, marriage, and persons may be found at #180, infra.

Summary: #180 Todd Haskins IV [7], a triple-great grandson of Henry Bater[2] (John Bater 1, Henry 2, Alice 3 Haskins, Todd Haskins 4, Todd, Jr. 5, Todd III 6, 7) married #67 Anne Bater[6] (John Bater 1, Henry 2, John 3, Martin 4, John 5), and had issue (3) Jane[8], Joseph[8], and Todd V [8]

Other Problems, and a Decimal System

As mentioned, very often you will know of many generations of names, yet have little or no information whatever concerning a large percentage of them. There is a commonly used decimal-like numbering system to show such people and their place in some family line. This numbering method is 1) usually used as an appendix with references there to chapters in the narrative, and 2) written with a minimum of detail and without symbols revealing discussion elsewhere concerning any of the individuals. As an aside, be careful to note that in decimal systems there is no place for information about spouses who are not related to the family by blood.

Here is a portion of the descendancy chart of Thomas (c. 1675-1758) and Anne Griffith (c. 1682-c1760) Drake, employing that system and beginning with one of their great grandsons, Dr. William K. Drake[4] (Thomas 1, Lazarus 2, Drury 3, 4). Dr. William is the first entry shown, and his number—**1.4.8.8.**—reveals to you that he is the 8th child of the 8th child (Drury [3]) of the 4th child (Lazarus [2]) of #1 Thomas Drake [1] and his wife Anne Griffith:

1.4.8.8. Dr. William K. DRAKE (1824-1882) = Susan Cole (1828-1896) (See Chapter VII for a discussion of this line.)
  1.4.8.8.1. Mary Alice DRAKE (1851-1859) d.s.p.
  1.4.8.8.2. Ida A. DRAKE (1854-1923) = **Isaiah Staley**
  1.4.8.8.2.1. Lorenzo (Ren) Clare Staley = _?_, died young
  1.4.8.8.2.1.1. Artho Staley
  1.4.8.8.2.1.2. Darrell Staley (killed WW II)
  1.4.8.8.2.1.3. George Staley = _?_
  1.4.8.8.2.1.3.1. etc. issue unknown
  1.4.8.8.2.2. Robert Staley = Priscilla _?_
  1.4.8.8.2.2.1. Priscilla Dean Staley d.s.p.
  1.4.8.8.2.3. Grover Staley = Clara Melcher Kibler
  1.4.8.8.2.3.1. Gerard Kibler (adptd) = _?_
  1.4.8.8.2.3.2. Gladys Kibler (adptd) = _?_
  1.4.8.8.2.3.2.1. Howard _?_
  1.4.8.8.2.4. Howard Staley = Clarice _?_
  1.4.8.8.2.4.1. Miriam Staley = _?_ Brinkman
  1.4.8.8.2.5. Eva Staley = 1.) Harley Norton
  1.4.8.8.2.5.1. Bobby Norton
  1.4.8.8.2.5.2. Lyle Norton = _?_
  1.4.8.8.2.5.2.1. etc., issue unknown
  1.4.8.8.2.5.   = **2.) Russell Wise**
  1.4.8.8.2.5.3. **Barbara Jean Wise** = Paul Baird
  1.4.8.8.2.5.3.1. _?_ Baird (son)
  1.4.8.8.2.5.3.2. _?_ Baird (daughter)
  1.4.8.8.2.6. Grace Pearl Staley = Walter J. Kerr
  1.4.8.8.2.6.1. Marilyn Virginia Kerr = _?_
  1.4.8.8.2.6.2. Betty June Kerr = Roger K. Burke
  1.4.8.8.2.6.2.1. Roger Michael Burke
  1.4.8.8.2.6.2.2. Patty Burke = Martin Row

1.4.8.8.2.6.2.2.1. Tara Lindsey Row
1.4.8.8.2.6.3. James W. Kerr = Polly Malone
1.4.8.8.2.6.3.1. Diane Eve Kerr = Roger Osbourne
1.4.8.8.2.6.3.1.1. Jessica Osbourne
1.4.8.8.2.6.3.1.2. Will Osbourne
1.4.8.8.2.6.3.2. Robin Kerr = Michael Burnett
1.4.8.8.2.6.3.2.1. Ian Burnett =
1.4.8.8.2.6.3.3. Amy Kerr = David Nezat
1.4.8.8.2.6.3.3.1. James Nezat
1.4.8.8.2.6.3.4. Walter James Kerr
1.4.8.9. John Drake =
1.4.8.9.1. A. J. Drake = Sallie Pender

In order to understand this simple system, turn your attention to the number for Dr. William Drake, "**1.4.8.8.**" It is the first entry in the list above. Notice that William's number—1.4.8.8.—also is included within every entry thereafter except the last two.

Now look at these last two entries, "**1.4.8.9.** John Drake" and "**1.4.8.9.1. A. J. Drake.**" They tell you that the writer has concluded the known descendants of W. K. Drake (1.4.8.8.), the 8th child of the 8th child, etc., and has commenced the listing for John Drake (1.4.8.9.), the 9th child of the 8th child, etc., and his first son, A. J. Drake, 1.4.8.9.1.

Notice that both W. K. and John both have the numbers "**1.4.8.**" within their individual numbers (1.4.8.8. and 1.4.8.9.). That fact tells you that they are brothers, and sons of whoever is "8" of "1.4.8." Since W. K. and John are numbers 8. and 9. after 1.4.8., you also know that they had seven other brothers and sisters—1.4.8.1., 1.4.8.2., 1.4.8.3., etc.

Then look at "1.4.8.8.**1.** Mary Alice Drake." Notice that she has her father's (Dr. William) complete number, to which the number "1" has been added, thereby revealing that she was the first child born to the marriage of Dr. Drake and his Susan Cole. As always, the *d.s.p.* means that Mary Alice died without issue.[3]

Next look at 1.4.8.8.**2.**, Ida Drake; she is the second child of W. K. and Susan (thus the "2" following her father's complete number). The " = " after her name reveals a marriage, following which her husband is identified as **Isaiah Staley**. Since here, as throughout this chart, WE ARE TRACING DRAKES, the first son of Isaiah and Ida— **Lorenzo**—is assigned his mother's complete number to which, once again, is added the number 1, since he is the first child of that marriage. Thus we have 1.4.8.8.**2.1.** for Lorenzo.

Next look at **1.4.8.8.2.1.3.**, George Staley (the third child of Lorenzo). It is said by family members that he married and had several children, however nothing is known of any of them. So he has the "= _?_" symbols following his name, indicating his marriage to an unknown woman, and then below his name, and showing the existence of known but unidentified children, is the number and word "1.4.8.8.2.1.3.**1. etc.**" So, through that indication it is revealed that, though unknown to the writer, there were such children. Should George Staley or his descendants look in the index under his name, they may be able to place themselves in this family line.

Finally, look at "**1.4.8.8.2.5. Eva Staley.**" From the marriage symbol (=) we know that she married **Harley Norton**, and from the "**1)**" appearing just before his name, we

---

3. From the Latin, *decessit sine prole.*

know that he was the first of more than one spouse. The two children of the Eva-Harley Norton marriage are then shown (1.4.8.8.2.5.1. and 1.4.8.8.2.5.2.).

Following those entries (repeating her number but without again giving Eva's name) the number "**2**)" appears, telling us of the second marriage of Eva, and of that husband's name, **Russell Wise**. Then, in her turn, appears Barbara, a child of Eva and Russell. Notice that Barbara, the child of Eva and Russell Wise, was assigned the number 1.4.8.8.2.5.**3.**, even though it was the first born of that marriage. The reason is that it was the third child born to Eva in the Drake line, and it is that line being traced.

So, in this system, to number a child, simply take the full number of the parent in the direct line from the first ancestor on the chart, to which we add the number that represents the birth order of that child. Accordingly, and as shown, since 1.4.8.8.2. Ida Drake (Staley) had Lorenzo (1.4.8.8.2.**1.**) as her first child, Ida's second child became "1.4.8.8.2.**2.** Robert Staley," the third "1.4.8.8.2.**3.** Grover Staley," etc.

This method is not only simple to write out, it is, as mentioned, eminently practical for use in an appendix. Notice though, unless you index this (and all other appendices, for that matter) it is of very little value to the readers, since they must read every entry to determine whether or not and where they might fit.

In spite of all that has been said, remember that much, if not most, of your narrative will not require numbering. If you are writing of the lives of ancestors, and telling stories of their wives, children, residences, lives, deaths, and burial places, such explicit numbering may not only be unnecessary, in some cases it may seriously detract from the stories being told.

So, at the beginning of any chapter (or anyplace else, for that matter) where there are to be many names or a confusing duplication of names, or if you think it necessary to provide an overall view of the families to be discussed there, number them in one fashion or another. Likewise, where there are many generations to be discussed, when the facts at hand are few in number, or where you feel a need to again remind a reader where this or that person fits in the whole family or story, make use of the numbering systems.

So much for forms, charts, writings, and numbering. If your work is to be both interesting and educational, you will be called upon to use all of the tools at your disposal. Still though, if any one of those devices does not clarify or add to understanding, do not use it; a chart that confuses is worse than no chart.

Summary as to Forms, Charts, Writings, and Numbering

Begin now to think of anecdotes told to you or written by others, and of family unit charts that contain detail as to marriages and brothers and sisters of your subjects. Think too of pedigree charts for use where only the barest detail is needed or intended, and of numbering methods that might provide overall perspective. And, whenever you have an idea as to placement or need for any of such tools, make a note, either in the narrative rough draft or in a file dedicated to that portion of your work.

Footnotes or Endnotes?

While the contents and style of footnotes and endnotes will be discussed later, whether to place such citations of sources and short explanations in footnotes (at the bottom of each page) or in endnotes (at the end of each chapter) is a proper subject in this consideration of format.

Where you place such notes is entirely a matter of preference, based upon what you feel will best meet the requirements and desires of your readers; not yours, theirs. There are no rules of importance in the matter, except that you be consistent. In making that decision (and it is important to remember that you can change your mind at any time before the final draft is completed) you should consider what effects both formats may have upon your readers.

Rather than disrupt the flow of your words, many of your readers will skip the notes. Thereafter, however, some will return to the narrative, reconsider your statements, and compare your sources with their own. Others—perhaps a majority— will never again think about those notes, whether at the end of the chapter or on each page. So then, what makes the difference where they are?

To those who, in the years to come, will use your work as a reference (and you hope they will be many in number!) it likely will be more convenient if the notes appear on each page; otherwise, whenever a reader questions your statements, wishes to compare your sources with his own, or seeks that little bit more of information, he must leave the course of the narrative, move the often numerous pages to the endnotes, read and consider that source, and then move back to the page where he was and there seek to regain the chain of thought. The only other choice you have given that reader is to wait until the chapter is read through and then to read all the endnotes at once, all the while moving to and fro the narrative; a most ineffective and frustrating method of study.

If the notes are on each page, your readers need only direct their attention to the bottom of that page, compare and consider the note, and then return the short distance up the page to the narrative. By shortening that time/distance factor, the flow and context of the narrative is more easily retained by the reader.

In addition to sources and authorities, occasionally you will have an explanation, an anecdote, or a quantity of information concerning one of the characters or subjects that is too brief to be used as an additional paragraph of narrative, much less an appendix. When such matters arise, they should be placed in footnotes, even if several sentences in length. Footnotes are better than endnotes here also, since once again flow needs to be maintained in reading. Notice though, if you have many such anecdotes or explanations, the result may be page after page where the space taken up by the notes is nearly equal to that occupied by the narrative, the net result being confusion and, again, a loss of the chain of thought. Consider omitting the information altogether if it is too far removed. You must decide where to draw the line—maybe you'll have enough material for another book!

So, as you write, think about the matter of where to place the notes, even though that decision need not be made until later. The form of the final draft will make the answer simple.

Conclusion

After all the text or narrative, and before the *How to Use The Index* and *Index* sections, is the place for the *conclusion*. The contents of conclusions are dealt with in Chapter 1 above. As to format, little need be said. Keep it short and simple and usually without footnotes, illustrations, and detail.

Appendices

Appendices almost always appear at the end of the writing, immediately after the conclusion. They may consist of any number of different types of materials. As with all chapters and sections, they should bear titles that are instructive and arouse curiosity. The partial table of contents shown here and on the following page is an example of a well ordered series of appendices.[4]

This table is instructive in its content. Notice that it has three (3) appendices that are ascendant in nature—"Some ancestors of..." (#1, #2, and #3); four (4) that speak of descendants (#8, #9, #10, and #12), one (1) that reveals the issue of an early marriage (#11), four (4) that are recollections of other writers and kin (#4, #5, #6, and #7), and two (2) that are abstracts and extracts of other sources; namely, records of cemeteries and of early courts (#14 and #15). If you wish, you may use letters instead of numbers, e.g., *Appendix N: Some Miscellaneous Cemetery Records....*

Materials Placed after the Appendices

Bibliographies, lists of references, and any tables, calendars, and lists of people, institutions, companies, or addresses are additional material that you might decide to include. As to these unindexed materials, just as with so many other considerations, there are no hard and fast rules, except that they be carefully captioned. Remember, when such sections are not indexed the only clues the reader has to their contents are the titles (captions) that appear at the top of each such section and in the table of contents.

So, perhaps even more so than in some other sections, give careful consideration to the titles of non-indexed materials. As always, your goal is to make your work a convenient and complete research source.

---

4. Paul Drake, *Now In Our Fourth Century: Some American Families*, (Heritage Books, Inc., Bowie, MD, 1994) (with minor changes for purposes of example).

Font Styles and Sizes

Too many writings done by amateurs employ exotic font styles. For the same reasons that we should not seek out cumbersome and seldom used words, we also should not select a font style that is unusual, seldom seen, or that causes our writings to be difficult, tedious, or tiring to read.

This book, like many others, is printed in *Bookman*, this paragraph is in 10 point type, and the indented and superscripted characters and paragraphs found throughout are in 8 or 9 point type. The paragraph below is in 10 point *Courier New*, a font also used by many.

There are several other acceptable fonts, and, once again, there are no rules about which to use, except, as said, leave the fancy typefaces to those who do wedding invitations and captions for paintings and diplomas. An examination of the following fonts will readily illustrate the wide variations in appearance:

Font style is important, and this is Brush Script MT.

Font style is important, and this is Brittanic Bold.

Font style is important, and this is Times New Roman.

Font style is important, and this is Arial.

The difficulties and eye strain encountered in reading in these fonts is apparent. So always avoid fancy type styles; the comfort of the reader is paramount.

Having considered format and content, it is time to move to other matters.

Chapter III: Evidence and Proof

"You cannot demonstrate an emotion or prove an aspiration."
John Morley, *Rousseau*

"For when one's proofs are aptly chosen, four are as valid as four dozen."
Matthew Prior, *Alma*

Genealogical narrative and family history are nothing more than a series of statements based on evidence of lineage and facts having to do with ancestors and kin, which evidence and facts you have gathered together in your research and set forth in an interesting (hopefully) and orderly fashion. When you write that your 4th-great grandmother was born on February 2, 1732, married on December 17, 1748, and died on June 5, 1817, since it is quite apparent to all that you could not have been present to witness those events, your reader will—must—infer that you have gained those dates from source records, and that you believe them to be true. By stating those facts and dates, you have set forth a statement concerning a conclusion you have reached from the evidence that you have uncovered about that person.

All statements concerning family and lineage are of that nature. Even where you personally witnessed events of which you write, you are stating facts that are evidence, the source of that evidence being your own memory. So it is that if you are to gather, state, and discuss genealogical evidence, a basic understanding of the matter is required.

Evidence

First off, we very much suspect that what we are about to describe as methods, approaches, and tests may be called by some, *common sense*. The problem is that, while perhaps true, that expression tells us less than nothing about how to explain and evaluate genealogical proof. To say that "common sense tells us" something or other is as useless as telling us that newspapers are hearsay; the listener knows not a whit more than he or she did before.

Indeed, so much foolishness has been written by genealogists concerning such words as *preponderance, secondary, circumstantial, contraindication, direct*, etc., that it is urged that you erase from your mind all ideas, preconceived notions, and labels that you now have concerning evidence and proof. Let us start with a clean mental blackboard, and move through some of the many genealogical sources with an eye to what values as genealogical evidence any of them may—MAY—be found to have.

It is critical that you remember always that every single fact, word, memento, monument, and state of being that in any way, no matter how slight, tends to prove some matter of lineage is evidence. And, the only difference between any two bits of evidence is in their quality, and not in their nature.

Even those matters that are glibly called *clues* are evidence, albeit sometimes of little weight, and the most distorted and remote family tale and tradition is every bit as much a piece of evidence as is a solemn and precise entry in a court record or deed book. The difference lies only in the weight to be given the clue or garbled tale, as opposed to that weight to be assigned to the court record; the former often unreliable and the latter surely quite the opposite. So, from here on you should consider as evidence any and all materials that give even the slightest direction to your search, and then diligently determine the weight to be given to those bits of information.

Proof

Proof is but an accumulation or aggregation of evidence; a collection of evidentiary facts of varying weights and value. When we say that something has been *proved*, we are saying that our little pile of evidence concerning that question has grown to such a size and weight—evidentiary value, probity—that a conclusion is apparent, warranted, and should be made by everybody who is reasonable.

So, how big does our stack of evidence have to be before we are able to say that it is clear and convincing, and that we have proved something? The answer to that question is easy when the evidence is clear and precise as to the question posed; quite usually we all would agree to its adequacy.

On the other hand, when the problem is a difficult one, and the evidence is not precisely on point or is only narrowly believable, reasonable persons may differ as to its adequacy in proving the statement. In these cases, whether or not the evidence offered is sufficient to constitute proof often depends upon who the judge is. How so?

Measures of Proof Required by Organizations

Generally speaking, in our writing we should strive to set forth a measure of proof as to each family connection that would satisfy the requirements of the more scholarly organizations. If, in order to gain admission to such a society, we are required to prove a birth year, and we have at hand a birth certificate issued by a state bureau of vital statistics, most everybody would consider the requirement satisfied. Almost everyone of ordinary intelligence would agree that this single document constitutes proof enough, even though there well may be errors in that certificate, since it, like all writings, was done by fallible humans.

If there was no such birth certificate, yet there was a Bible entry written ten years later by an aunt, and also an old letter from one cousin to another stating that the birth did take place as written in the Bible, while most would agree that the year is thereby established, that decision is up to the judge or board or panel or whoever of that society has been designated as the final arbiter. Thus, when others, such as the Colonial Dames, D.A.R., or S.A.R., are to determine the adequacy of the proof you have gathered, then you must seek out, study, and meet their required standards.

Societal and organizational standards (unfortunately) are sometimes set forth in some variation of the legal expression "preponderance of the evidence." Preponderance means nothing more than that the greater weight—a "preponderance"—of the evidence favors one conclusion over some other conclusion also at hand. If the evidence supporting one answer outweighs that supporting some other, then the argument having the greater weight is considered proven; one group of evidentiary facts "preponderates" over some other; not over ALL others, over only those others presented for consideration. *That amount of proof is not sufficient to conclude matters of lineage.*

To demonstrate that a preponderance of evidence is inadequate for any serious researcher, one need but consider the following example: Suppose you want to prove that Mary had only one brother, John. Next, suppose that you have two (2) documents; an affidavit from John saying that he was Mary's only brother, and a letter from an aunt stating that she thought there were additional brothers. If a mere preponderance of the evidence is required, then we would have to say that you have proved that there was only one brother, since surely an affidavit from the brother himself would outweigh—preponderate—over a letter from some aunt. Silly? Of course; the matter is not yet proven either way. So, preponderances simply are not enough.

The inadequacy of a "preponderance" in matters of genealogy being apparent to everyone, in their attempts to solve the dilemma and permit an understanding of their requirements some organizations have ruled that their applicants must submit an "overwhelming preponderance," "a preponderance with contrary findings distinguished," "a preponderance with no contraindications," etc., etc. Such definitions are extremely difficult—indeed, impossible—to apply, the reason being simply that the word preponderance means that one pile of evidence outweighs some other pile, and to add modifiers to the word brings only contradictions of terms.

Most of the examiners of proof of the more careful and demanding of the organizations, such as the N. S. S. A. R.[1] and N. S. D. A. R., give very careful consideration to whether the evidence presented indeed does "preponderate" in favor of a suggested relationship. If it does, they take the further and most sensible intellectual step; since it would be impossible (and surely non-productive) to undertake to refute all other possiblilties, they look to the quality (and quantity, it must be admitted) of the totality of evidence shown in favor of that suggested kinship. If, upon that consideration, they are satisfied that the evidence is clear and convincing and, moreover, there are no more satisfying alternatives, the matter is considered settled; the relationship is said to be proven for their purposes. Even here still, the rule is easier to state than it is to apply, since evidence that is quite convincing and eminently clear to one researcher may be less so to another. Notice, however, that a rule that "proof must be clear and convincing" surely is more understandable than a rule that "proof must be by the weight of the evidence with other possibilities distinguished."

Finally, while the law in criminal cases requires that guilt be established "beyond a reasonable doubt" (not ALL doubt, mind you, only "reasonable" doubt), that rule surely does not work for our purposes, since events of the distant past almost never are so clear and well defined. To suggest that ALL doubt must be eliminated or ALL other possibilities distinguished is simply silly, and even more surely impossible. Human affairs can not ever be ascertained to that degree of certainty, not even our own paternity!

Measures of Proof Required by Ourselves

It is said by a few that if you are not seeking admission or recognition by someone or other, then you need only satisfy yourself concerning sufficiency of the proof offered. But, is that all you must do, really? The answer is no. As researchers and writers, whether or not we are to be judged by others, whether or not our proof is to be scrutinized by outsiders or by only our own family, we have the solemn duty to provide that quantity or measure of evidence that intellectually honest, sophisticated, and sincere people would accept as sufficient.

Stated otherwise, and aside from all the poorly defined labels such as preponderances and contraindications, etc., the proof we offer and write of must be such that reasonable and intelligent genealogists—all the while aware that no proof ever can be absolutely certain—would be satisfied that, while other answers may come to mind, the conclusions stated are the most compelling of the possibilities that flow

---

1. For the following definition of a most difficult, subjective and tedious concept, we are in large part indebted to Ms. Susan Acree, Genealogist/Examiner, N. S. S. A. R., Louisville, Kentucky.

No. *163.159*

APPROPRIATION. }

Bounty Act July 11 1862, 75,
Pay or Rolls. 23.75
$98.75

TREASURY DEPARTMENT,
SECOND AUDITOR'S OFFICE,

April 29 , 186*5*

I certify, That I have examined and adjusted the claim of

John E. McCann decd Priv D 13 Cav. Trimbles

and find there is due *him* from the United States the sum of *Ninety Eight*

dollars and ___ *75* ___ cents, being for

Pay &c from Muryt to June 27 1864 & the
Bounty of $100. under Act July 22 1861.

as appears by the account and vouchers herewith transmitted for the decision of the Second Comptroller of the Treasury thereon. To be paid to *William W. McCann Father of*

deceased or *his* order, by any Paymaster of the Army, in the
district of the claimant's residence. *Tenn*

E. B. French
Second Auditor.

Second Comptroller's Office,

$98.75

May 6 , 186*5*

The above claim of *Ninety-eight*

dollars and *75* cents is admitted.

Second Comptroller.

[Should this Certificate be assigned, the blanks for date and the Paymaster's name will not be filled until the Certificate is taken up as a voucher by a Paymaster.

The blank for the amount will be filled at time of transfer, and the receipt signed by the original payee. The form for transfer on the back of the receipt will be filled with the name of the assignee, dated and signed by the same person who signed the receipt, in the presence of two witnesses. All these signatures to the assignment will be made before and attested by a Notary Public or Justice of the Peace—the officer before whom the original affidavit of applicant for arrears of pay was made, if possible.]

Received this *third* day of *August* 186*5*
from *L. T. Thruston* Paymaster *Ninety eight*
dollars *Seventy five* cents, in full of the above

Witnessed by—

Geo R Adrian

James N. Craig

} *William W. McCann*

Here from the Civil War military records of John E. McCann, available through the National Archives, it is learned that John served in the "13th Cav(alry, known as) Trimbles", and that he was killed or died on June 27, 1864. Moreover, it is here shown that his father, William W. McCann (who was literate), was the beneficiary and received the sums due John at his death, namely $98.75, about $3000 in 1996 money.

from the evidence gathered. Nothing further is required of you (as if that were not burden enough!).

Evidence: Qualitative Examples

All evidence is absolutely neutral until we decide how we will use it. The genealogist has not been born who can state the value or reliability of this or that source unless and until you state what it is that you would prove through the use of that material. Any single bit of evidence may be very powerful in proving one proposition, yet equally weak if tendered as proof of some other matter to which it speaks.

As an example, a Civil War discharge certificate of your ancestor may not be spoken of as reliable, unreliable, or somewhere in between until you state what it is that you seek to prove through the use of that document. If you intend to use it to establish that the soldier named there served during that war, the paper is very powerful evidence, almost incontrovertible in fact. Notice though that if, instead, you propose to use that identical discharge paper to prove the spelling of the surname of that veteran, the document is considerably less convincing; we all know that if the soldier was illiterate or was not present when the certificate was written, the discharging officer or some bystander supplied the spelling. And finally, if you were to undertake to establish the patriotism of that ancestor the evidence provided by the same discharge paper is very weak indeed, since he probably was drafted and had little choice as to his participation in the fighting.

Perhaps more than any other bit of family material one could imagine, a recently uncovered, handwritten, single sentence letter vividly illustrates that every item of genealogical evidence must be scrutinized carefully, and may have widely varying degrees of value, reliability, and weight depending completely and entirely upon what it is that you hope to prove by its use. That letter read simply:

"Nebraska Territory
June 23, 1853

My Dear James:

Judge Cole has informed me that Father is dead, and I thought you would want to know.

Love
Betsy"

What all does that letter prove? Read it again. The careful researcher will notice that this simple letter is very powerful evidence and reliable to the utmost degree in proving several things; namely a) that Betsy was in Nebraska during some part of June, 1853, b) that she knew and had some measure of affection for someone named James, c) that she had gained information from a Judge Cole, d) that her father was dead prior to the date of the letter, and e) that Betsy was literate.

Notice however, that as to whether or not the father had died shortly before the date of the letter or, instead, had by then been dead for some number of months or even years, the evidentiary value of the letter is much, much less. Similarly, while the letter provides some evidence that James was alive when it was written, it is not conclusive as to that fact; considering that it was 1854, he may have died before the letter without Betsy having learned of his death. Finally, whether James was Betsy's brother, even though again the letter is some evidence as to that fact, the matter is not established; the evidence is clearly insufficient to prove that fact.

Consider too: it stretches our imagination to say that the letter provides evidence as to whether the judge lived nearby or far away. We are unable to say even whether the judge wrote or spoke to Betsy. Significantly, as to where James lived, considering that in the 1850s there were no automobiles or telephones, the letter is substantial evidence that he did not live in the area of Betsy's residence, yet were the letter written one hundred years later—in the 1950s—we would be near certain that he lived at some distance, otherwise surely she would have phoned James, driven over to relay the message, or asked someone else to tell him when next they met.

Then too, look again. Rather than having been of the judiciary, could "Judge" have been a given name, as it sometimes was? Finally, if you knew, in fact, that Betsy and James were brother and sister, is there evidence here that James was estranged from the family? From the father? From Betsy? Perhaps, but we are unable yet to make any conclusions as to those matters; while some evidence is present as to all those questions, more is needed before proof is established. All that from a one-sentence letter.

So, never speak in the abstract about reliability or value as evidence of this or that source of information, unless you also reveal what it is that you hope to prove through the use of that material. As another example, do not tell your reader that a county history is reliable or unreliable, unless you also state what it is that you are seeking to prove with that book. As we shall see, among many other matters, county histories are often very reliable in the maps they contain, in confirming the presence or whereabouts of some of the people named therein and their occupations, and as to lists of public and elected officers and officials.

Evidence and Reliability: General Considerations

The earth is not populated by liars, nor has it ever been. For the most part, your ancestors usually told and wrote the truth as they perceived it to be, just as you do. How, then, do we determine the worth and reliability—the probative value, as it is called—of the evidence we uncover?

First, since we usually know what it is that we seek to establish, we decide what portions of a writing will be used to prove that fact and, at least for that moment, ignore the balance of information contained in that source. For example, if using a birth certificate to establish a birth date, we pay little heed to the statements written there about birthplaces of the parents of the dead person. Similarly, if using a military discharge to establish a birth year, we ignore the unit or regiment, the physical description of the soldier, and the place of discharge, yet note carefully his or her age on the date of that certificate and the place of birth (in order to later confirm our deductions). So, having in mind what you want to prove, select the portion of the evidence before you that will assist in that proof.

Tests of Evidence, Generally

Having determined what portions of the evidence are critical at the moment, how do you measure the evidentiary—probative—value, the reliability and believability of those words or portions? You do it by considering: 1) the motives or incentives that likely encouraged the actor or writer to be accurate (or inaccurate) in setting forth that portion that speaks to your question, 2) the capacity and opportunity (or lack of the same) of that author or maker to know or ascertain and to understand the true facts, 3) the probability of loss of memory, that is, the likelihood of unintentional error by reason of the passage of time, 4) the constraints or requirements—intellectual, social, religious, legal, or occupational—that likely served to increase or to decrease the accuracy as to those facts.

Those tests will serve in your consideration of all genealogical evidence, and examples are everywhere. Always, always remember, though, that those factors are only helpful AFTER you have determined what portions—what particular words—of the document might assist you in the proof of the matter at hand.

Tests of Evidence: 1) Motives

Notice that genealogical materials found in newspapers or publications other than those dedicated to genealogical studies sometimes are suspect because the motives at play usually were to make a profit through popular interest, and were not to write good genealogy. Then too, the editor of those publications may not have had an opportunity to know of the true facts; he or she likely accepted it as written by a staff person.

As examples, in matters concerning family history the writings in the North Carolina Genealogical Journal are quite likely to be more accurate and reliable than those in the daily newspaper. The reason is simply that the motive in publishing NCGSJ is to provide a place for well researched family matters, while the motive at play at the newspaper office is to provide knowledge of facts and events to a wide and varied audience, and to do so at a profit.

No matter how honest both are, NCGSJ sells genealogy, while the newspaper sells news of a much broader nature. Remember though, as to some specific question of lineage that appears to be answered by an article in such a journal, careful as he or she may have been (and usually is) and proper though the motives at play doubtless were, the editor and staff probably had little or no opportunity to otherwise confirm the materials submitted.

Tests of Evidence: 2) Knowledge and Understanding

If establishing matters of birth and parentage, we trust the writings of a mother, a father, or their other children, simply because those folks probably had the greatest opportunity to know of the true facts. And, we also think—rightly or wrongly—that they are not likely to lie concerning such matters. So, even though one can imagine many situations where others would have had a better opportunity to know the truth of it all, in the absence of a showing of such other circumstances, when we seek to know what children were born to particular parents we trust the statements made by the immediate family. We do that, even though at the same time and in the same writings those parents or relatives might speak of other matters such as military service or the private affairs of the parents or children, about which they may have had little or no opportunity to know the real truth.

Just as in the above consideration of preponderances, where we were concerned with whether Mary had more than one brother, we decided that the brother would know better about his siblings than would the old aunt. We believe that, not because we think brothers are more honest than aunts, but because we suspect he had a greater opportunity to know the truth. But, he may not have.

Similarly, as to having understood an event, we think that descriptions are more believable if the person doing the describing was beyond childhood. Simply stated, we do not fully trust a small child to understand or comprehend things. It is not that we presume a child to be dumb or ignorant, or that we think children are generally unreliable or prone to lie, it is that, until shown otherwise, we question their capacity to comprehend all that they see and hear.

That same reasoning applies to tales told by folks who were not there when an event took place. We do not trust their version of the events because we suspect that the best sources of the facts are the persons who were present at the time. So, while your grandmother may have been an extremely intelligent and absolutely truthful person, her stories concerning tales told to her by her grandmother sixty years ago when she was a child are probably less reliable than accounts of the same events told at the same time to an adult.

Tests of Evidence: 3) Memory Loss

Human experience tells us that even the most quick-witted and observant people forget; that time clouds memory and befuddles all of us now and then. Thus, in the example above where the woman related a tale told her by her grandmother, that story may be unreliable, not only because that woman was not there when the event occurred and so had no opportunity to know the truth, but also because she may have forgotten some of the details.

Likewise, an 1851 birth written into a Bible published in 1864 is not as reliable and trustworthy as that very same entry would be if found in a Bible published BEFORE the birth, say in 1845. Since the 1864 Bible was not printed until fourteen years after the birth, the entry had to have been made at least that number of years after the event. So, if a Bible was published after the date of a birth, death, marriage, baptism, etc., that is entered there, while that entry may, in fact, prove to be absolutely reliable, the passage of the years before such an entry possibly could have been made causes us to be a bit less trusting of the writing. Again, the human propensity for forgetfulness and inaccuracy bring distrust. We presume that the nearer the date of a writing to the date of the event, the more reliable the writing is, since the element of forgetfulness is less likely to have intervened.

Tests of Evidence: 4) Oaths and Other Constraints

We must examine all records, written or otherwise, with an eye to intellectual, social, religious, legal, or occupational rules that tended to favor reliability, accuracy, and truthfulness (or the opposites of those). As an example, we presume (whether rightly or wrongly) that God-fearing people are less likely to tell lies, hence records of the church or pertaining to church ceremonies—baptisms, marriages, funerals, etc.— are less likely to carry elements of intentional dishonesty. While, indeed, there may be errors of other kinds—forgetfulness, lack of opportunity to know and understand the true facts, etc.—we trust that, at the very least, church clerks, rabbis, pastors, and other persons having religious duties have a strong inclination toward accuracy, candor, and honesty as they write their entries and records.

So, if your search brings you to a record of some church activity where the actors likely had in mind their respect for the Almighty or for the church and its institutions, it is reasonable to presume such writings to be more reliable than where those forces were not at hand. But notice that an entry in the records of a church business meeting or concerning who was on the church softball team may not deserve the same measure of respect.

Similarly, we usually trust the words of court entries simply because we feel that courts are truthful; they must be, we think, otherwise our society would have collapsed long ago. While, in fact, some particular court order or entry may have been made under corrupting influences, we think that such usually was not the case, and so we assign a high measure of accuracy and reliability to these records.

Notice though, a writing by the same judge or court official having to do with his or her personal affairs or concerning the character of some other person may not be under the same constraints as to honesty and accuracy, and so are not quite as reliable, we suspect. A judge's court order reciting the names of the children of a dead person probably is quite believable, yet his general statement made over coffee that "...those children were not well educated" would require additional substantiation if we were writing or speaking of some particular one of those children.

A legal document or deed bearing an affidavit or acknowledgment is of a similar nature. Such a writing has a double dose of accuracy and reliability built in. These instruments usually invoke the Almighty and, in addition, are signed by those who have been solemnly warned concerning the laws prohibiting false oaths. Quite reliable, we think.

Nevertheless, those portions of the same documents that speak incidentally of matters that were not significant, or that the parties were not asked about, might have forgotten, or might not have had an opportunity to know the truth of, are not to be trusted any more than the same words in a document to which no oath was required. If a pension application sworn to by Evan Haskins relates that he enlisted in the army on May 4, 1777, was wounded at Germantown, and that he spent three weeks recuperating at his cousin's house on the Skippack Road, the enlistment date and the name of the battle in which he was injured likely are quite accurate. However, the statements as to where his cousin's house was located or how long he was in recuperating may be much more imprecise (perhaps even meaningless), even though equally and solemnly sworn to; the accuracy of those words was not important in the application.

Even within a single sentence, words may carry varying values as evidence. A deed that stated that land was purchased by "Thomas Drake of Isle of Wight County, a son of Richard Drake" is quite reliable and believable as to the father-son relationship, however we cannot be nearly as certain whether Thomas lived in Isle of Wight at the time of the deed, or simply stated that he was from there as a way to differentiate himself from some other Thomas Drake. Similarly, all researchers occasionally have encountered the terms "Sr." and "Jr." being used, not to show a parent-child relationship, but rather to distinguish between a younger and an older person having the same name who were in the same area or community, and that is true of women as well as men. Still again, to what extent do the specific words prove what we seek to prove?

An affidavit by an eyewitness stating that "...after killing John Smith as he was milking his three cows, Richard Jones stole one of the cows" may be absolutely accurate and precise as to the identity of the thief and murderer. Note though, were we called upon to prove the number of cows owned by Smith at his death, that affidavit might be much less reliable, depending upon whether or not the witness had the opportunity to know whose cows were being milked and whether that was the whole of Smith's herd.

It is commonly believed that when engaged at our occupation or profession we often are inspired (or bound) by higher standards of care and truthfulness than when at home or at play. The writings of an accountant at work are more likely to be checked and double-checked than are words of that same person while he or she was standing in line at the supermarket. An 1855 "school bill" submitted by a teacher for lessons given to an ancestor's child is more likely accurate as to that child's schooling, name, and presence than are notes of the same teacher concerning who was at a school picnic on the same date. In the matter of the bill the teacher was trying to do a thorough job and was acting under the dictates of the law that reports and invoices be accurately set forth, while, as to the picnic, neither of those constraints were at play.

When, as often happens, our purpose in citing a "death certificate" is to prove who the parents of the dead person were, the date and cause of death shown in that certificate are not significant to us. Notice, though, that the statements about parents may not be as reliable as the statements that tell of the death and its cause. Why? Because, as to all facts other than the date, time, place, and cause of death, the physician who completed the certificate probably wrote down information supplied by others and, as likely as not, had no first-hand knowledge as to those other matters.

As to the facts that were told to him (the parents, their residences, places of birth, etc.), the physician, no matter how observant, skilled, and honest, fails the test of having had the opportunity to be certain. Moreover, the usual constraints of his profession and the law were not applicable when he wrote about those parents; he did not need to be absolutely accurate in those matters, as he did when stating the time and cause of death. So, as to parents, birthplaces, etc., even though found in a formal and certified document, the reliability may be substantially decreased.

By way of summary, while all facts that in any way whatever, no matter how slight, tend to establish kinship are evidence, we must be careful to separate out and individually weigh every scrap of such evidence, whether sworn to or not and even within the same sentence. In addition, we must set aside all labels, and our decisions about the reliability and weight to be given each bit of evidence must be based entirely on the same tests that are a part of every intellectual exchange, namely 1) the motives or incentives at play, 2) the capacity and opportunity of the author or maker to know and understand the true facts 3) the likelihood of loss of memory, and 4) the constraints or requirements that served to increase or decrease accuracy.

Finally, you should notice that, just as we said we would, we have discussed the nature of evidence and proof in a rather complete fashion over several, several pages, and yet used not one label. We spoke nowhere of "primary sources" or of "double hearsay" or of "circumstantial evidence" or of "contraindications;" those terms simply were not needed, by us or anyone. So too should you write.

Writing about Evidence and Proof

So, having established that such and so was true, how do we write out—state—that proof? We write it in the simplest fashion possible, without any labels or legal jargon.

It will very much serve your purposes to read the following paragraphs from a recent family history work. Here the author first establishes—proves—that a man named Owen Griffith performed a number of legal activities that involved friends, neighbors, and relatives. Then, the writer takes the further step of using those established facts—that evidence—to prove that Owen was a man of standing and reputation among his contemporaries and in his community:[1]

---

1. Drake, *Now In Our Fourth Century*, Chapter 3, "Owen and Mary Huntt Griffith."

"...We found no record of Owen's activities for the three-year period following the William West affair. Thereafter, however, he again came upon the scene. On Wednesday, 15 May, 1680, Owen assisted in effecting the division of the estate of John Daniell, a man of some standing in the community,[2] and that same spring he 'proved' the nuncupative will of Matthew Walkley, thereby revealing his presence at the death bed of, and likely friendship with, that citizen.[3]

...during the following year (1681), he acted as security for the administration of the estate of Robert Edwards, whose widow—Mary Huntt—soon would become his wife.[4] Then, on Saturday, September 9, 1684, Owen appraised the estate of Edward Rogers,[5] who perhaps had patented land as early as 1637 in Isle of Wight,[6] and whose will had been witnessed by the same Thomas Gany identified above.[7]

Early in 1685, Owen divided the estate (identified and totaled the assets in order that the same then might be proportionately distributed to those entitled) of Dorothy Bond, the widow of his acquaintance, Major John Bond, Bond having been referred to in that record as "Gentleman", notwithstanding his previous public humiliation.[8] It will be remembered that in 1666—nearly twenty years before then—Bond had witnessed the lease from Luke to Owen, and therein commented concerning the lack of sealing wax.[9] Then, in 1688 Owen appraised the estate of John Hole,[10] who was a "gentleman from Devon,"[11] and whose wife Mary was the daughter of the now familiar and prominent Arthur Smith.[12]

So it is that from the repeated selection of Owen as a person having the standing with and confidence of the wealthy and upper class gentlemen-planters mentioned, we may conclude that he was well known and enjoyed a measure of respect from his contemporaries...."

Notice that twelve footnotes were created, in none of which explanation or comment was given or needed; the fact that Owen was selected by others to perform those specific legal duties that number of times is proof that he was held in high regard. While any one of those activities might be interesting to his descendants, the sole purpose for their use here was to demonstrate that measure of public respect.

Should the reader want to investigate Owen's activities further, the sources cited provide the avenues to that additional research. Finally, observe that note #8 refers to a subsequent footnote (#20), and note #10 states a fact that, while surely of interest to John and Dorothy Bond and Arthur Smith descendants and students, has only a remote connection to the subject of Owen Griffith.

---

2. *Wills and Administrations of Isle of Wight County, Virginia*, op. cit., p. 20

3. Ibid., p. 21

4. Ibid., p. 71 (1681). Also see p. 4 (1698)

5. Ibid., p. 24

6. *Seventeenth-Century Isle of Wight County, Virginia*, op. cit., p. 78

7. *Wills and Administrations of Isle of Wight County, Virginia*, op. cit., p. 72

8. See Note 20, supra

9. *Seventeenth-Century Isle of Wight County, Virginia*, op. cit., p. 24

10. *Wills and Administrations of Isle of Wight County, Virginia*, op. cit., p. 29. Hole owned land adjoining Arthur Smith, *Seventeenth-Century Isle of Wight County, Virginia*, op. cit., p. 599

11. *Seventeenth-Century Isle of Wight County, Virginia*, op. cit., p. 599

12. Ibid., p. 251

The intellectual exercise employed above in proving Owen's reputation is quite similar to that performed every time you write something like,

> "Grandpa Tom Roberts was a kind person who loved children. To my knowledge, he never failed to lend a dollar or a helping hand. On many occasions he gave candy to all of us grandchildren and to our friends, took us fishing whenever possible, and by owning more horses than anyone ever needed, he kept the whole neighborhood well supplied with horseback rides."

With Owen, the task was to prove that he enjoyed a higher station in life. Here, the proposition being established is that Grandpa was kind and loved children.

Owen's stature was established by proving that he did many things that people of elevated standing do. Grandpa's kindness was proved in the same way, by showing that he acted like a kind person. With Owen, your proof was court records. With grandpa your proof also was records, your memories from having been there.

Just as you did not know Owen and so had to cite sources other than your memories, so too with Grandpa, had you not remembered him. In that case, you would have had to cite some relative's recollections or letters, a newspaper article, some church records, photos, etc. Those outside sources, as with Owen, would have been recited in your foot- or endnotes (see them below), and the above story about Grandpa might then appear as:

> "Grandpa Tom Roberts was a kind person who loved children.[13] He never failed to lend a dollar or a helping hand.[14] On many occasions he gave candy to all of the grandchildren and to their friends,[15] took us fishing whenever possible,[16] and by owning more horses than anyone ever needed, he kept the whole neighborhood well supplied with horseback rides.[17]"

Early on in this chapter we discussed the question of how big a pile of evidence had to be to prove something or other. With that in mind, let us look once more at only those words that were pertinent to establishing Owen's reputation:

> "...15 May, 1680, Owen assisted in effecting the division of the estate of John Daniell, a man of some standing...

> that same spring (1680) he 'proved' the nuncupative will of Matthew Walkley, thereby revealing his presence at the death bed of, and likely friendship with that citizen...

> during...1681, he acted as security for the administration of the estate of Robert Edwards...

> on September 9, 1684, Owen appraised the estate of Edward Rogers...

> in 1685, Owen divided the estate... of Dorothy Bond, the widow of... Major John Bond... 'Gentleman'...

---

13. See Appendix 12, "Recollections Of The Children Of Thomas Roberts", pp. 401-433
14. *Old Marion Methodist Church Review* (pub. by the church, 1906), vol. 2, pp. 23.
15. Letter of September 25, 1903, Ida C. Roberts to Edith Uncapher, the same in the family collection
16. See series of photos of fishing trip with children, now in possession of Bethany Drake, and "Fishing Prowess of Roberts," *Marion Star* newspaper, June 2, 1902, p. 3
17. See *Diary of Brittany Drake, 1920-1928*, the same in the family collection.

in 1688 Owen appraised the estate of John Hole...a 'gentleman from Devon.'"

Was that enough proof? Surely it is. How much less would have been enough? The activities stated took place over eight years; suppose we had stopped after the 1684 event. Would that have been sufficient? Suppose we had used only the last two events where his activities were in the estates of "gentle" people? Enough? The answer is: there is no sure answer.

Ask yourself again, "Who is to be the judge?" If it is an organization, we must seek out their standards and requirements and undertake to meet those. If it is the community of genealogists—family historians—then we must state all the proof we have, and hope that reasonable and intelligent people of that group will find it clear and convincing. And finally, if the judges are to be ourselves, then satisfy that panel as well, whatever it takes.

In summary, gather all you can, weigh it carefully, state it clearly and concisely without any labels, and then ask yourself: would intelligent and reasonable genealogists find this amount of evidence sufficient? If the answer is yes, assume it is true, and say so. If the answer is maybe, tell your readers that you are not sure, and that more research is needed. If the answer is no, do not call it proof at all; tell the readers that while some facts are known, no conclusions may yet be drawn. We will say no more; you will know when there is enough, and when there is not.

But, did we miss any of those needed bits of evidence?

Chapter IV, Part 1: Gleaning What We Missed;
Courthouse, Family, and Non-Genealogical Sources

"Gleaner: One who gathers anything slowly and laboriously"
Johnson, *A Dictionary of the English Language*, 1755

All of us who decide to write family history find that we have overlooked or forgotten facts learned long ago. Thus arises the need to review the files, and again consider the records, writings, mementos, photos, and memorials of our ancestors. For that reason, we here revisit the most common of these sources, and suggest that upon review, you will rediscover much of value.

Remember, the careful writer must be a careful researcher. No matter how talented you may be in creating narrative, if your underlying data is not complete and accurate, your writing will not conceal that shortcoming.[1]

Documents and Writings Made Under Oath

Perhaps the most misunderstood of all genealogical sources are writings—documents—that "are notarized" or "have been recorded." Somehow, we feel that upon the fixing of a notary seal, or by taking a writing to the courthouse for recording, magic takes place and all doubt, dishonesty, forgetfulness, and error are thereby brushed away. Nonsense; as mentioned briefly earlier, the contents of acknowledged—sworn to, made under oath—writings must be tested for reliability and truth just as all other documents.

The only difference between sworn and unsworn writings is that the former bear visible evidence that the persons signing them had been warned that they should tell the truth insofar as they knew it or suffer the penalties of the law for falsely swearing to a document. As with all other words (written or spoken), the question of forgetfulness by the signers, the considerations as to motives, and the inquiries as to whether or not those persons could have known and understood the truth of the matters still are present and must be considered and weighed.

Deeds

The information often nearly hidden in deeds, be they warranty, mortgage, or trust, or quit-claims, can be so important and revealing to the astute genealogist that a few pages should be dedicated to the subject.

When studying deeds, whether "trust" deeds, "mortgage" deeds, or any other, you must remember that the Latin suffixes "-or" and "-ee" frequently appear here as in many other legal writings. For our purposes, it is sufficient to know that the suffix "-or" usually refers to the actor or person bringing about or causing some legal activity or result, and the suffix "-ee" refers to that person upon whom or to whose benefit such action was taken. Thus, a grant*or* is a seller of land. That is, he conveys—transfers—title, and a grant*ee* is a buyer, one who receives the benefit of that transfer, i.e., he usually gets title to the land.

Similarly, a mortgag*or* conveys title to land as security for a debt, and the mortgag*ee* gains that title to keep until the debt is paid; a less*or* gives over a use of land to a

---

1. A number of valuable sources are identified by Leland Meitzler in his fine article, "New and Little Known Resources for the Genealogist," *Heritage Quest*, March/April, 1995, Issue #56, p. 35 et seq.

less_ee_; a lienor files—"takes"—a lien against a lienee; and a vendor sells some asset or goods to a vendee or buyer, on and on. So much for suffixes; watch out for them, as they reveal who is doing what.

Some History of Deeds

The conscientious researcher must know something of the history of legal documents, especially deeds, and in that regard it is important to remember that land was of the utmost significance, especially to poor English speaking colonials who had never had the opportunity to own any. For that reason, the requirements of the law concerning deeds transferring that most precious and coveted asset—land—were carefully set forth and widely observed. Therein, and NOT because they bore acknowledgments or were recorded, are the reasons for the high degree of reliability of the information found in deeds.

So, deeds are instruments of transfer, very formal in style and written in a precise manner, that contain certain well defined clauses and sections, and are executed (signed), acknowledged, sealed (in early times), and delivered. Deeds serve to document and confirm that the parties have transferred some ownership in land, one to another.

After gaining title to land through the formality of a deed, the new owner—the grant_ee_—usually sees to its recordation at the courthouse. It was not always that way: in the early days, in old England (from which we gained most of our rules concerning land ownership) and in the American colonies as well, there were no recording statutes, and original deeds were carefully preserved, quite usually in a "deed box."

By early in the eighteenth-century, however, and in part by reason of the vastness of this land and the distances, hardships, and dangers often encountered in traveling to and from county seats, the colonial legislatures required that the counties' clerks (also called registers, registrars, prothonotaries, etc.) should copy into a permanent record book all deeds presented to them for that purpose. When this "recording" had been done, a buyer was protected against unscrupulous sellers who might again sell the same land to another buyer and then disappear into the frontier.

Notice too, once recording was accomplished the original deed became almost insignificant, since even if it was stolen, lost, or destroyed, the copy made at the courthouse pursuant to the recording laws was available to all with any interest. (As an aside, deed boxes almost totally disappeared from American estate inventories after our people became accustomed to and trustful of such recording activities.)

Partly by reason of the long history, and partly for the reason that it was necessary that deeds be written in a style readily recognizable to the clerks who recorded them (and to the aid and comfort of modern genealogists, it must be said), deeds came to have the precise form mentioned. In fact, you could copy, word for word, a deed of 1750, substitute your names and a description of the land transferred, and find it quite understandable and acceptable by modern lawyers, judges, and registers of deeds.

Names and Occupations in Deeds

Near the beginning of the deed text will appear the names of the seller(s) and the buyer(s). In the early days, it was at that place that marital status and the occupation of the parties usually were stated, for example, "Todd Haskins, joiner, and Diane Drake Haskins, his wife, Grantors, do hereby grant, bargain, sell, assign, transfer, and convey unto "James Smith, husbandman, Grantee, all their right, title...." It is there that you may gain very reliable evidence of the exact names, occupations, and marital status of the grantor and the name of his spouse at the date of that deed. Notice, however, that the wording of that deed clause will tell you nothing of the marital status of the grantee, since early deeds usually were made only to the husband.

Particularly in early deeds, notice that if the husband alone owned the land that was being conveyed, then the wife's name usually will not appear in this granting clause. However, that wife almost always will have disposed of her rights (usually "dower" derived by virtue of the marriage) at the end of the deed and in a separate clause, to which she too "swears."

It is important to remember that even in the earliest days of the American colonies, no one would ever buy land without the wife of the seller signing away whatever rights she might have in that property. Because of that need of all buyers, and since men truly held dominion over women in those times, it was a requirement that a women be taken aside, placed under oath, and asked whether or not her signature was given willingly and without duress.

Those requirements provide powerful evidence that where no wife appears in an early deed, there was none; there may have been one earlier or later, but at the date of the deed there almost certainly was no spouse. As an aside, notice that here is an instance where the absence of evidence—no signature—is powerful evidence of a fact.

Consideration in Deeds

In reading deeds (whether from 1660 or 1960), at the very beginning you will find the familiar expressions "in consideration of the sum of ___(so and so)___, the receipt and sufficiency of which is hereby acknowledged...." Those words tell you what was exchanged or paid or given over to the seller by the buyer for the property. You may find "love and affection" as that consideration, or a sum of money, or tobacco, or six hogs, or anything else that was recognized as valuable by both buyer and seller.

What about money? While in early times the legal currency here was English, some of which was always in circulation, the Mother country well knew the advantage of forcing the colonies—including this one—to constantly be in a position of trade deficit. As a result, we always owed England more than she owed us, and there was an ongoing shortage of even that "coin of the realm."

Since commerce and trade, of course, demanded that there be something to exchange for land, goods, or anything else of value, the colonies and even merchants sometimes printed or coined their own money. In addition, we also used the currency of the other colonies, of Holland, Spain, and France, and even that of the Indians (wampum). When there were none of these monies available, our people were forced to trade goods, commodities (and receipts for the same) and anything else of value for land or other things they wished to buy.

This wide variation in the kind and worth of the "money" being used at any given time and place meant that our people sometimes could not trust it; they often were not at all sure that they could spend it away once they had received it, particularly if that currency was from another colony or country. Now under the common law, a sale of land sometimes could be overturned—rescinded—if the consideration paid to a seller "failed"—turned out to be worth nothing or substantially less than the seller reasonably believed it to be. So it was that our ancestors nearly always stated in the deed the type of currency or other thing of worth used by the buyer as purchase money, just in case it did turn out to be valueless or almost so.

Therein are the reasons that the consideration stated in a deed may be very valuable to the genealogist. As but a few of the many examples that might be given, if a deed stated that the buyer paid "Proclamation Money" it may be that he was from North Carolina, no matter what the location of the land purchased, since that was a currency of the Carolinas; if the consideration was "tobacco and cask," it probably was paid by a buyer who lived in a tobacco growing colony or was a trader or merchant in that "weed;" and if "New York Gold Coin" was paid, the buyer may have been a resident of that place just before the sale. As now, money usually was paid at the place of the bargain, and in land sales, it almost always was paid at the place where the deed was signed (executed), and that place usually was where the land was situated.

In transactions between people of the same community or area, the risks were minimal that the "money" paid would be less valuable to the seller than it was to the buyer, and so we often see deeds containing the term "current money," meaning current to both buyer and seller. So, the consideration stated often is reliable evidence as to residency of both buyer and seller at the date of the deed.

Land Descriptions in Deeds

After the names of the buyers and sellers (grantors and grantees) and the consideration, deeds describe the tract being transferred. Through descriptions, you can map lands of ancestors; through those maps you can visit those tracts; and through those visits, perhaps more than in any other way, you can feel that you are in contact with those who once lived there. It is because of that importance that we here will spend extra time and thought.

Other than descriptions of lengths and directions of boundaries, there are two commonly used methods of describing tracts of land. They are 1) by *Lot Number* (Lot #, In-Lot #, Out-Lot #, or subdivision Lot #), and 2) by *Section, Township and Range*.

In the "lot" method of description, a city, town, village or other relatively large area of land is divided into tracts of various sizes, known as "lots," which then are assigned numbers and drawn on a on a *plat, plat map*, or *subdivision map*. That dividing (subdivision) and numbering is done (for profit or not) by the governmental body, individual, or company that owns the land.

Such lots are then sold off (hopefully), with the purchaser thereafter using as a description the lot number and the plat, the title of the plat, or the title of the subdivision. Thus, when you learn that in 1854 Dr. W. K. Drake purchased "Out-Lot 8 of the Village of Arlington," or that your ancestor Cheryl Bater bought "Lot 6 of the Jones Addition to the village of Radnor," it is an easy matter to seek out the tax assessor, local surveyor, or county engineer, and ask directions to that property. When you do so, as always, procure a map of the area, mark the land on it, and include it as an illustration in your writing.

On the following page is a partial map (the center and eastern part) of the Village of Nevada, Ohio, dated 1879. Observe the examples of subdivisions. Appearing just to the right of the center of town (obliquely labeled "Nevada") someone named "Cook" divided a small parcel of land into a series of numbered lots (see arrow #1), and to the north of Nevada (at arrow #2) a citizen named "Mr. Laughlin" did the same.

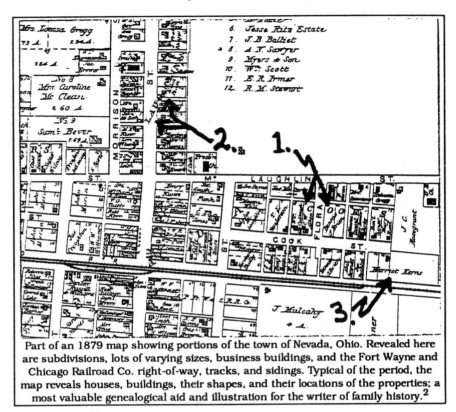

Part of an 1879 map showing portions of the town of Nevada, Ohio. Revealed here are subdivisions, lots of varying sizes, business buildings, and the Fort Wayne and Chicago Railroad Co. right-of-way, tracks, and sidings. Typical of the period, the map reveals houses, buildings, their shapes, and their locations of the properties; a most valuable genealogical aid and illustration for the writer of family history.[2]

"Harriet Kerns" also owned land within the Cook Addition (arrow #3). To describe her land within the village, we need but say or write that she owns "Lots 75 and 76 of the Cook Addition to the Village of Nevada," and all would know where that land is and be able to locate it on a map, either current or historic. Notice too that she owns land just to the east of those two lots, the same unnumbered, hence probably described by their position within a *Section*.

The second method of describing land—Section, Township, and Range—is also commonly found and easy to use. Large portions of the United Sates were surveyed, divided, and described by this method, a good example of which may be seen on any land map of Ohio.

You may find that an ancestor gained land through the *Homestead Act*. Therein, in 1862, in order to relieve the cities of the problems that came with a burgeoning population, encourage settlement and development of the vast tracts of public lands that provided no tax base until settled, and assist the "common man" to elevate himself and his family, Congress provided that any head of family over 21 years of age could either gain 160 acres of such land after five years of continuous residence and the payment of a registration fee (usually from $26.00 to $34.00), or could earn tracts of varying sizes by a six-month residency and a payment of $1.25 per acre. Thereby tens of thousands of Americans were encouraged to undertake farming operations, some of which "family farms" still remain occupied by descendants of those original settlers. Any incidence of "homesteading" in your family may provide immensely interesting background for your narrative.

Range is the term given to the series of numbered *townships*, each Township within each Range also being assigned a number. Ranges are bounded by their north-south

2. From *Atlas of Wyandot Co., Ohio* (Harrison and Hare, Phila., 1879) p. 81.

lines and by the township boundaries within each range. For example, Crawford Township of Wyandot County, Ohio, is **Township 1 South, Range 13 East**. Be observant, however, since most Ranges have townships numbered the same as those of most others, and almost every Township has Sections numbered the same as in all others. As but one of many examples, Township 1 South, Range 13 East has a Section #8, and so does Township 2 South, Range 14 East, as does Township 3 South, etc.

Within each township (almost always) there are 36 *Sections* of 640 acres (one square mile) each, for a total of thirty-six square miles per Township.[3] These sections, as stated, are numbered, and are divided into quarter sections of 160 acres each (1/4 of 640 = 160), and quarters of quarter sections of 40 acres each (1/4 of 160 = 40). Even beyond that, a partial section may be divided into even smaller portions.

Now look at another partial map. It shows the same village of Nevada in smaller scale (notice again the railroad), and also maps part of Antrim Township (*Township 3 South, Range 15 East*, see arrow #1).

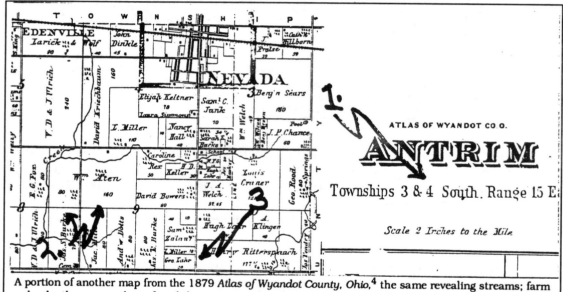

A portion of another map from the 1879 *Atlas of Wyandot County, Ohio*,[4] the same revealing streams; farm lands, the owners thereof, and the acreage within the tracts; roads; villages (Edenville and Nevada); a railroad; a school in the upper left corner of Section 10; and a pond ("pool") in the lower right corner of Section 3. The value of such maps to genealogical writings can not be overstated; they are superb.

In the above, notice arrow #2, at Section #9 (section numbers are almost always shown in the very center of the section), and look at the land of "Wm. Aten" shown there. Aten owned the northwest quarter of that Section (north is always straight up, unless the map states otherwise). Now look to the left of that land, where he is also shown to own the east half of the northeast quarter of Section #8. His deed description would be:

> "Situated in Wyandot County, Ohio, and being the northwest quarter of Section 9, Township 3 South, Range 15 East, and also the east half of the northeast

---

3. The word Section is usually capitalized when used in the description of a particular tract of land, as are Township and Range.
4. *Atlas of Wyandot Co., Ohio*, op. cit., p. 33.

quarter of Section 8 of the same Township and Range, consisting of 240 acres more or less." [5] or

"Being the northwest quarter of Section 9, T3S, R15E, and also the east half of the northeast quarter of Section 8 of the same Township and Range, being 240 acres, more or less."

Since Sections almost always have been 640 acres, and quarter sections 160 acres, you can tell from looking at the map (without reading any deed description) how much land Aten owned. Finally, notice that George Lahr owned land in the lower right portion of Section 9 (arrow #3). You now should try to write a description of his tract.[6]

So, whether a tract of land is described by "lot" or by "Section, Township, and Range" it is a simple matter to locate that tract on a recent land map, and it is equally easy to drive out there. Enough, then, of descriptions by *Lots* or by *Section, Township and Range.*

Land Revealed by Boundary Description

If not written by 1) designating a lot and subdivision plat or 2) by stating a Section, Township, and Range, your ancestors' lands will be described by stating lengths and directions of boundaries and the quantities of acreage believed to be contained there. Almost all early deeds used this last method.

There were two ways of stating lengths and directions of boundaries. First, even well into the nineteenth century, usually because the citizens were accustomed to it and there were few surveyors at hand on the fringes of settlement, the descriptions in many deeds were set out in "metes and bounds" (metes being an early rendering of the word "meets"). An example of a line being described in metes and bounds would be "...from an ash tree in the southwest corner of the churchyard, south along the main road to the southwest corner of A. J. Drake, thence along a line of trees west to a red oak in the bank of Town Creek...."

In later deeds and now, when surveyors were available and greater accuracy was desired than that provided by metes and bounds, land was described by the other method—"courses and distances." That expression means a measure of *distance* (usually poles, rods, or feet) along lines—*courses*—described by points of a compass. A courses and distances description might read, "...from an iron pin in the northwest corner of the Dan Carner tract, thence south, fifteen degrees east, two hundred poles to a pile of stones, thence, south, 22 degrees west...." As we shall see, and to the pleasure of genealogists, sometimes the old metes and bounds points and lines will be mixed in with courses and distances.

It is important for you to remember that most descriptions, whether in "metes and bounds" or in "courses and distances" commence with a point 1) somewhere in or at the corner of another property line 2) in a creek or river bank, or 3) in or at the edge of a road or other well established landmark. After relating the starting point, the description will then proceed around the perimeter of the tract, either in a clockwise or in a counter-clockwise direction, but not both.

---

5. It might be abbreviated as "NW1/4, Sec. 9, and E1/2, NE1/4, Sec. 8, T3S, Range 15E"
6. It would be "The south half of the southeast quarter of the southeast quarter of Section 9, Township 3 South, Range 15 East, being 20 acres, more or less" or "S1/2, SE1/4, SE1/4, Sec. 9, T3S, R15E, 20 acres.

To plot a tract of land, you have to read the description. If written in early English or otherwise obscure, you must translate it, just as you would all the other words in such documents. To do that, make a few copies of the description, and then read through it, highlighting the words you do recognize. Reread it, again attempting to understand the letters, characters, and words not recognized at the first reading, and again highlighting what is recognized. Continue with rereading several times, and you will find that you soon will come to understand what was said.

Suppose that the deed to your ancestor for a house and tract of land contained the following courses and distances description (notice that some of the metes and bounds points and lines also are included, even though they are unnecessary):

"Beginning at a point in the center of the old Meeting House Road, thence North 20 degrees East a distance of 160 feet to an oak tree, thence North 30 degrees East a distance of 160 feet to the southeast corner of the A. J. Drake tract, thence North 85 degrees West along the line of said Drake tract a distance of 160 feet, thence North 55 degrees West a distance of 28 feet to a creek bank, thence South 30 degrees West along the east side of the creek a distance of 160 feet, thence South 5 degrees West 160 feet to an old fence corner, thence South 81 degrees East 142 feet to the place of beginning, containing 1.2 acres, more or less."

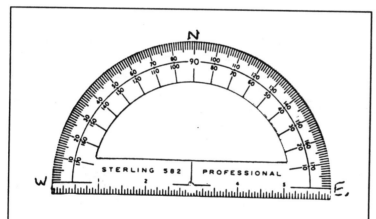

An ordinary grade school "protractor" used by genealogists to plot lands owned by ancestors. Notice that North is at the top, East is at bottom right, and West is at bottom left. For now, you will use the degree marks, however you will ignore the printed Arabic numbers.

Now draw that tract: Start with a blank sheet of ordinary graph paper and an inexpensive protractor, both of which may be purchased at any school supply counter (opposite). For this example let one inch (1") equal 40 feet (so one fourth inch (1/4") equals 10 feet). Depending on the size of your paper, you could have selected any other ratio of distance to measurement; 1" could have equaled 1 *pole* or 2 poles or 50 feet or 100 feet, or whatever (a pole is 16 1/2 feet, and so is a *rod*).

Next, place a dot (see next page) in the bottom center of your paper. That will be the starting point for the drawing. Assume that point is the center of a clock, and notice that east (90 degrees) is always 3:00 o'clock, south is always at 180 degrees—6:00 o'clock, west is 270 degrees—9:00 o'clock, and north is always at 360 or 0 degrees—12:00 o'clock

The first words—first "call"—of the description above is

"Beginning at a point in the center of the old Meeting House Road, thence **North 20 degrees East** a distance of 160 feet to an oak tree...."

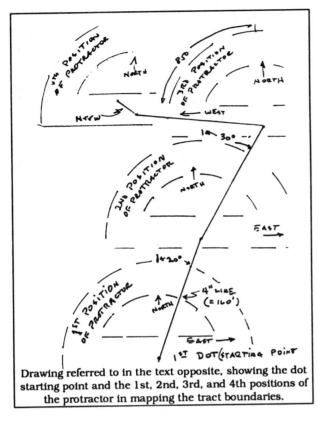

Drawing referred to in the text opposite, showing the dot
starting point and the 1st, 2nd, 3rd, and 4th positions of
the protractor in mapping the tract boundaries.

Now and always, you will place the protractor on the paper with the flat part lying in a straight line from left to right (from 9:00 to 3:00 o'clock). Place the protractor center point (it may be a little hole) on your starting point dot— "1st POSITION OF PROTRACTOR" on the drawing, left.

You must now find the call given, *North 20 degrees East.*" To do that you will first look north and then move toward the east. So, look straight up the protractor to 12:00 o'clock—north—and then count down to the right around the circle for a total of 20 degrees toward 3:00, east (ignore the printed degree numbers already on the protractor, such as "80" and "100" etc.). After counting down that 20 degrees, you have found "North 20 degrees East." Make a mark there.

Move the protractor out of the road, and draw a straight line between the dot you first drew on the paper and your new mark. That line is given in the "call" as 160 feet long, and since you have decided that one inch will equal 40 feet, the line on your drawing will be 4 inches long (still "1st POSITION OF PROTRACTOR"). Make a dot at four inches on your line.

Consider the new dot at the end of the 4 inch line as the new center of your clock. Place the center of the protractor on the new dot, just as you did first, again and always with the flat side of the protractor being straight from left to right (3:00 to 9:00 o'clock)—"2nd POSITION OF PROTRACTOR" on the drawing above. Now draw the next call, which is given above as

"...thence **North 30 degrees East** a distance of 160 feet to the southeast corner
of the A. J. Drake tract,...."

So, again, look to 12:00 (north) on the protractor, then look down around the curve to the right (toward east) for a total of 30 degrees, and make still another mark; that is "North 30 degrees East." Again remove the protractor, and draw a line between the dot at the end of your last line and the new mark. Once more, since the call says 160 feet, your line will be 4 inches long. Make another dot at four inches along this line. The next call is given as:

"...thence **North 85 degrees West** along the line of said Drake tract a distance of
160 feet...."

Again, place the protractor with the center at the latest dot ("3rd POSITION OF PROTRACTOR" on the drawing above), and you have a new clock center. Now look to north (12:00) on the protractor, but instead of looking around the curve to the right like before, look down around to the left, since that is toward west—toward 9:00. Look

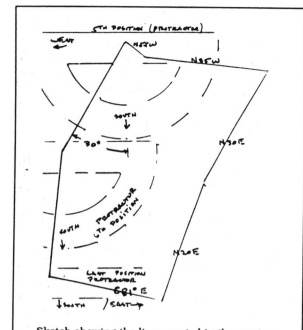

Sketch showing the lines created in the previous drawing, and also showing the 5th, 6th, and last positions of the protractor in completing the sketch.

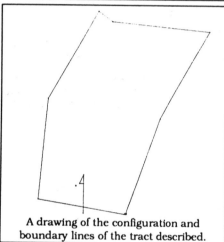

A drawing of the configuration and boundary lines of the tract described.

The same sketch with the additional facts from the courses and distances description.

around that circle a total of 85 degrees (almost down to the 9:00 o'clock position). You have "North 85 degrees West." Still. again, make a mark, move the protractor, and draw a 4 inch (160 foot) straight line between the last dot and this new mark.

Notice that the last call also tells you that you have followed the property line of a man named Drake. Since you did, you now know that he was a neighbor to the north of your ancestor. The next call says,

"...thence **North 55 degrees West** a distance of 28 feet to a creek bank..."

To make this short line, do as always: place the protractor over the new point ("4th POSITION OF PROTRACTOR" on the drawing above), look around to the west a total of 55 degrees, make a mark, and draw a line slightly less than 3/4 of an inch long (your call says 28 feet, and 3/4 inch = 30 feet). The next call is

"...thence **South 30 degrees West** along the east bank of the creek a distance of 160 feet...."

Now a variation is required. Since the first word of this new call is "South," you have to turn the protractor upside down so that the curved surface is downward ("5th POSITION OF PROTRACTOR on the new drawing below), with the end of your last short line as the new clock center. Since the call says "South 30 degrees West," you must look to the *south* (6:00 o'clock), and then count 30 degrees up around the curve from 6:00 toward 9:00 o'clock, the *west* side. Again the call is 160 feet, so make a mark at 30 degrees up from 6:00 toward 9:00, and as before draw a 4" line from the dot through the mark. The next call is:

"...thence **South 5 degrees West** 160 feet to an old fence corner...."

Since the call again begins with "South," with the protractor upside down and the center on the end of your last line (PROTRACTOR 6th POSITION), move up from 6:00 toward 9:00 a total of only 5 degrees, mark it, and draw still another

4" line. The next call is,

"...thence **South 81 degrees East** 142 feet to the place of beginning..."

Again, with the protractor upside down (LAST POSITION PROTRACTOR) count **up** 81 degrees from 6:00 toward 3:00 o'clock, since the call is *South* 81 degrees *East*. (Notice, since there always are 90 degrees between north and east, between east and south between south and west and between west and north, you could also have counted **down** 9 degrees from east toward south and gotten the same line.) You have completed the drawing and it should appear as here on the left (previous page).

Now, with the complete deed description again before you, draw in the other information given there. The property line description began at a point in a road called "Meeting House Road", the next line ended at an "oak tree," and the next went to the "corner" of someone named Drake. The next line went west and followed the south line of that Drake tract, and then there was a short line north and west to a "creek bank." Following that, the line followed the east bank of that creek for 160 feet, and then left the creek and went toward an old "fence corner." The drawing should appear like that on the lower left, previous page.

Now that you have the drawing showing all the known facts, lines, courses, and distances, you quite probably will be able to locate that land on a current map of that county, and you now are in a position to go out there and photograph the site as it appears today. You also have the makings of several interesting stories. Even if it can't now be located (and that would be unusual), context has been added and an interesting drawing is available to use as an illustration in your book.

Suppose, instead, that you come upon an earlier deed that described the land as follows:

"Beginning at a point in the center of the old Meeting House Road, then north and east along a line of trees a distance of 10 poles to an "y" shaped oak tree, then along the old line of Alexander a distance of 10 poles to the southeast corner of the land of A. J. Drake, then generally west and north along Drake's line a distance of 10 poles, thence north west a distance of 2 poles to a creek, thence generally south and west along the east side of the creek a distance of 10 poles to Haskins' line, from there along Haskins' line generally south a distance of 10 poles to a fence corner, and then generally east and south a distance of 9 poles to the place of beginning, containing $1^7/_{10}$ acres, more or less.

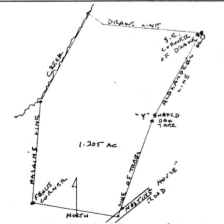

A complete sketch of the example tract. Included here are the courses and distances description and the landmarks written in the more recent deed, as well as the old metes and bounds points as found in the earlier deed. The result is a superb and meaningful illustration for inclusion in your book.

If you now look at your drawing and read the old metes and bounds as you do, you will find that it very nearly matches the more accurate courses and distances calls. So, add these old calls to your drawing, and the whole of your information will result in a delightful sketch such as that shown here to the right. (Try doing the rough metes and bounds drawing for yourself; it will be excellent practice.)

When you are unable to make a drawing of a tract or locate the land on a modern map, it is worthwhile to go to the office of the county surveyor or county engineer (who may have an office of their own or be located within the courthouse) in order to gain help. While the land did not move and is yet where it was when the original deed was written, the boundaries may have undergone several changes over the years. In addition to name changes, old creeks may have been dammed up or changed courses slightly, other tracts of land may have been added or taken away from the original, and new roads may have been built and old ones abandoned.

Despite such changes, that local engineer or surveyor often will find enough in the description to tell you about where the tract was located. If that fails, you have lost only a little time. If it succeeds, you will be richly rewarded.

If that officer can locate the area of the land, by all means purchase a modern map from his office (they will be quite inexpensive), and carefully highlight the tract thereon. Remember, just as when working with all other courthouse or library personnel, DO NOT bore them with some long tale about your ancestors; they are working, and quite usually have no time for (nor interest in) such stories. Also, do not forget that the location of lands of ancestors also calls into play the locations of nearby early churches and schools, possible sources of further family information.

Other Clauses in Deeds

In most deeds, immediately following the description, the words appear that tell lawyers (and you) the type of interest—the extent of the ownership—being transferred. That portion of a deed (called the *habendum clause*) was usually written, for example,

> "To Have and to Hold the above described thirty acres unto the said Robert Marston, his heirs, executors, administrators and assigns, in *fee simple absolute....*"

The expression, *fee simple absolute*, means simply that the seller is transferring all of that title that may be transferred under the law of the time. That is, he or she is transferring the entirety of the rights owned, whatever they may have been under the law of that day.

That expression might have read quite differently, and to a much different effect. The habendum clause in a deed of 1747 from William Hines to his daughter Sarah Hines read,

> "To Have and To Hold the said 147 acres to my daughter Sarah Hines *and to the heirs of her body....*" [7]

By directing that the land was being conveyed to Sarah **and** the heirs of her body, old William attempted to create an interest that had long been favored by land owners, yet equally frowned upon by taxing authorities. He was transferring a land in *fee tail*— an entailment.

Such devices were attempts by landowners to maintain land in the immediate family for all time to come. Notice that if that entailment had been given full force and effect, neither Sarah nor any of her descendants could ever have sold that land, since, then and now, all owners must join in a deed, and the vast majority of her co-owners—the "heirs of her body"—were not yet born, nor are they, even today.

---

7. Sarah Hines Drake was a triple-great grandmother of the author.

Even long before the days of the Hines deed and the myriad others like it, owners attempted to restrict future transfer by other words and provisions such as

> "To Have and To Hold unto (the buyer) *so long as* The Old Brick Church shall stand *and no longer....*"

Notice here, as with the "fee tails," had such restrictions as this been considered valid and the land transfer viewed as lasting as long as the Old Brick Church stood (it still does, even yet in Virginia), the title to that land would have remained in the heirs of that original grantee even now. Moreover, if that "so long as" provision were valid, when that old church finally does collapse—perhaps a thousand years from now since it is on our *National Register of Historic Places*—the land would revert to the hundreds of thousands, if not millions, of then living heirs of the original seller (grantor).

Land being sacrosanct in an Englishman's mind, the early judges (in addition to the taxing authorities mentioned) thought such a precious asset should not be so limited.[8] So, as did the *fee tails* like that given to Sarah Hines, such long term restrictions upon the sale of land all have been ruled invalid, either by the courts or the legislatures.[9]

Warranties in Deeds

If the deed is a warranty deed (and most were and are), following those clauses mentioned above that define the type and extent of the land interest being transferred will appear the *warranties*. Warranties are just that; the grantor warrants —guarantees —the adequacy and extent of the interest being sold or conveyed, and promises to legally defend the grantee, should anybody assert any claim that would be contrary— would hinder the "peaceable enjoyment"—of the interest that the grantor sold or transferred to the grantee. A deed without warranties was (and still is) like buying a "pig in a poke;" you may or may not gain those rights you thought you were buying.

Such warranties, though widely varying in wording, had (and have) very precise meaning to lawyers and judges and, in early times more often than now, were called into effect by reason of claims by others to ownership of some or all of a tract that had previously been transferred—deeded—to someone. For our purposes as genealogists, it is only necessary that we be aware that warranties usually contain the words "warrant" and "defend" and read similar to the following:

> "...and the said grantors for themselves, their heirs, successors, executors, administrators, and assigns do warrant that they will protect and defend the grantees against any and all claims...."

Should you uncover a deed <u>to</u> an ancestor, and yet find no later deed <u>from</u> him to another person for the same tract, in addition to the possibility that he still owned it at death and so no deed was required, be alert to the possibility of a lawsuit (of which below) that set aside the earlier transfer by reason of either a failure of the warranties or of the consideration as mentioned above. So, read the warranties; they may provide a story or two.

---

8. Those having interest in early limitations on transfers of land should first consult the headings "Rule Against Perpetuities;" "Entailments;" and "Fee" in either *Black's Law Dictionary* or *Ballentine's Law Dictionary*, both of which may be found in most libraries.

9. A court order terminating restrictions upon future transfer was called a "docking" order, and, after such a proceeding, an entailment was said to have been "docked." Georgia abolished entailments in 1750 and Virginia in 1776, followed shortly by almost all other states.

A gold mine for the family historian: Here is the signature page of a New Hampshire warranty deed from Jeremiah Veazey to Winthrop Marston, dated January 7, 1741/42 (the 13th year of the reign of King George II), a copy of which would be obtainable from the recorder's office of that county by simply looking up either Marston in the grantee/reverse index or locating Veazey in the grantor/direct index. James Marston and Jabor Smith were witnesses and Smith also was a justice of the peace. Someone noted (faintly visible written vertically, in the lower right margin) that the land was located "two miles W of Deer Hill." and consisted of thirty (30) acres and Notice how the year is written, that style revealing that March 25, rather than January 1st, still then was viewed as the beginning of the new year, as it was until after 1752.

Signers of and Witnesses to Deeds

Finally, in examining deeds, you should carefully note all signators—those who signed it for whatever purpose, including the notary or person administering the oath. Deeds always have been widely used, and in the days when travel was on foot or horseback, if the deed was not executed at the courthouse, nearby neighbors or friends quite usually witnessed the signing of such documents. So, signatures often are valuable clues as to relationships with neighbors and friends, as well as family members of ancestors.

Then too, widely accessible throughout the colonies were persons such as notaries public, justices of the peace, magistrates, and others who were authorized to administer the oaths contained in deeds and other "notarized" documents. Remember, however, if the deed was signed while the parties were in town on business or during "Court Days," assumptions concerning relationships may not be valid; just as we do, they may have had people at the courthouse or in the lawyers' offices administer the oaths and act as witnesses.

Recording Deeds

Deeds, mortgage deeds, deeds of trust, and quit-claims all are recorded and indexed in a time tested way, 1) in the names of the grantors and 2) in a separate section of the index volumes, in the names of the grantees, as well.[10] Accordingly, when searching for deeds simply make your way to that place in the courthouse where the land records are kept (ask any employee where they are; they will know what you are talking about), and upon entering that room, ask the person in attendance to direct you to the deed indexes (or indices, as you prefer).

Use of Records Concerning Deeds

Records indexes are nearly the same in all American courthouses, they usually contain explanations in the beginning of each such volume, and are easy to use. Generally, the only information you will need to know to use an index are the first couple of letters of the surname, and the first initial of the given name.

Notice, however, that minor variations in indexing do exist, and if, after carefully reading the instructions and making a diligent effort to understand, you are still unable to work with the system, do not hesitate to ask those in attendance if they have a moment to show you how to do it. They usually will help you, if you ask politely.

Remember as said, that it was not always required that deeds be recorded. Recording was (and, in some places remains) an option and an advantage, particularly for buyers. It was (and is) advantageous because, once recorded in the county where the land was located, the whole World was on notice that ownership had been transferred from one person to another on some certain day. Upon recording, a buyer was protected against an unscrupulous seller who might sign a subsequent deed for the same land. The result was that most folks recorded their deeds, however if the element of trust as to the seller's intentions and honorable conduct was strong, deeds sometimes were not recorded.

---

10. In some States of the Union "grantor indexes" are called "direct indexes" and "grantee indexes" are called "reverse indexes."

Incidentally, upon arrival at any office in the courthouse in which you intend to do research, you should ask if there are any special rules for the handling of the records, such as whether or not you should re-shelve the books, who makes copies, etc. If they have rules, good genealogy manners requires that you abide by them.

Absence of Recording of Deeds

The absence of some deeds from the records, and the occasional failures to record discussed above, have given rise to a lot of nonsense by family researchers. There were many reasons other than a mere failure to record to account for a deed not being present in the records.

How so? In the early days, aspects of the ancient laws of *primogeniture* prevailed almost everywhere.[11] The law was clear as to who got title to land when a parent died, and virtually everybody knew about it.

As but one of the myriad examples that might be given, when a seventeenth-century father died without a will, leaving two sons, a daughter, and a widow, all knew that the son (the eldest son, whenever there was more than one) automatically and at the moment of death was the new owner of the father's lands; the widow, younger son, and daughter receiving portions of personal property, income, and money, if any. As a result, no deed was required; the land had been transferred to that son as a matter of law. (Notice that the dead man could not have signed a deed anyway, and because the law had been such for a thousand years and more, the courts felt no need to do it for him.)

Similarly, if that inheriting son also died intestate with similar heirs, the land again went to his eldest son, and once more no deed was executed or necessary. Instances of land passing by intestacy for several generations are well known to all experienced researchers.

One more example: The only positive evidence yet found as to any land owned by William Huntt, who died intestate in Virginia in 1668, is a court entry made some fifteen years later that approved the action of his administrator in conveying "land of William Huntt to William Parker." Moreover, since there also seems to be no deed <u>to</u> Huntt from anyone at any time, he probably had gained ownership of that land through the intestate death of his father. The result is that because of those deaths without wills, there are no deeds of record either to or from Huntt, nor should there have been. Those deeds did not go unrecorded, as some might suggest; they never existed.

So, before giving up a search for land owned by an early ancestor, search the records to see if, perhaps even many years later, children or grandchildren transferred—"deeded"—property that appears not to have ever been conveyed to them. That land may have passed to them without a deed ever having been executed.

Mortgages and Deeds of Trust

In most family history discussions, "deeds of trust" are considered to be the same as "mortgages," and rightly so. Still though, some differences are present.

---

11. In New England, the eldest son received a double share, otherwise the children inherited equally, those provisions having been abolished by 1798. Primogeniture was abolished in Georgia in 1777, in North Carolina in 1784, in Virginia in 1785, in Maryland and New York in 1786, in South Carolina in 1791, and in Rhode Island in 1798.

A mortgage is a document very similar to a deed; formal, acknowledged, witnessed, and almost always recorded. Mortgages set forth the terms and conditions by which one person (the mortga<u>gee</u>) extends credit or loans money to another (the mortga<u>gor</u>), and in return, and as security for that loan of credit or money, the owner of land transfers legal title to the lender.

The difference between a mortgage and a deed of trust (sometimes imprecisely called a "mortgage deed of trust") is that in the former the legal title is transferred to the lender, and in the latter the title is conveyed to a third person agreeable to both the lender and the borrower, that person to hold the title to the property *in trust* pending payment of the debt. In both documents—mortgages and deeds of trust—upon payment of the debt and the interest, the land is transferred—"released"—back to the person who borrowed the money; that is, back to the mortgagor in a mortgage, and to the grantor in a deed of trust).

Almost without exception, mortgages and deeds of trust contain the terms and conditions by which the debtor may regain the title, and releases confirming satisfaction of those conditions were (and occasionally still are) noted in the margins of the recorded mortgages. Thus, even though it would seem that a new deed back from the mortgagee to the mortgagor would be needed, such is usually not a requirement, and the date upon which the final payment on the mortgage was made will be found in those margins.

Early Mortgages

In the early days there were almost no banks that were in the business of loaning money to common folks to buy land (or anything else). So it was that lenders very often were relatives, close friends. Moreover, since, then as now, we tend to maintain confidentiality in matters of personal business and money, the witnesses to mortgages likewise were very often chosen from among relatives or friends.

Recordation of Mortgages

Mortgages are recorded and indexed as are ordinary deeds; in the names of the mortgagors (grantors, in deeds of trust) and in the names of the mortgagees (grantees, in deeds of trust). These indexes should be searched just as we do deed indexes.

In the early years, mortgages usually were placed of record with the deeds. Not so recently, however. With the tremendous increase in the number of home loans and mortgages, the deed records became too many in number, and the result is that there now are separate volumes for the two categories of documents, both indexed in the same manner.

Deeds of Partition, Quit-Claims, and Leases

There are three (3) other classifications of documents involving land titles that are of importance to family historians. They are the *deeds of partition, quit-claims* (often imprecisely called "quit-claim deeds"), and *leases*. All usually have to do with rights to land owned by heirs and family members.

Deeds of partition and quit-claims are best understood through example: Suppose that your mother died, and then your father, both without a will, and as a result you

Here from the deed records of Rockingham County, New Hampshire, is an 1805 quit-claim from Jonathan Marston, "husbandman," to David Marston, "joiner." The deed conveys Jonathan's fractional interest in the home and land of his deceased father, Winthrop Marston, and also mentions that Samuel Marston was a brother of Jonathan. Here is proof of the occupations or callings of the parties (Jonathan, a cattle breeder or farmer, and David, a woodworker), proof of the father-son relationship of Winthrop and Jonathan, proof that old Winthrop lived on that Brintwood property at death (which land now would be easy to identify through the land records of Rockingham County), and proof that Jonathan's wife on that date was names Mary. Notice also that Ezekiel Godfrey and Joseph Godfrey signed as witnesses to the deed and that Ezekiel was a justice of the peace. Truly a treasure trove for the researcher.

and your four brothers and sisters (five people, in all) are now the owners of 500 acres of real estate.[12] The interests of all of you in that land are said to be "undivided."

Next, suppose that all have agreed that you are to have the farm and pay each of the brothers and sisters one-fifth (1/5) of the total value for their undivided share. You have the property appraised, they all find that appraisal satisfactory, and you pay them. They then execute a quit-claim. By doing so, they literally have *quit*— abandoned—their claims against the land, thereby transferring their undivided four-fifths of it to you (remember, you already owned one-fifth). You take that document to the courthouse, record it, and everybody is happy.

Based upon an agreed value, you and your siblings have entered upon a voluntary relationship, a *partition* of the worth—not the land itself, the worth—of the whole tract; everybody now has been paid a sum of money equal to value of their one-fifth interest. Note, in addition to bringing about total ownership in you, that quit-claim will forever more provide evidence to your descendants that you had the four siblings who were named (along with their spouses, if any) in that document.

As before, since husbands and wives of owners also must sign away their interests, where no spouses are shown in a quit-claim you have very reliable evidence that they did not exist at that date. Then too, while the possibility of error does exist as to how many siblings you had, as to that number the quit-claim is proof enough for anybody until otherwise shown.

Next, suppose that you wanted the land, but you and the others could not agree on the worth of the property, and one of your brothers also wanted it. You might then file a lawsuit seeking a *partition*; a determination by a court of the value of the property, one fifth of which value each of you would then be entitled to. If, after that determination, all of you still are unable to agree that you should have the land and pay those others, the court could order a sale (public or private), at which you may buy the land or not, as you see fit. If you are the highest bidder, you will gain the land and again will be required to pay your brothers and sisters for their 4/5th interests.

If your brother outbids you, you will join the rest and receive one-fifth of the proceeds. That lawsuit and sale would be concluded by a court order stating the facts, the nature of the dispute, the sale, and the proceeds derived. That order also would reveal the court's findings as to 1) what children were born to the dead parents of you and your siblings, 2) who of those children survived the last parent to die, and, 3) if any further children had previously died, who their heirs were.

After making those determinations, it is likely that the court would order that a deed of partition be executed by you and your siblings, the same revealing those findings and facts and transferring the land to whoever of you bought it. Notice that the result of that legal action is the same as in a voluntary transfer, however here it was done pursuant to court action and order.

In deeds and court orders such as these mentioned, in addition to learning the names, ages, and usually the whereabouts at the time of the court action of all the children of the dead parents, you also will know where the land was located, how much it brought at sale, and who bought it. Through knowing those facts, once again it should not be difficult for you to trace the land down to the present.

---

12. Do not forget that in colonial times it may not have been that way; the eldest son usually inherited the land.

Should one of the parties refuse to sign—execute—the deed of partition, the court order (or "entry") would be recorded, would act as a deed from that person, and usually would be found in the grantor (or direct) index under the names of each sibling who sold (even any who would not sign the deed), and in the grantee (or reverse) index under your name if you bought the property; a genealogical gold mine indeed.

It is important for you to be aware that had there been a sixth child who died before the last parent, your interest would be one-sixth (1/6) instead of one-fifth (1/5), and the heirs of that deceased child [13] would be entitled to their proportionate part of the one-sixth that their dead parent would have inherited. Heirs such as these are be said to receive their share *per stirpes* (by the stock).

So, quit-claims are similar to all other deeds in what they accomplish; they transfer some interest of one or more persons to some other person or persons. Still though, quit-claims may differ substantially in the motivation for and provisions of the document. For example, you could this day execute a quit-claim to another person for the whole of your home town, and while surely ludicrous, that document would be perfectly legal and quite recordable.

That unusual state of affairs arises out of the fact that in a quit-claim you state that you convey whatever interest you may own, and you make no warranties whatever concerning the quantity or quality of that ownership. A quit-claim says: "If I own anything—and I am not saying that I do—I hereby transfer it to you."

Quit-claims, even though they may not be true deeds (since they may be intended to convey little or nothing and deeds always intend to convey something of value), are recorded in the deed volumes and indexed, both as to grantor and as to grantee.

Quit-claims may be executed many years after an event, and may have been signed by only one of many heirs or descendants. Another example: suppose that 1) your husband is dead, and that many years ago 2) his grandfather and all that grandfather's children including your parent, agreed that 3) one of those children—a sister—would continue to farm the old home place.

The grandfather then went west, never wrote, and died, following which—over many years—4) all those children of the old man died, 5) all of whom had children and grandchildren. 6) The grandchildren of the sister are still farming the land. Since you are a widow of one of the many grandchildren of that old man, you probably stand to inherit some of whatever your husband would have received, and since there were no deeds, sales, or purchases by anyone, anywhere along the line, your husband likely would have owned an interest in the farm, difficult as it might be to measure now.

A lawyer has contacted you, and he wants to pay you for your interests, whatever they might be; there now are many heirs of those grandparents of your husband, and the lawyer must gain all rights owned by anybody before he can clear the title. He will ask that you sign a quit-claim. You would be in favor of a quit-claim since, without a lot of time and expense you cannot be sure what percentage you do own, and so would not be willing to execute a deed in which you guaranteed—warranted—anything. Remember, as said, a quit-claim simply says "I don't know what I own, but if it is anything, I hereby transfer it."

---

13. There are no deaths without heirs; if no relatives are ascertainable, the state is considered an heir and inherits the assets.

Also notice the subtle difference between quit-claims and partition deeds. In the partition deed example, all knew (or the court was able to establish) what portion everybody owned. However, in the quit-claim situation there probably were claimants, like you, who had no idea what percentage they owned, and whose percentage might be so small as to be next to worthless, yet all of whom would be asked to sign in order that the lawyer might be confident of the title.

So, quit-claims often are very valuable in learning of lineage or siblings of ancestors. Still though, the researcher must be ever watchful of quit-claims signed by those who *might* have been an heir, yet in fact were not. Also, as in our example, be aware that a quit-claim signed by an ancestor does not necessarily mean that he or she ever lived on the land or even saw or knew anything about it.

Leases were (and are) writings that state a relationship in which someone—a less*ee* (remember the Latin suffix "-ee")—gains rights to the use of land, and often a house[14] located on that land, while another person (the less*or*) receives money or something else of value as payment (consideration, "lease rental") for that use and occupancy.

In early times, as now, the presence of a recorded lease may not reveal where the ancestor lived; he or she may have needed additional land to farm, even though they had no intention of ever living there. So, if you find an ancestor as a lessee in a lease that includes a house, do not halt your search for deeds revealing ownership of other land by that same ancestor. Notice too, since travel was limited to horseback or foot, if there is recorded both a deed to land and a lease for other land, the ancestor very likely was engaged in farming activity and lived on one of the tracts and close by the other. (Be aware however, though few in number, there always have been land investors—speculators—that bought and sold land, not for its use to them, but for the potential profit they might make.)

Leases are very interesting, often telling us much about lifestyle. As an example, a seventeenth-century, twenty year lease of Virginia land from Paul Luke to Owen Griffith stated that every six months Griffith was to pay as lease rental the sum of "500 pounds of tobacco and cask,"[15] and also was to deliver to Luke a "fatt capon on each Lady Day."[16]

That lease also revealed that Griffith had the right to use the "twenty foot by thirty foot dwelling house thereon" and to "fall, saw and maul"[17] any or all trees on the land. Notice the dimensions of the house—600 sq. feet—and there probably were two floors, for a total of 1200 square feet. Seldom are early leases found that are not equally interesting and valuable in adding color to the life story of that ancestor.

Other Early Land Transactions

As we know, business was not always conducted as it is now, and the genealogist must always be aware of these differences. In early England, and in the American colonies, there was a means of transferring land quite distinct from the deeds to which we are accustomed today. That method was known as "lease and release," and many instances of the procedure are to be found in our early records.

---

14. The word *messuage* was commonly used, meaning a dwelling house plus small buildings necessary to it, such as a privy, kitchen building, smoke house, well house, etc.
15. The expression "tobacco and cask" meant that a container adequate for the bulk and weight of the tobacco was to be provided by the debtor as part of the payment.
16. March 25, the first day of the new year until September of 1752.
17. Meaning that Griffith could cut down, use, or dispose of the timber as he saw fit.

In a lease and release transaction, a lease for one year for some stated amount of money (usually nominal) was made, with the buyer-to-be acting as a lessee, thereby resulting in the owner (lessor) remaining "seised" of the property, subject to its *use* by the lessee for that year. At that point, the even then ancient "Statute of Uses" operated to legally join—attach—the possession (the seisin) of the land to the lessee's "use" of the land. By virtue of that joinder of interests in the lessee, it was legally possible for the owner to release to the lessee that lessor's remaining interests as well as the reversion that was to have taken place at the end of the one year term.

The releases in such "lease and release" transactions usually were signed on the day following that of the lease itself. By those actions, the two instruments—lease and release—merged to act as a conveyance, and a transfer of ownership was accomplished just as if a deed had been executed and delivered.

Thus it is that what may appear in the records to be a lease may, in fact, be a deed in its effect. Note too, the release may not be of record, it having sometimes been noted only on the original lease document margin, as discussed earlier. For that matter, neither may have been recorded.

As in the matter of intestate deaths such as those discussed above, in lease and release transactions there were no unrecorded deeds; no deeds were ever made. So, when you find a recorded lease with a minimal lease payment from someone to a very early ancestor, look for a release in the margins of that lease or in the records immediately following. If you do not find a release, look in the records for the following years for a deed for the same land from the ancestor to someone else. That later deed may be the only evidence as to that previous ownership.

Miscellaneous Legal Writings

Over the centuries, lawyers and judges have devised many different documents that serve as evidence of this or that contract, transaction, or relationship, many of which resulted in recorded or recordable writings. In addition, in order that still other important records be safely kept, the clerks and the legislatures have permitted or ordered that some writings be recorded, even though these sometimes were quite informal and without acknowledgments (so-called *notarization*).

Some examples of this group of writings would be discharges of veterans; some liens; tax matters; some chattel mortgages; automobile titles; partnership and corporate documents; declarations of status; divorces; records of county commissioners, aldermen, or boards of education meetings; records of monies paid to citizens for work done; records of road and bridge work; records of ferries, toll roads and toll bridges; many court orders and entries, especially those that affect title to land; and still other materials in one courthouse or another. All are worthwhile, and many provide valuable information not otherwise recorded concerning ancestral families.

A word as to automobile and tractor titles is necessary. Advances in the manufacture and use of the gasoline engine during the first half of the twentieth century made ownership of an automobile or tractor a matter of considerable importance and interest, and for the common man, at least, such were investments

Approved by the Attorney General, July, 1923

BILL OF SALE, in Duplicate

NEW MOTOR VEHICLE

Gen'l Code, Sec. 6310-5

Know All Men by These Presents, That: _Ideal Garage_

Residing at _Prospect Ohio_

the Grantor___, do___ hereby execute this Bill of Sale in Duplicate and deliver to: _____

Sam Seiter Senr Jr

Residing at _Prospect Ohio_

the Grantee___, the possession of the following described Motor Vehicle:

Manufacturer or Maker _Ford Motor Co_ ; Manufacturer's (Factory) No. _494620_ ;

Engine or Motor No. _494620_ ; other numbers _____

Horse Power _22_ ; Description of Body _Black_

Make _Ford_ ; Type _Truck_ ; Model _T_

Other number or marks of identification thereon on or appliances attached thereto, _____

It is mutually understood that the contents, execution, delivery, acceptance or filing of this "bill of sale" in no manner affects or governs the rights, title and interest of either the transfer or transferee in and to the vehicle herein described or referred to, or in and to any chattel mortgage, note, paid or unpaid purchase price, lease, lien, insurance policy, conditional sales contract, or any contract or agreement collateral or otherwise of any kind whatsoever, concerning such vehicle, the sole purpose of this "bill of sale" being to comply with Sections 6310-3 to 6310-14, inclusive, of the General Code of Ohio, and in order to evidence the fact that possession of such vehicle has changed on this day.

IN WITNESS WHEREOF, the said _Ideal Garage_

Prospect Ohio

ha__ hereunto set __ hand this _21_ day of _Dec_ 19_25_

Witnessed by

A. N. Emberton

E. Waag.

Ideal Garage

Roy R. Nyland Mgr

Grantor___

Grantee___

OATH

The State of Ohio, _Marion_ County, ss.:

R. Nyland being duly sworn says that __he is

the Mgr of the Ideal Garage the grantor___ of the within described

Vehicle and that the statements in the foregoing Bill of Sale are in all respects true and correct as __he verily believes.

Sworn to before me and signed in my presence this _21st_ day of _Dec._ 19_25_

R. Nyland

Edward Waag

Notary Public

Marion County, Ohio.

1. Here insert the name and residence, giving City, Village or Township, County and State, with street and number, if any, or postoffice address of each Grantor.

2. Here insert same as to each Grantee.

3. Here insert, if so, "Agent of_____ (give name)."

Early in the twentieth century, automobile purchases were of much greater significance than now, and the instruments of such purchase were more formal. Here is a copy of a bill of sale yet maintained in the Marion County records at Marion, Ohio, for a Model T truck purchased new in 1925 by Sam Seiter of Prospect, Ohio. It was all of 22 horsepower, was black, and was purchased by Sam from "Ideal Garage." How interesting for Sam's descendants.

second in size only to the home or farm. The result is that auto and tractor titles and the *chattel mortgages* involved in the purchase of such vehicles were much more descriptive and important than now. Chattel mortgages were the documents, (now called "financing statements") that were similar to mortgage deeds and served to evidence loans secured by personal property.

These chattel mortgages bore witness to addresses, sellers, buyers, mortgage holders, make and model of vehicle or machinery, and sometimes even the marital status of the buyer. Accordingly, when in the courthouses of the counties in which they lived, you should always ask if any records remain of early chattel mortgages and titles to automobiles or other vehicles. Where they do exist, they are quite usually indexed in the name of the owner.

As to many of such miscellaneous papers and the names appearing there, courthouses maintain a "Miscellaneous Index." You must examine that index for the years during which an ancestor lived in that area; your people will appear, as often as not.

Loose Papers

Finally, throughout the early years (and still) many documents and writings have been created to meet some legal need and then, for one reason or another, have been left at the courthouse. Because many of those old documents were not recordable and indexable as "miscellaneous," yet appeared to be too important to destroy, they were stored, often for centuries.

Such old writings usually are now called "loose papers." If not previously forwarded to the states' archives, such materials often may yet be found in the courthouses to which they were taken or in which they were created those centuries ago. Perhaps no better example may be found than the wonderful collection of such writings yet housed in the Sussex, Virginia, courthouse, beautifully indexed by the Honorable Gary M. Williams, Clerk, and available (under supervision) for hands-on examination by sincere researchers.

Usually, unlike those of Sussex, loose papers are not yet indexed, and often are not yet even placed in chronological order. Accordingly, where indexed, you have a vast source of incredibly interesting genealogical materials at your disposal just for the asking. Where not indexed, yet placed in chronological order, you will find it most rewarding to read through those documents for the years during which an ancestor lived in that county. Where not indexed or placed in some order, sometimes the workers of the Church of Jesus Christ of Latter Day Saints (Mormons) have microfilmed these materials and made the same available through their Family History Centers.

Tax Records

This is not a course in tax record research, and many good books have been written concerning that most interesting area of study. Nonetheless, you must re-think your past efforts, and if you have passed over such records, you should return and tie down those loose ends, where possible.

People have been taxed as long as government has existed. And taxation has not always been bad. To name but a few benefits, remember that protection of the people has been brought about, wars fought in defense of countries, and sheriffs and firemen

[Bill of Sale of the Personal property of Joseph W Robinson Dec, Sold on the sixth day of January A.D. 1853]

	# cts
Negro Boy Levi	Sarah D Robinson 1,195 00
Negro Boy Frank	Sarah D Robinson 1,125 00
Negro Boy Jordan	Dr. J Thomas 1,150 00
Negro Boy Alexander	Jos W Robinson 570 00
Negro Girl Hannah	Sarah D Robinson 300 00
Negro Girl Easther	Jas Prewitte 550 00
Negro Girl Ann	Sarah D Robinson 600 00
One Cary plough	Sarah D Robinson 1 00
Lot of Plough Stocks	Sarah D Robinson 2 00
One sweep and Two scooters	Sarah D Robinson 1 00
Box of Sundries	Sarah D Robinson 25
One Grind Stone	Sarah D Robinson 1 00
One Shovel and Two Hoes	Sarah D Robinson 25
One Falling Axe	Sarah D Robinson 50
One Lot of Pots	Sarah D Robinson 1 00
Lot of Kitchen Furniture	Sarah D Robinson 50
One Four Horse Wagon and Harness	A M Creigh 145 00
One Mare and Colt	Sarah D Robinson 60 00
One Mule Rush	A B Cooper 70 00
One Mule Belt	W R Ran 56 00
One Mule Nick	G Turner 42 75
One Brood Sow	Perry McGammon 2 00
One Stock Fodder	Sarah D Robinson 2

The probate records of Shelby County (near Memphis), Tennessee, yielded this first page of the account of the 1853 public sale of the assets of Joseph W. Robinson (deceased). Robinson's estate included seven (7) slaves varying in worth from #300.00 for the "...girl Hannah" to $1195.00 for the "...boy Levi." It is interesting to note that most of the slaves were purchases by Sarah Robinson, probably the widow or a daughter, the others bought by Dr. Thomas and James "Prewitte." Note too that a "four horse wagon and harness" brought $145.00, that sum being twice what the mule names "Rush" brought ($70.00). A brood sow fetched only $2.00. How interesting such information would be to your readers!

KNOW all Men by these PRESENTS, That we *Moses Baskins of Lancaster & John Gray of Carlisle, Cumberland County & Province of Pennsylvania Yeomen*

are firmly held and bound unto the Honorable *RICHARD PENN*, Esq; Lieutenant Governor and Commander in Chief of the Province of *Pennsylvania*, and Counties of *New-Castle, Kent*, and *Sussex*, on *Delaware*, in the Sum of *two hundred* Hundred Pounds, good and lawful Money of *America*, to be paid to the said *RICHARD PENN*, Esq; his certain Attorney, Executors, Administrators, or Assigns; To the which Payment well and truly to be made, We bind ourselves jointly and severally, for and in the whole, our Heirs, Executors and Administrators, firmly by these Presents. Sealed with our Seals. Dated the *twelfth* Day of *August* in the Year of our Lord One Thousand Seven Hundred *and Seventy three*

THE CONDITION of this OBLIGATION is such: That if there shall not hereafter appear any lawful Let or Impediment, by Reason of any *Pre-Contract, Consanguinity, Affinity*, or any other just Cause whatsoever; but that the above-mentioned *——us Baskins with Eunes Richardson ——*

may lawfully marry; and that there is not any Suit depending before any Judge Ecclesiastical or Civil, for or concerning any such *Pre-Contract*; and also if the said Parties, and each of them, are of the full Age of Twenty-one Years; and are not under the Tuition of his or her Parents, or have the full Consent of his or her Parents or Guardians respectively to the said Marriage; and if they, or either of them, are not indented Servants; and do and shall save harmless and keep indemnified the abovenamed *RICHARD PENN*, Esq; his Heirs, Executors, and Administrators, for and concerning the Premises; and shall likewise save harmless and keep indemnified the Clergyman, Minister, or Person, who shall join the said Parties in Matrimony, for, or by Reason of his so doing; then this Obligation to be void, and of none Effect; or else to stand and remain in full Force and Virtue.

Sealed and Delivered in the Presence of *Moses Baskins*

Gilbert ——— John Agnew *John Gray*

From the "Loose Papers" of Cumberland County, Pennsylvania, here is a 1773 "marriage bond" by which Moses Baskins and John Gray of Carlisle, both described as "yeoman" (meaning they did then or had previously owned land), agree to pay £200 "lawful money of America," should it later be discovered that at the date of this bond there was some legal impediment to the marriage of that Moses Baskins to "Eunes" (Eunice) Richardson. Notice that the bond is payable to Richard Penn (son of William), "Commander In Chief" of Pennsylvania, and also reveals that both Baskins and John Gray probably were literate.

CUMBERLAND-COUNTY. *ſſ.*

GEORGE the Third, by the Grace of GOD, of *Great-Britain,* *France* and *Ireland* King, Defender of the Faith, &c.

To the Sheriff of *Cumberland* County, GREETING :

WE command you, that you take *Edmond Huff and John* ~~~~~~~~ *we have commanded you* *Huar both taken of your County Yeomen*

if *they* ſhall be found in your Bailiwick, and *them* ſafely keep, ſo that you have *their* Body, before our Juſtices, at *Carliſle,* at our County Court of Common Pleas there to be held the *twenty-five!* Day of *April* next, to anſwer *John Gally of ſuff* *ſ* *In plea on the Caſe* *ſ*

And have you then there this Writ. WITNESS *John Armstrong* Eſquire, at *Carliſle,* the *twenty-fifth* Day of *January* in the *twelfth* Year of our Reign.

John Agnew

No. 25 To April Term 1772

John Gally ⎱ Nº Cap. baſe
⎰
Edmond Huff &
John Hart ——

N.B. *R. Kenshel*

Huff lives near Capt. Pattersons & *Hart lives on Cocholamus*

Wilson

In the days when we were citizens of Great Britain and had kings and queens, as now, sheriffs were ordered to take those actions necessary to effectuate courts' orders. Here, from the "Loose Papers" of that county, is a 1772 (the twelfth year of the reign of King George III) "capius" directing the sheriff of the county of Cumberland to find Edmond Huff and John Hart and to physically bring them before the court. John Gally has alleged that those men were guilty of "trespass on the case"; probably meaning that they had not done as promised in the matter of a debt owed Gally. Interesting and most valuable to the family historian/genealogist, on the reverse (above right) the clerk of the court has told where the two men lived; Huff, "near Capt. Pattersons", and Hart, "on the Cocholamus."

have been paid. Poor farms and homes for the aged were created, as were courts, and roads, bridges, and ferries have been built. The list of benefits derived from taxes, past and present, goes on and on.

Still though, not only have we been taxed, we have been taxed on everything imaginable. Whenever a government thought that some property or asset did, could, or might produce income or benefit, it has been considered for taxation. The list is unending: government has taxed real estate, of course; whiskey, beer, rum, and wine; tea, chocolate, and coffee; cattle and almost all other animals; crops; buildings; businesses; ships; vehicles—horse drawn and otherwise; bank accounts; ownership in companies and other associations; and, perhaps the most hated, we have been taxed upon income derived from the very assets upon which we already were being taxed. In short, at one time or another, some government someplace has taxed almost anything you can think of.

Onerous though they sometimes were (and are), taxes required that accounts be kept. Where such accounts have been preserved, they are incredibly valuable sources for genealogists.

Where they yet exist, tax records are easy to locate. Your first stops or calls always should be the local genealogical or historical society and the local library. Probably more so even than the courthouse employees, they will know what tax records have been saved, where these are now kept, and whether or not the same have been abstracted. Indeed, your visit or call there may save you many hours of travel and search, especially if the old records have been destroyed, abstracted, or previously sent off to the state archives or other repository.

To the extent that tax records are available and not abstracted, you probably will be called upon to visit the courthouses. While their titles may and do vary from state to state, virtually every county and town (or city) government maintains offices for collection of personal property taxes and for a real estate tax assessor, a county clerk, and a county treasurer. Once you have arrived at a courthouse, simply ask anyone working there where the tax records may be found.

Within the tax offices, inquire as to 1) what records have been kept for the years during which your ancestor lived there, and 2) what indexes are available for those records. As with the deed indexes, tax indexes are usually simple and self-explanatory. However, as with deed and mortgage indexes, these may vary slightly from courthouse to courthouse. As with other indexes, if after diligently trying, you are unable to understand an index, politely ask if the clerks there have time to assist you, and if so, listen carefully, and then thank them. As always, remember that courthouse employees are not there to do your research; help, yes; do your work, no.

Not all tax records have indexes. Still though, since tax matters almost always were kept in chronological order, you are not at a great disadvantage. Simply take your time and carefully examine the ledgers for the years in which your ancestor lived in that area. If you don't know what years those were, you haven't done your homework, and should not be there yet anyway.

If the tax records have not been abstracted and have been forwarded to the state archives or some other repository such as a local or state museum or library, it will be necessary that you visit there. The other alternative is to make use of the resources available through your local Mormon Church *Family History Center*. In summary, if you have not exhausted tax records still in existence for the areas where ancestors lived and worked (and most of us have not), do so as you write and work on other aspects of your book; you still have time.

A quick note here: many libraries and research institutions (such as the National Archives) have on-line computer "home pages" that list the type of records they hold. You may still need to go to that place or to your local library in person, or to make your requests in writing, but at least you will have some idea of what is available. "On-line" services also contain genealogy directories of people who may be willing to share information with you, which you can then "download" for your own records.

Now, back to tax considerations. Even if you have already done tax record research, your need now is to glean from them facts about and a picture of daily life. Notice again that land tax payments reveal ownership of land, thereby sending you to the deed indexes for knowledge as to where the land was; ownership of a lone cow or a lone horse and no other animals tells you that the ancestor probably was not working as a farmer and may have been a shoemaker, blacksmith, storekeeper, joiner, cooper, etc., that clue sending you to the newspapers of the day for ads. A tax paid on an "ordinary" or "inn" surely sends you to county histories, newspapers, and court records; taxes paid for a boat or bridge reveal ownership of a small ferry operation or a toll bridge; and early taxes on a vehicle—wagon, hack, dray, etc.—lead you to similar sources that reveal occupations as carters, teamsters, or small transportation business owners.

In summary, review your tax record research notes. If you have overlooked what they reveal concerning the day to day affairs of an ancestor, rethink the matter. Here is context, just for the taking.

Other Non-Genealogical Writings as Sources

It is important that you consider again that once you have moved backwards in time to that point at which no memories, tales, or traditions have been passed down and no witnesses to the events yet remain, you are left with bare dates and names; to most folks who are not genealogists, very uninteresting material indeed. The result is that in you must re-create the background—the setting or context—during which those ancestors lived, and non-genealogical writings are sources for doing that.

Non-Genealogical Writings as Background Information

In addition to background materials, bits of genealogical evidence often are found in books and writings that do not have family history as their purpose. As one example, Bruce's *Economic History of Virginia in the Seventeenth Century* (mentioned previously) has an excellent index listing many of our very early Virginia ancestors, their activities, beliefs, and surroundings, and thereby providing a most worthwhile source; that, even though Bruce had little if any intention of publishing a "genealogy book."

As an example, suppose you know only that an ancestor was born in 1840 in Edgecombe County, North Carolina, lived there until her marriage in 1865, and then moved to Ohio with her husband and children, where she died in 1915. Those naked facts are of little interest to other than genealogists. However, if you add a few non-family facts gathered from history sources, writings, and articles easily located at any library, a tiny window will be opened through which the vital place of your family in the great play of history will become visible.

Of the vast quantity of general information available about North Carolina, you might mention that at the time of the birth of that ancestress in 1840 Edgecombe was, as now, a place of very hot and humid summers and long, damp winters; where tobacco and pigs were the main farm products, and quaint and pretty little Tarboro was the county seat; where boat traffic and commerce moved up and down Tar River carrying trade goods to and from Albemarle Sound; where the well attended "Primitive Baptist" church was just a mile up the road from the family farm; where blacks and whites lived and worked together peacefully as they had done for generations, despite the conditions of servitude that most of the former had suffered; where folks still remembered when General Cornwallis and his Britishers passed through on their way to Yortown; and where aged veterans of that glorious conflict then still lived, rocking under the shade of the great trees and spinning tales for grandchildren.

Similarly, works such as the series titled the *War of the Rebellion* (Government Printing Office, Washington, D.C., 1901, 128 vols.) provide vast quantities of both genealogical and non-genealogical information within certain time periods or during certain events. Studies such as Winston Churchill's *History of the English Speaking People*, and Samuel Eliot Morison's *The Oxford History of the American People*, speak of the history of segments of mankind, in this case our own.

Likewise, the myriad books having some particular aspect of daily life as their subject matter serve as sources for information you may need to bring understanding to and render interesting the lives of ancestors. A history of the Pennsylvania "Dutch" lifestyles or a study of nineteenth-century farming methods can provide a wealth of background material for your book, as well as the settings within which to relate tales of ancestors. Byrd, in his writings known as *The History Of The Dividing Line Betwixt Virginia and North Carolina*, provides a truly delightful view of the lifestyles of some of the earliest settlers in tidewater Virginia, as well as of those farmers in the earliest of the North Carolina counties that border the Old Dominion.

On and on. The sources are almost limitless. Simply decide what years you need and what subjects you want to discuss—styles of houses, wars, cooking, transportation, religious activities, court activities, animals, farming, Native Americans of that period and place, etc.—then go to the library and search for or ask the reference clerk for suggestions as to books that deal with those topics and periods.

Cemeteries and Churches

You must review your findings from churches and religious affiliations. As we all know, most folks went to church in the early days. They did so 1) because they were God-fearing, 2) because the law often required it, and 3) by reason of the pleasure and social value of such meetings and gatherings. So be sure to mention all known church affiliations of ancestors discussed in your writing.

Draw the locations of their churches on your maps, and whether or not those churches are still in existence, drive out there, take pictures of the setting, and inquire of the pastors or other church officers as to the whereabouts of records of births, baptisms, communions, deaths, and even of meetings of deacons and the like. Wherever these records do still exist, you should seek them out and make copies (if permitted) for use as illustrations.

Remember that the folks who were named as witnesses, sponsors, and participants in baptisms, christenings, confirmations, and dedications of children were often relatives of the child—parents, aunts, uncles, grandparents, etc. Likewise, God-parents usually were relatives. Even if they were just friends, sponsors and participants at religious ceremonies had SOME relationship to or association with the family.

You might want to mention to your readers that because often many children were born to a family, ceremonies such as christenings, dedications, and baptisms were commonplace, and by reason of the time consumed and the difficulties of moving about on foot or by horse, folks normally did not travel long distances for such ordinary events. Therefore, it is reasonably certain that the sponsors and witnesses at such events resided in the nearby neighborhood.

If an old church once attended by ancestors is no longer active, visit a nearby church (preferably of the same denomination) and ask the whereabouts of the records, or of the last record keeper, of the now inactive congregation. When the records are not to be found locally, ask the name of the old church and approximate year that activities there ceased. You can use that information upon your next visit to the state archives.

Then, when at the archives, inquire as to the location of any regional repository for that religious denomination. Two examples are sufficient: in Nashville, Tennessee, and Rochester, New York, you will find substantial collections of materials and records pertaining to many early Baptist congregations, and the American Jewish Archives are located in Cincinnati, Ohio. Likewise, and simply for the asking, many other repositories of church records are free and open to us.[18]

Incidentally, in the early days the best records were kept by the Quakers, Lutherans, and Catholics, to which list, after about 1850, one may add the Mormons. Remember too that Orders of Sisters (nuns) often owned and operated schools, and their valuable records of students and activities sometimes may be uncovered simply by inquiring of parish priests in the areas of ancestors' homes.[19]

Cemeteries

Finally, and of great importance, especially for photos to be used for illustrations, remember that many churches maintained cemeteries, the records for which are often kept locally with the other church documents. So, inquire of the pastors, clerks, or members of the congregation concerning such facilities and records.

Locate all cemeteries on the maps to be included in your book, and be sure to include the names by which they are known, e.g., "Bishop Cemetery," "Pleasant Hill Cemetery," etc. Remember, since walking horses and mourning people moved at only about three miles an hour, ancestors nearly always were buried within two or three miles of their homes, if not in a private cemetery on the family property. Just as now, very few persons were buried off by themselves even within those cemeteries.

Note all information found on every family grave marker, and make notes of the dates and names found on the headstones immediately surrounding those graves. Do not forget that many cemeteries once were churchyards, even though that fact may not be apparent now. So, just as you sought church records, inquire of folks living nearby as to whether or not there ever was a church there. If so, attempt to learn its name, again for use later when visiting church records repositories or the archives.

---

18. An excellent article, by Charles F. Rehkopf, concerning the uses of church records and a list of sources may be found in *Ancestry*, July/August, 1994, "Using Records in the Archives of Religious Organizations," pp. 5, et. seq.

19. A partial list of orders of nuns are listed in Paul Drake, *What Did They Mean By That? A Dictionary of Historical Terms for Genealogists* (Heritage Books, Bowie, MD, 1994), pp. 154, 155.

In doing cemetery work, remember that most headstones deteriorate in a few score years, and within your lifetime grave markers that are now difficult to read will be illegible and lost forever. For that reason, "rubbings" are important, and where the inscription or decorations are unique or interesting, such rubbings may be reduced in size and used as illustrations

Sometimes rubbings are difficult to make because the carvings in the headstone are difficult to read. That problem often may be solved by simply brushing away the dirt and debris with a soft bristle (not metal) scrub brush. After brushing, place a sheet of thin brown wrapping or meat paper tightly over the stone, and thoroughly rub red or blue carpenters' chalk (available in every hardware store) or dark crayons over the paper.

Where no rubbing is intended, an easy way to make faded inscriptions more legible is to spray the stone with aerosol shaving cream, and then quickly wipe over it with an ordinary small squeegee such as are used to clean windows. The old writing often will be quite visible for a few seconds. This method works particularly well if you intend to take a photograph of the stone.

In early times, particularly in the tidewater counties from Maryland south, there was no native stone from which to make cemetery markers, and only the wealthy had the means to have stone shipped in from the other colonies. For these reasons, many of your southern ancestors were buried with markers made of wood that have long ago turned to dust.

Then too, even in those settled areas where stone was available merely for the taking, stone carvers either had not yet arrived or charged unaffordable fees for their services. So it was that the men of the family often made monuments to the dead with a piece of ordinary field stone and a "cold chisel," often inscribing only the initials. Nevertheless, even these sometimes are rendered legible by the use of chalk and paper or shaving cream.

If the cemetery has an office and record keeper (usually called a "sexton"), ask if you may search any index to interments that they may have kept. Check such indexes for all persons who had the surnames you are studying. Do so, and make notes, even if you think they are not related to you.

Many cemeteries have log books or journals, often kept in the work shed, in which researchers have recorded their names, addresses, and the names of the families for whom they were searching. Carefully note those names; not only may they be kin and become friends, they are potential buyers of your book.

If there is no cemetery office, ask a neighbor for the name of the caretaker, grounds keeper, or person who mows the grass, and then inquire of him or her. Such folks often know many important details concerning families buried there and of others like you who have visited and inquired after specific families and names. Mowing a cemetery time after time lends a considerable depth of knowledge, hence such folks often will know quite positively if a family name is not familiar to them, thus saving you much time and also revealing that you probably are in the wrong cemetery.

Having spoken a little of archives and libraries, let us re-examine some sources that typically are found only there.

Chapter IV, Part 2: Gleaning What We Missed
Libraries, Archives, and Archival Type Sources

"Beware of the man of one book."
Isaac D'Israeli (1766-1848)

Censuses and Enumerations, Generally

The researcher of American families must always strive to maintain an overall perspective of our history. To that end, it is appropriate to divide our history into two periods, 1) the colonial period 1607-1775 (the first permanent English-speaking settlement at Jamestown, VA, until the beginning of the American Revolution) and 2) the years since 1775, during which we have been an independent nation, the United States. That division might be stated in another way: 1) the years during which we were for the very most part English men and women (Britons), and 2) the years since, throughout which we have been proud to be Americans.

Censuses and Enumerations, State and Local

A definition is necessary. Even though in genealogy most of us usually use the terms interchangeably, strictly speaking a *census* is an enumeration of a group of people, to which has been added data concerning age, sex, names, etc., while an *enumeration* is a numbering—a mere count—and is generally said to not include information other than an identifier, such as the head of household, address, religious affiliation, etc.

However you use the terms census and enumeration, in addition to the familiar *Decennial Censuses* of the United States government, there have been many of both taken. Since the beginning of civilization, if taxes were to be collected and existing social orders understood and maintained, governments had to have information as to who lived where, how they earned a livelihood, what they owned, what their station in life was, and what their needs were.

So too, the states and colonies, and even our counties, cities, and some religious groups, especially in the early years. These bodies, in their desire to maintain a tax base and a bank of vital statistics, frequently counted their people and the age groups to which they belonged, measured and listed their assets (especially those upon which a tax might be levied as discussed above), and located these citizens geographically. Those many and varied lists are so well known to experienced genealogists that no further explanation is here needed; who has not encountered the *Visitations* of old England and the tithables lists of the early American colonies?

Such enumerations, censuses, and lists—variously available at the National Archives, states' archives, and at genealogical libraries all over the country—contain many different categories of information, depending entirely upon what it was that the sponsoring colonies, states, and political bodies sought to do or learn. As with so many other records, now that you propose to write you must reconsider these sources.

Decennial Censuses Re-examined

While the twenty (20) Decennial Censuses sponsored and taken by our government (thirteen of which are now open to us[1]) surely are the best known and most used listings of our people, many other and similar "censuses" have been made. As have we all, it is likely that in more than one of these sources you have overlooked or failed to note what are important details, now that you have begun the process of writing.

One of the many details to be found in enumerations or censuses (whichever term you use) is the full name of the enumerator, the census taker. That name is usually found, if not on each page, then at least at the beginning and at the end of his or her forms—work sheets. These workers almost always lived near the people they listed (usually within a day of walking) and are ancestors or relatives of someone, perhaps you. So always make a note of and consider those names as potential kin.

In the many enumerations where the heads of household are listed in alphabetical order, after examining the same for the surnames you seek, make it an ongoing practice to look at the very end of that listing. In early times there were no word processors, typewriters, carbon paper, or effective erasing materials for ink. Thus, if after alphabetizing and writing his final list an enumerator learned that he had missed persons who should have been included, rather than undertake the very considerable task of re-writing the whole list, the missing names usually were included at the very end, quite out of alphabetical order. One example will suffice, even though there are myriad such instances; the 1790 list for Fairhaven, Vermont, is written alphabetically, yet following the final entries in that list you will find the families of Abraham Utler, Hezekiah Keeler, Cornelius Brownson, and Davis Quevy, in that order.

To advanced researchers, no instruction is required in the problems encountered in early spellings, phonetic or otherwise. Nevertheless, one should always be aware that given names also were misspelled, albeit less often. Again, one example is enough; the 1810 census for Bucks County, Pennsylvania, lists Revolutionary War veteran Claudius Martin as "Martin, Cloudy S"; a quite understandable error, yet the latter appears alphabetically (Clo) far from where one would seek the word Claudius (Cla), thus requiring great care by the researcher lest old Claude be thought not present.

Then too, do not forget that quill-pen writing with sometimes poor quality ink has resulted in portions of letters being indistinct or often missing, and small blobs of ink mistakenly may be interpreted as portions of such letters. The name William K̲. Drake once was abstracted as William R̲. Drake as a result of a small smudge of ink at the top of the "K." in the original, causing it to appear very much like the letter "R."

Finally, by way of general considerations, note that over the decades many census pages have been renumbered, sometimes several times. So, if you are unable to locate an entry on the page revealed by an index, always look about and in all the margins of that page and on the following and preceding 2 or 3 pages to determine if you have inadvertently moved through the microfilm or volume using a pagination that was later abandoned or revised. While errors do sometimes appear in indexes, usually the entry thought to be missing will be found by simply reexamining the page-numbering. Where considerable confusion is brought about by such a re-numbering, advise your reader of the problem by comment in your foot- or endnotes.

---

1. The census of 1890 was destroyed by fire, and those after 1920 are not yet open to the public; a Decennial census is opened 72 years after its taking.

Citing of Decennial Censuses

A word must be said concerning citations of authority from one of the censuses. The purpose of all citations, is to provide a means—precise directions—by which your readers may seek and examine the same information that you used.

In the case of the First Decennial Census (1790), most of us use the copies that have been bound and published, either by the U. S. Government Printing Office or by private publishers such as "Reprint Co." of Spartenburg. In citing any of these volumes, the method is the same as that used with all other books, e.g., "*Heads Of Families, etc., 1790, Pennsylvania* (U. S. Government Printing Office, Washington, 1908), p. 138, second column, 19th family."

Where microfilm is used, no matter for what census or year, examples of one of the several acceptable methods of citing would be: *Seventh Decennial Census* (1850), Pennsylvania, Microfilm M432-0784, p. 24, dw. 55, fam. 63, "H. Neff"; or *Tenth Decennial Census* (1880), Pennsylvania, Microfilm Roll #T9-1103, p. 56, dwelling 524, family 535, "Carner, Charles". (For further information regarding proper methods of citing, consult a good reference guide, such as the *Chicago Manual of Style*.)

Decennial Censuses: 1790

The census of 1790 (again, to the purists, an "enumeration," since only the names of the heads of households were stated) is properly called (and cited) "Heads Of Families, At The First Census of the United States Taken In The Year 1790."

The researcher of the 1790 lists, and, for that matter, of all early lists, always should be vigilant and bear in mind that the early census takers were not well paid, and not always conscientious and careful. They often were not good spellers, particularly literate, or skilled at penmanship, and they sometimes were not well liked, knowledgeable, or even sober. Many were called upon to work in what we would now view as the deep backwoods, and it was not uncommon for them to encounter incredibly bad roads and equally difficult weather, loss of direction, reluctance or outright hostility by those interviewed, and big, mean dogs. Indeed, considering the immensity of the task they undertook in those times, we cannot help but wonder how they succeeded as well as they did.

It should also be remembered that those questions in the schedules that sought information above and beyond the mere names and numbers of members of the households sometimes were considered by both the enumerators and those being questioned as 1) nobody's business, 2) questions that could be answered with something less than honesty and candor without a great risk of punishment, and 3) quite unnecessary. Unfortunate that is, too, since the advanced researcher looks at these very columns for those tiny bits and scraps of evidence that others have overlooked or ignored. So, seek out what is there stated, and do not make assumptions based on the occasional absence of information where it should have appeared.

The careful researcher also will keep in mind that one must look elsewhere than the 1790 national censuses for ancestors then living in what was or would soon be Delaware, Georgia, Kentucky, New Jersey, Tennessee, and Virginia; since those schedules were destroyed when the British burned Washington during the War of 1812. Moreover, even though the Virginia state censuses, tax lists, and enumerations made in 1782, 83, 84, and 1785 help immensely in the absence of the 1790 lists, those lists that have survived the years include only thirty-nine of the seventy-eight counties then existing.

In working with the schedules of 1790 and other early lists, it is apparent that some are set forth, rather than in alphabetical order, in the order in which the enumerator encountered the dwellings as he moved through his assigned district. To our great advantage, that style of listings reveals neighbors of ancestors.

Moreover, in those lists that are not alphabetical, the appearance of the same surname in close proximity to an ancestor may reveal the presence of a child, brother, or parent; in earlier times, children often built a house and remained on or very near the "home place." Notice also that if an ancestor had no sons or had sons who moved away, oftentimes the daughters and their spouses were those who chose to live nearby, especially since daughters frequently cared for aged parents. So it is that the careful researcher will note names of adjoining or nearby neighbors with surnames other than that of an ancestor, since they may be in-laws of that ancestor.

As always, historical perspective must be maintained. Most folks lived in the country, in rural areas on what now we would view as small farms; yet notice that a village of considerable size may be platted and developed on only a hundred or so acres. Thus, since census takers, as now, worked along the streets and roads, either one side at a time, or back and forth across to the houses, the names of immediate neighbors of ancestors living in villages more rarely provide clues to kinship. As an example, W. L. Midlam of Marion, Ohio, whose name and family appear in the 1900 census on Prospect Rd., Ed Carner, his brother-in-law, who lived on Carner Ave., and Oscar Midlam, his father, who lived on Lake St., all were within a three minute walk of each other and visited at least every other day or so, even though that proximity is in no way apparent in the lists. So, do not presume that persons of the same surname were not related simply because none seemed to live close together in an enumeration of a village or city.

Decennial Censuses: 1800 and 1810

The type of information contained in the Decennial Censuses of 1800 and 1810 is the same. What often is overlooked, or viewed as little more than interesting, is that the number of slaves living on the property is set forth. That residency may reveal something of the calling and affluence of the landowner. But, beware that rented or loaned slaves also were included if they lived there, and such business relationships were common. Moreover, in early times, children of slaves often were sent to the homes of aged or ailing parents in order that those parents be assisted with life's difficulties. Accordingly, be careful with assumptions about ownership of slaves until further evidence (tax lists, etc.) proves such ownership.

The 1800 and 1810 listings also have a category called "All Others." "Others" were those whose residence was with that head of household and were not at liberty to leave, and included such as apprentices, redemptioners, and other "bound"[2] servants, i.e., persons who were not "free." When considering such non-family members, remember that farmhands, children who were "fostered out" to that family, and others who were not bound by some condition of servitude—that is, they were "free"—were enumerated as though they were members of the family.

---

2. For our purposes here, "bound" means "apprenticed to another."

Decennial Censuses: 1820

Next after the itemization of the ages of the family members, the 1820 Decennial Census sets forth the number of members of the household who were not yet "naturalized," i.e., were not citizens of the U.S. Note here that children born of U.S. citizens, or born in this country to non-citizens, have always been citizens because of that birth, and, except for the period 1798-1802 when fourteen (14) years of residency were required, all persons who had lived here for a period of five (5) years or more were eligible to apply for citizenship.

A listing in this column as not yet naturalized should take you to the local courthouse, since many entries revealing naturalization appear in the recorded materials at the county level. If the surnames you seek there do not appear in the deed or "Miscellaneous Index," simply ask the clerk to direct you to any other indices that might contain entries having to do with citizenship.

As one example, the deed records of Delaware County, Ohio, reveal that on Friday, 26 July, 1844, thirty-four year old Richard Roberts (a successful, devout Welsh farmer residing in that county) appeared before the court and was naturalized. By including a photo of that old courthouse and describing a typical hot Ohio July day, Richard's horseback, wagon, or buggy trip from the farm to the courthouse those many years ago becomes a poignant and most enjoyable passage in the story of that family.

Following the column having to do with citizenship, the 1820 enumeration tells of occupation or business activity by reflecting the measure of participation of the head of household in 1) agriculture, i.e., those who grew or tended living plants or animals, e.g., husbandmen, sheepherders, or farmers, 2) commerce, i.e., those who worked or dealt within the stream of trade, e.g., agents, traders, factors, shippers, or haulers of merchandise, and in theory including such callings as cartmen, teamsters, canal boatmen, owners and operators of ferries, tugs, boats carrying goods or people for hire, etc., and 3) in manufacturing, i.e., those who created goods or products, e.g., millers, gunsmiths, foundry and forge owners and operators, coopers, distillers, shoemakers, cabinet and furniture makers, wagon and wheelwrights, etc.

So, be very observant of numbers listed in those columns. Evidence of an ancestor's calling is there, to be confirmed through other sources such as tax lists, membership applications for societies, crafts guilds, and Masonic organizations, listings, ads, and notices of occupations in newspapers, and passages in county histories that speak of the adequacy or location of services available in the villages and towns of the area.

Still in 1820, the "Free Colored" living on the premises were counted; unfortunately, they were not named. Those persons were blacks who had been born free or were emancipated by their owners or by act of the legislature of that territory or state.

In that regard, notice that in 1820, and even later, many former slaves lived in the northern and what we now consider the "free" states. Slavery was not abolished in Pennsylvania until 1780, in Connecticut and Rhode Island until 1784, in New York until 1785, in New Jersey and Massachusetts (the latter by court decision) until 1786, and in all of the Northwest Territory (the future Ohio, Indiana, Illinois, Michigan, Wisconsin, and Minnesota) until the Ordinance of 1787.

After gaining their freedom by whatever means, many former slaves "hired out" to whites, and were paid some combination of money, food, and housing. Once again, here is revealed something of the activities of the family, and also of what the home

No. 3

The United States,

To E. C. Francis Capt. 54th O. V. Infantry

ON WHAT ACCOUNT	COMMENCEMENT AND EXPIRATION		TERM OF SERVICE CHARGED		PAY PER MONTH		AMOUNT		REMARKS
	From	To	Months	Days	Dollars	Cents	Dollars	Cents	
PAY.									
For myself,									
For...	March 14th 1862	August 20th 1862	5	20	60	00	340	00	
For 1 private servant not soldier			5	20	10	00	71	33	
CLOTHING.									
For 1 private servant not soldier									
FORAGE.									
For horses			5	20	2	50			
SUBSISTENCE.									

	No. of days.	No. of Rations per day.	Total En. of Rations.	Post or place where due.	Price of Ration. cents.		
For myself for	173						
For 1 private servant not soldier	173	5	865		30	259	50
						798	33

RECAPITULATION.

Pay ....
Subsistence ....
Forage ....
Clothing ....
Amount ....$

I HEREBY CERTIFY, That the foregoing account is correct and just; that I have not been absent without leave during any part of the time charged for; that I have not received pay, or received money in lieu of any part thereof, for such part of the time therein charged; that I actually owned, and kept in service the horses, and employed the private servant, as charged for...

DESCRIPTION OF SERVANTS.

NAMES	COMPLEXION	HEIGHT		EYES	HAIR
		Feet.	Inches.		
Allan Smith	Black	5	9	Grey	Black

RECEIVED of ...

Quarter U. S. Army, this 20 day of ... 1862 the sum of Seven Hundred Ninety eight dollars and thirty three cents, being the amount and in full of said account.

(SIGNED IN DUPLICATE) Eli C. Francis

A. A. Q. M. 54th Oh. Reg't

A unique document, a copy of which entries may be obtained through the National Archives by the use of their Form NATF-80. Here, Captain Eli C. Francis, of the 54th Ohio Volunteer Infantry in the Civil War, is compensated for his expenses and for those needed for his maintenance of a Negro servant. It reveals the rank of Capt. Francis and his above ordinary station in life, and also shows his pay as a captain ($60.00 per month, $2400.00 or so in 1996 money), the sums he received for his "arms, clothing, etc." ($10.00, about $400.00 now), and the $2.50 per month he received as partial reimbursement for his expenses in keeping his servant, Allan Smith (about $100.00 in present-day money, 1996).

scene might have been on any given day. When the activity engaged in by the members of the family was agricultural, those free blacks doubtless were farm workers, and when the occupation was manufacturing, such persons, humble as their origins may have been, likely worked alongside the owners and—whether realistically or not—considered themselves to be "free." Not to be forgotten was the common practice of utilizing the services of the women of those black families as domestic help, as governesses, and as "wet nurses."

It is interesting that even the children and grandchildren of free black families lived and worked openly as servants even down to the end of the Civil War. Among the many officers compensated for their expenses in maintaining black "servants" during that war were Capt. Eli Francis of the 54th Ohio (see illustration, p. 94) and 2nd Lt. Isaac Lytle of the 148th Pennsylvania, the servant of Francis having been "Allan" Smith, and that of Lytle having been Thomas Miles. So, never overlook that column, since there may be found evidence that, upon follow-up, will be of great interest to your readers.

Decennial Censuses: 1830 and 1840

The type of information contained in the enumerations for 1830 and 1840 is identical, and here, for the first time, we find clues to the ages of those listed as "over 45" in earlier listings. Notice that those persons appearing in 1830 at ages between 40 and 50, or in 1840 at ages between 50 and 60 (born 1780-1790), would have appeared in the 1790 census as "under 16," and those over 60 in 1830 or over 70 in 1840 would have been in the "over 16" column of 1790.

Additionally, since the females of 1790 were simply counted, regardless of age, and those of 1800 and 1810 were listed relative to 16- and 26-year age groups, the approximate ages of some wives may be extrapolated from the 1830 and 1840 schedules. Perhaps equally important, fathers of extreme age and aged and widowed mothers of the heads of households or their spouses, frequently appear in the advanced age columns, thus often explaining the absence of those persons elsewhere as heads of households.

As in prior years slaves are listed here, thus again indirectly reflecting callings, affluence, or stations in life of families, particularly in the South. Then too, as in the examples above, "free colored" again were revealed, as were "foreigners not naturalized." The considerations mentioned above should again be taken into account when working with these columns.

Notice too that pensioners of the U.S. are shown in the enumeration of 1840. These are most valuable bits of evidence, and reveal that the named persons will be found elsewhere in the records of the government, e.g., the records of veterans and of former office holders or employees of government. Notice that these "employees" might be census takers in the near area.

Decennial Censuses: 1850

The census of 1850 is well known to all genealogists, since therein, for the first time, all persons within the households were named. What is often overlooked, however, is the other information provided in the schedules for this year.

For the first time, the existence of more than one family within the household is apparent. Where the dwelling number is the same in two or more consecutive entries, yet the family numbers are different, the researcher is made aware that the dwelling was either a multi-family structure, or, more often, that two separate family units lived under the same roof, each to some extent legally and financially distinct from the other.

In earlier times, as now, government did not enjoy the complete trust of the citizenry, and poll—"head"—taxes were not uncommon. For those reasons, a head of household usually would be quite specific in who was or was not within his or her charge, lest that head of household later be considered to have additional responsibilities for those residents, e.g., taxes, duties of care, etc. So, where there are multi-family households, be aware that the heads of each of those families will likely be found in other records, independently charged with or enjoying other obligations or benefits.

The census for 1850 also had a column in which the "color" of the household member was to be set forth. Persons of as little as one-sixteenth African blood were to be listed as "colored." (Then too, American Indians were occasionally shown as "colored.") That column was placed in the census in deference to the miscegenation statutes of the several Southern states. Thus, where an ancestor is listed as colored, the extent of that mixture may have been large or small.

Also stated in the 1850 breakdowns of families are the occupations of all household members. Notice that while a wife might be expected to appear "keeping house," a daughter or other member might be engaged in some other calling that would be taxable or otherwise noticeable by government. Moreover, in addition to the usual callings of men that may lead the researcher to other sources, where a woman is shown as a milliner, musician, teacher, dressmaker, seamstress, etc., the local newspapers of that immediate time period should be examined for advertisements that might shed light on the life of that person, all to the immense enjoyment of your readers.

Notice too that where a young man or woman appears with small children, and no spouse seems to be present within the household, the local newspapers and court records should be examined for the period preceding, thereby perhaps revealing a death, estate, divorce, criminal charge, or abandonment. Remember, not long before the date of that entry those spouses were someplace! Remain aware, however, that husbands often placed their families with relatives and "went west" seeking land or employment, after which they sent for the family. So, be careful about making presumptions.

The 1850 lists reveal the value of all real estate owned by the persons named. Those values can be misleading, however. It was no great crime to incorrectly state the worth or your property in a census, and so those with an inclination to be boastful, and an equal number who felt a need to conceal their true worth from the world, often told of values in excess of or less than the true worth. Still though, as the people being counted chatted with the census taker, they usually could learn what their neighbors had stated as the value of their respective holdings, and because of that factor, some folks stated values that were not too far from true worth.

Accordingly, no generalizations can be made, and the values set forth after your ancestors' names may or may not provide meaningful clues concerning the relative affluence of the community, the neighborhood, and that family.

Never forget also that where a value is given for real estate in a Decennial Census, you have powerful evidence that somewhere—almost certainly in the local courthouse

—there is a recorded deed or mortgage for that land. Copies of those deeds are very important by reason of their content, and often also make interesting illustrations for your book, especially if written in early English or in a foreign language.

Despite how interesting such census stated values may be, the real estate tax lists for that same period usually provide a more meaningful number, and should be searched out. Bear in mind, though, that throughout history the tax value has almost always been some percentage less than the retail or market value of property; voters demanded it of their elected tax people.

Next in the 1850 schedules is a column that reveals birthplaces of individuals named. Little need be said to the experienced researcher in this regard, but do remember that if a foreign country is shown there, you may find that person appearing in prior passenger lists and in naturalization records during his or her lifetime.

Following that is a column that reveals whether or not a person had married during the preceding year. While the experienced researcher has utilized these columns repeatedly, remember that you will here gain knowledge of a time period positive for your search in government or church marriage records for further information concerning that couple.

Next is the column reflecting whether or not that person attended school within that year. Note here, where the person said to have attended school was over sixteen, you should look at records of colleges and "academies" in the area, and where the family was wealthy and the person attending school was a female, the local girls'—ladies'— academies should be checked. Such records, if not still housed in that school or in the local library, usually will be found at the state archives. The completeness of such records is sometimes most gratifying. The 1882 record of a "grade"—report—card of Ohioan Maggie Belle Carner yet remains; she received "A"s and "B"s, except in mathematics, wherein her marks were "C"s, all of interest to her descendants.

Significantly, next is that column that reveals literacy. Notice that where illiteracy is stated, particularly in male heads of households, you have an indication that in prior censuses and other records requiring signatures or acknowledgments someone else provided the spelling, which, in turn, led to variations. On the other hand, where literacy is shown, you have a clue for searches in schools or among tutors in the areas of prior residences during the younger years of that person.

Finally, a column for the enumeration date is set forth. That column was intended to reveal the date upon which the information was gained, if that date was other than the one at the top of the page. So, notice that if no one was home when the census taker arrived and he or she interviewed the household at a later date, the date at the top of the page was not correct as it related to that family and their precise ages. Indeed, that date may be as much as several months after the date upon which the enumerator first came by.

All too often, the careless researcher has been in error by as much as nearly a year through calculating an age without regard to the date given in this column. That is particulary true where the age of a child was stated as less than one year.

The final column in the schedules of 1850 is titled "Remarks." That column served to reveal conditions such as "idiot," "feeble-minded," "in prison," "would not answer," or such other comments as the enumerator thought necessary in addition to the information previously stated. One should closely examine that information column for leads as to circumstances or to other records.

Decennial Censuses: 1860

The 1860 schedules are identical to those of 1850, except that in 1860 the value of personal property also was stated. As with the real estate, these estimates were sometimes subject to boastfulness or to concealment. Nevertheless, station in life sometimes, and affluence often, are revealed. Remember, crops in the ground were listed as personal property (sometimes having a value in excess of the worth of the real estate), just as were cattle, machinery, tools, and household goods. As before, a search of the tax records of that county is indicated whenever personalty is declared to have more than the values stated for nearby neighbors.

Decennial Censuses: 1870

All the information sought in 1860 was again gained in 1870, and more than in any earlier census, that for 1870 gives assistance to the genealogist. After the columns of 1860 discussed above, the next query concerned whether or not, first, the father and, then, the mother were foreign-born.

Suppose that the person listed in 1870 was then 40 years old and not foreign-born. Then, if either parent was foreign-born, the careful researcher will know that the immigration took place before 1830, the birth year of that child (1870 less 40 equals 1830). Moreover, if only one parent was foreign-born, then the marriage (if there was one) of that couple took place here (unless the American traveled back to the "Old Country" for the wedding - a rare occurrence, except among the very wealthy) not only before 1830 (the calculated birth year of the child), but subsequent to the immigration of the foreign born family member.

Whether foreign-born or not, since the childbearing years of a woman start at about 15 and almost always end by age 55, that mother was probably born sometime between 1775 (1830 less 55) and 1815 (1830 less 15). Note too, by deduction we may be sure that the marriage took place during that same period of time, before which the migration of the spouse most likely occurred.

Thus is illustrated a very important aspect of research: the elimination of records, the determination of what records we need NOT examine in our search for some line. In the example above, we need only to search the immigration records for a man of that surname before 1830 and after about 1760, since the father could not have come after 1830, and almost surely was not more than 70 when the child was born.

Further, as to marriage and church records, we would need only to search from 1775 until 1830 for a marriage of that surname, and as to birth, of course, we need but look from about 1825 until 1835, thereby accounting for errors in the stated age of the child shown in the census. Notice the myriad volumes we have eliminated and the hours saved through simple deduction and thought. You do not have time to waste, especially now; the records to be re-examined are too numerous.

The next column of the census sets forth the month during that calendar year that a person listed was born or married, thus bringing to your calculations (and those of the government) a greater measure of accuracy. Then, as in 1860, whether or not the person was in school that year is revealed. Next, and again as previously, literacy is revealed.

Following literacy, the 1870 schedules reveal whether or not the person named was eligible to vote. "Eligible" is the key word, and it usually was determined by the legislatures of the states.

Despite the efforts of the states of the old South to deny blacks the power of the vote and equal treatment under the law, land ownership as a requirement had been gone for some years and, in theory, at least, universal suffrage was at hand. While those folks came into the rolls of voters, thousands of ex-Confederates, especially former military officers and high ranking Confederate government officials, were denied that right, and as to those citizens Congress reserved the right to review each case.

That denial of the franchise continued throughout the period 1865-1872, and even in that last year, the amnesty granted the former Southerners continued to exclude some 500 of the highest ranking of that group. Accordingly, the 1870 census rolls, especially those of the Southern states, may reveal much and provide many interesting stories concerning previous Confederates.

In addition, those adjudged as lunatics or feeble-minded were ineligible, as were felons and others convicted of crimes against the government. So, note this column, and realize that a mark there likely will lead you to some very interesting family history.

Finally, be aware that the 1870 census is of the greatest importance to researchers having African heritage, since all persons then living who had been slaves are listed for the first time by their full names. (Emancipation, though declared in 1863, was not accomplished until the Civil War ended and the 13th Amendment was ratified.)

Decennial Censuses: 1880

The years immediately following the census of 1870 saw the birth of a realization by our government that we had reached maturity as a nation and a position of great strength in the world. Moreover, the rapid—indeed, explosive—growth of our industrial machine gave rise to great wealth and its attendant exploitation of the masses, and to a new and growing middle class.

For those reasons, coupled with the growing humanitarian attitudes of the "thinkers" and a demand by the infant sciences for information of all sorts, we began to be aware that vital statistics were critical to government; we decided that only with what was then viewed as in-depth knowledge concerning our citizenry could we administer to our people and solve the growing social problems. One of the results was the new census schedules designed for 1880.

From 1880 through 1920 (and on to now in the "closed" censuses) the "Enumeration District"—street, precinct, township, village, etc.—is stated at the top of most pages or at the beginning of each enumerator's schedules. If you seek copies of pages of such censuses from the National Archives, you must use the required Form NATF-82, and that "district" must be stated. Incidentally, while the employees at the archives will not search censuses for you, they will copy specific pages of any "open" Decennial Censuses if you provide 1) census year, 2) state or territory, 3) county, 4) township or other subdivision, 5) name of head of household, 6) page number, and 7) enumeration district.

Copies, such as are available from the National Archives, make superb illustrations for your book. You may need to obtain copies from them, especially if those available to you are of lesser quality, or if you question an abstract and want to view the original.

In 1880—for the first time—age was noted with some precision. The schedule asks for the month of any births that took place in that year, and the ages of all on May 31, again, of that year; both, most helpful bits of information to genealogists who have long struggled with the extrapolations required by the earlier schedules.

Notice too that questions about age posed by enumerators in such a precise way required the persons being interviewed to give no small measure of thought to the answer, thereby providing to the answer a measure of credibility not usually achieved earlier. For that reason, in determining birth years, many experienced researchers consider the 1880 schedules more accurate and reliable than any prior ones.

Significantly, the relationships to the head of household of all persons residing in that home are set forth, thereby revealing siblings, in-laws, cousins, fostered children, hired hands, etc., to a substantially greater degree than in prior schedules. By reason of those entries, many "same name" cousins and other relatives are easily distinguishable.

Thereafter, the schedules relate marital status through use of the words *single, married, widowed, divorced.* Further, and again of importance to the family historian, whether or not a person named was married during that census year (1880) is revealed.

As in prior schedules, the occupation was again set forth in 1880. Following that column appeared a space for "Miscellaneous Information." As before, it is there that one often finds descriptive words (many of which we would not now use) such as "amputee," "crippled," "blind," "disabled," "unable to work," "imbecile," "lunatic," "idiot," "quarantined," and still others used by the enumerators to describe conditions or handicaps. Virtually all such terms lead the researcher to further records.

Still again, the literacy question was asked, and following that, to the ever increasing pleasure of the researcher, the place of birth of the individual is listed, as is that of his father and of his mother. Therein, lingering questions of who was an immigrant ancestor often are resolved.

The matter of whether or not Joseph Midlam (1788-1854) was an immigrant ancestor is illustrative of census entries that raise questions that may not be resolved, except through other sources. In the 1880 schedules, his sons, Oscar and John Midlam, independently of each other, stated that their father, Joseph, was born in England. However, the two sisters of Oscar and John - daughters of Joseph - stated to their respective enumerators that Joseph was born in this country! Where here is the reliability?

As to all of the four children of Joseph, no ill motive is apparent or likely, no constraints of a social or economic nature seem to be at play, and the problem does not seem to be one of probable loss of memory. So, the question seems to be, who had an "opportunity to know the facts"? The real truth of it remains uncertain, and the reader is free to conjecture, just as do Joseph's descendants today.

Decennial Censuses: 1890

The census of 1890 was almost completely destroyed. To our great misfortune, except for a few counties of Virginia and New York, no schedules remain.

Decennial Censuses: 1900

As we have seen, an ever increasing amount of data was sought and supplied by the Decennial Censuses, and the 1900 schedules are a bonanza for the family researcher. By that year and the arrival of the new century, in addition to once again assigning numbers to dwellings and families, the schedules called for house numbers and street names. Thereby was provided knowledge of the precise places of residence of the families. By utilizing this information, at least in those cities and towns where a city directory was compiled, almost all "same name" problems may be eliminated. Additionally, those addresses render school systems and schools attended and their records easily identifiable, not to mention police, tax, voting, and property records.

Notice though, it is wise to visit the offices of the city clerk or similar officer in order to be sure that the addresses have not been changed or the streets renumbered. If there seems to be no clerk who knows, seek out the mayor's office and there ask who would have knowledge of such changes; somebody should know.

Following the names and relationships to each other, the exact birthday and the age at the date of the enumeration are set out. Then, after marital status, the schedules give the number of years married for those shown to be so, which information, by simple subtraction, will lead you to marriage records of the appropriate prior years.

Significantly, the next column relates the number of children born to all females listed, and goes on to state how many of these were yet living in 1900. Those statistics are a boon to both statisticians and researchers interested in family medical history.

Following that, again the researcher will learn of the birth places of all listed, and their parents, and the year of immigration for the foreign born. Notice too, since former slaves are not distinguishable from any other citizens, the information concerning the birthplaces, parents, and siblings of these folks is extremely valuable and almost nowhere else to be found. (Any person who had been a slave had to be at least thirty-five in 1900, since Emancipation took place in 1863, and the Civil War ended in 1865.)

Next will be found the number of years that person had been in the U.S., and whether or not he or she was naturalized, again sending the family historian to appropriate records for such proceedings.

After the column revealing occupation, the number of months during that year that the person was unemployed is revealed, that data revealing much concerning seasonal works, hard times or illnesses (or ambition).

Thereafter, to a greater extent than in prior schedules, literacy is revealed, and the number of months spent in school during that year are set forth. Next there are columns revealing the ability to read, to write, and to speak English, those entries speaking volumes concerning the propensity of the elderly to cling to the language of the old countries.

Finally, and leading the researcher directly to the deed, mortgage, real estate tax, lien, assessment, and miscellaneous records, the schedules ask whether or not the home was owned or rented, whether or not it was mortgaged, and whether the property was a farm or otherwise. Little wonder that the careful researchers seeking ancestors of the early 20th century make as much effort to view the 1900 schedules as the older family historians do those for 1850.

Decennial Censuses: 1910

The 1910 schedules include the same categories of information found in those from 1900, with a few refinements in some matters. Where, in 1900 (and earlier) as previously, we learned whether or not the person was married, here we learn the duration of the existing marriage. Additionally, while in 1910 we learned whether or not the person named spoke English, here we learn what other language he or she knew; very important to those seeking countries of origin.

As in 1900, the information concerning ages, marriages, birthplaces, and numbers of births to parents of those enumerated is of the utmost value to those having African lineage. Then too, the 1900 schedules are expanded upon by relating, in addition to occupation, the nature of the business in which the person worked, and whether or not he or she was an employee, employer, or working on his or her "own account"—on commission, by piece work, or acting as an independent contractor. Thereby are opened up avenues to many other sources of data, such as corporate and business records, labor unions, and newspaper advertising. Note too, that it was at this precise period that photographs became commonplace and quite inexpensive, many ordinary folks having even taken it up as a hobby.

While at the taking of the 1910 census those who were engaged in farming, in theory at least, were required to fill out or answer questions concerning a "farm schedule," tragically those schedules have been lost. It seems that they disappeared about 1915.[3]

There too, and for the first time, the presence of both Confederate and Union army and navy veterans was revealed, leading directly to the archives for veterans' pensions and service records; to the records of the G.A.R. (Grand Army of the Republic) and U.C.V. (United Confederate Veterans) and associated organizations and societies (both local and statewide); to regimental histories; to local newspapers, particularly at patriotic holiday seasons; and to local museums and historical collections. If you find that a veteran was a member of a G.A.R. or U.C.V. post, it is wise to stop in the local antique and curio shops, there seeking G.A.R. or U.C.V. medallions, many of which are yet (1996) to be found at reasonable prices.

Closing the 1910 schedules are questions concerning whether or not the person was partially or completely blind, deaf, or "dumb,"[4] again adding greatly to the medical history of a family. The last column on the page, as in prior years, is for "comments." Again, such now socially incorrect words as "crippled," "bedridden," "amputee," etc., often appear and provide additional facts previously unknown.

Decennial Censuses: 1920

At this writing, the last census open to the public is that for 1920, having been made available—"opened"—in 1992, seventy-two years (the average man's lifespan) after it was taken, as the law required. That Congressional deference to the feelings and

---

3. This information was obtained by the author from the Library of Congress in 1994.
4. Dumb, meaning "could not speak."

desire by the citizenry for privacy now has been undermined, what with all agencies of government, not to mention the private credit agencies, etc., having liberal access to these and most other "private" records. Nevertheless, that vestige of a consideration for our desires and feelings remains in place, and the census of 1930 will not be opened until the year 2002.

The 1920 schedules were similar to those for 1900 and 1910, however the wards and precincts set forth for each individual quickly lead the careful researcher to the voting and poll records of the time, thereby once again adding background to the story of your family. All too often, voting and registration records are overlooked. Where they do yet exist, considerable information is often found, especially concerning those who sought public office and having to do with the political leanings of individuals and neighborhoods.

Then too, details of nativity and languages spoken is somewhat expanded over prior years by requiring 1) that the country of birth be stated, and 2) whether or not the language of that country was considered to be the "Mother tongue" of the person named. Background and attitudes are suggested by those answers, and should be added to your story.

Finally, as in 1910 and 1900, the information to be gained through the 1920 schedules is of the greatest importance to those with Black lineage. Indeed, 1920 has been said to be the most important stop for Americans with African roots.[5]

As should be apparent by now, you must review the census schedules, especially having to do with persons of whom you know little else. If nothing more, you will gain illustration materials.

Veterans' Records

Even though you probably have in the past, whenever "talking family" with any relative, again ask if they know of traditions or tales concerning wars in which any members of the family fought or were otherwise involved. As with family traditions, war stories often carry down through a family for numerous generations. Why search such records again? Two reasons: 1) You probably missed military service or contribution by some relative of whom you will be very proud, and 2) the records of all veterans provide detailed information not to be found anywhere else.

Remember that the available records vary from war to war, and to a considerable extent (even for the very early wars) such records are still in existence. Copies of many of the same may be procured through the archives, either state or National or both.

For state records, send a large SASE to the state library for the state or colony from which the veteran is thought to have gone to war, or in which he or she is thought to have lived after that war, with a request for such forms, schedule of fees, and requirements that they may have concerning veterans' activities. (See appendix for addresses.) If information is sought from the National Archives, write to the Reference Branch, U.S. National Archives, 7th and Pennsylvania Aves. NW, Washington, D.C. 20408, and request six or so sets of *Form NATF-80*, which are free of charge.

---

5. Those having interest in Afro-American genealogy and family history should make contact with the Afro-American Historical and Genealogical Society and the Association For The Study of Afro-American Life, the offices of which are in Washington D.C., and the Schomberg Center for Research in Black Culture, in New York City.

BRIEF in the case of *Jonathan Meacham*
of *New Salem* in the State of *Massachusetts*
(Act 7th June, 1832.)

1. Was the declaration made before a Court or a Judge? *In open court*

2. If before a Judge, does it appear that the applicant is disabled by bodily infirmity?

3. How old is he? *Seventy Six years*

4. State his service, as directed in the form annexed.

Period.	Duration of Service.			Rank.	Names of General and Field Officers under whom he served.
	Years.	Months.	Days.	As a	Gen.
In 1775		6		Private	Col. Woodbridge and Capt. Meacham & King
1775		3	15	"	Capt. King
1777		2		"	Col. Root and Capt. Izask
1777		2		"	Col. Williams & Capt. Goodale

In May
In Nov.
Feby
June

5. In what battles was he engaged? *15 months service* *Bunker Hill*

6. Where did he reside when he entered the service? *New Salem, Mass.*

7. Is his statement supported by living witnesses, by documentary proof, by traditionary evidence, by incidental evidence, or by the rolls? *Four living witnesses and traditionary evidence*

8. Are the papers defective as to form or authentication? and if so, in what respect? *correctly authenticated*

I **Certify** that the foregoing statement and the answers agree with the evidence in the case above mentioned.

Examining Clerk.

Here from the National Archives through the use of their Form NATF-80 is one of the pages available to all having to do with the Revolutionary War record of Jonathan Meachum of "New" Salem, Mass. By noticing here that Meachum was at Bunker Hill (fought on 17 June, 1775), and that he was in Capt. Goodale's Company of the regiment of Col. Williams, through the use of a battlefield map it would be relatively easy to locate where on that battlefield that unit fought. By so doing and taking a photo of that location or area as it now appears, your reader will find the whole matter of Meachum and the American Revolution vastly more interesting. Notice also that Meachum gave his age as of the date of the application for pension, thereby providing reliable evidence for deducing his birth year.

Just as the states have their own requirements, the National Archives insists that NATF-80 forms be used to gain any military records of any veteran or dependent. As with so many clerks and public servants, all archives employees are busy, hence it is wise to order the blank forms now in order that you may have them on hand as you write.

Once you receive the blank forms NATF-80, since a separate form must be submitted for both of the categories of records that you want searched, it is necessary to complete two (2) forms for each veteran. Those categories are, 1) the military records, which include the activities and movements of the veterans during the wars, and 2) the service connected sales of land and *land grants*, also often referred to as the *bounty land* records. (Again, states' archives may have different requirements and forms.)

If you want both categories of National records (and you always do), complete two forms NATF-80 as fully as possible for each veteran and return them. Likewise, if you seek records of widows' pensions and benefits, NATF-80 forms must be submitted for those. Upon receipt by the Archives of your completed NATF-80s, the folks there will do the records search for that ancestor, and if he or she is found in either or both of the categories mentioned, you will be notified that the records have been located. Thereupon, you will have thirty days within which to forward the nominal fee required for copies of those records; usually, $10.00 is required for each category of records found. When sending in the forms, be sure to tell them that you want copies of all the papers in the file, otherwise they will select what they think appropriate and important and you may not receive all the available information.

Concerning those two categories mentioned, it is important to remember that, commencing in colonial times, continuing through the Revolution, and nearly until the twentieth century, land or a right to land quite usually was given as one of the rewards for military service. In fact, grants of land to veterans and others continued on through the *homesteading acts* of both the states and the federal government, and finally ended in Alaska and Minnesota in the early 1980s.

Thereby, as with other inexpensive land settlement programs, veterans and the adventuresome were induced to take their families and clear and settle portions of the vast wilderness that yet remained on this continent. All such governmental efforts resulted in records and record keeping that will be of great value to your writing.

So, throughout most of our history, land rights and other benefits have been granted to veterans, and then, after their deaths, certain of those benefits also were granted to their survivors, especially widows. Since the methods used for recruiting our early (usually volunteer) veterans frequently were quite informal, very often little or no record was kept by the government of the names of individual soldiers or even of their units. Accordingly, later it often was impossible from the records alone to determine who should receive pensions, land, and other benefits, and who should not.

Thus it was that after being placed under oath, veterans who sought such rewards (and their widows, dependents, and witnesses, as well) were required to give complete statements of those facts that rendered that person eligible. These sworn statements often listed the birthplaces, ages, residencies before, during, and after the wars, marital status and names of wives, names of dependents, brothers and sisters, and sometimes even the parents of the veterans, as well as the military units in which they served, and their battles, wartime activities, and movements; genealogical gold mines, truly.

Concerning the records of veterans, it is important to remember that until mid-1818, only those Revolutionary veterans who were "maimed" or seriously disabled were awarded pensions. From then until 1828, a veteran had to demonstrate very reduced means—poverty—in order to qualify for a pension. That latter requirement resulted in affidavits and lists setting forth the total belongings owned by the veterans, which lists are delights to read, and serve beautifully as illustrations. Following that law, after 1828 all of the yet surviving veterans were pensioned. Finally, in 1836, veterans' widows also became eligible for monthly pensions.

Because of these requirements, many Revolutionary veterans received no pensions, and so they often escape detection by the researcher. Why? Because if a Revolutionary veteran died before 1818 and was not maimed or disabled during service, or if he died between 1818 and 1828 (between thirty-five and forty-five years after the end of the war) and was neither poverty stricken nor maimed, his name will not appear anyplace in the pension records, even though his widow's name might well later appear.

So, where then will he be revealed? He likely will be found within the land awards—grants—records, since his right to land[6] was not dependent upon his age, physical infirmity, or financial condition. So it is that the "bounty" land records may be the first and only record of the military service of an ancestor that the researcher will find in the National Archives.

Caution: Since land warrants owned by a veteran had value and legally could be sold by him, they often were. Further, such warrants sometimes were converted into land, whereupon the land itself was sold. So, rights to land warrants or the unsettled land resulting from such warrants may never have provided a residence for a veteran ancestor. Indeed, he may never even have seen the property, yet still appear of record to have been an owner. Accordingly, you must not presume that an ancestor lived on a tract simply because he had a warrant for it or because he once "owned" it.

On the other hand, many a soldier was granted land, cleared it and built a house there, raised a family, lived out his life, and found his final resting place near the house or in the orchard. So, be very careful in making assumptions based on land warrants in the name of ancestors.

In summary, unless you know when a veteran died and have knowledge of his physical condition and economic status, it is well to seek out both forms of records mentioned—1) land records files and 2) the combined pension and military activities files. Remember, while any veteran not maimed, who also was not poverty stricken and who did not live to extreme age, died without ever appearing in the pension records, if his widow was alive after 1836 she may appear in those very records.

Incidentally, widows' pension files are every bit as complete as the veterans' files. Indeed, from the standpoint of genealogical information to be gained, widows' claims are often more informative than are those of the veterans, since widows' claims rested entirely upon kinship, and not upon military service, and so required proof of marriage, sworn statements concerning residences, children, etc.

It also is important to note that the during and after all wars, particularly the Revolution and the War of 1812, the state and federal governments usually have permitted citizens to file claims for property destroyed by acts of war, for non-military

---

6. More precisely, his rights to receive *warrants* that might then be traded for land or sold, as the veteran chose.

services rendered, and for materials or supplies furnished the armed forces. Thereby will be revealed the locations, residences or areas of contribution of ancestors, thus leading the researcher to the libraries and courthouses of those places. Many such claims have been the subject of numerous writings and books found in nearly all large libraries. As with other library searches, you likely will start with the *card catalogs*.

Not all existing veterans' records (especially those of the Revolution and the War of 1812) are housed in the National Archives. Many was the soldier who served in combat in a unit of the state *militia*, rather than in any "national" military unit. Such militia records very often were retained only in states' archives.

Accordingly, if you do not find an ancestor in the national records, yet because he was of military age you suspect that he did serve, you must search the records of those states (and colonies) which either existed or were carved out of those that did exist at the time of the war being researched. Again, it is best to commence with the card catalog at the library under "veterans" or under the names of the wars.

When searching for Revolutionary veterans and their families, keep in mind that most large libraries have the very fine indexes to the records of the Society of Daughters of the American Revolution (*D.A.R.*), which contain thousands of names of patriot veterans, as well as names of myriad descendants, who by reason of the service of their ancestors, are now or were once affiliated with that organization or sought to be so associated.

The magnificent library of the D.A.R. is in Washington, D.C., and is open to the public. So too is the fine library of the Society of Sons of the American Revolution, located in Louisville, Kentucky. Remember, though, that those records do <u>not</u> contain the names of every single veteran. If no descendant of a veteran ever sought membership in any of those organizations, his or her name may not appear in their records.

If you do find that an ancestor was a veteran of the Revolution, you are eligible to be considered for membership in the S.A.R. or the D.A.R. Further, there are many other societies and organizations for which you may be eligible as a result of the military service of an ancestor in that and in other and later wars (Order of the Cincinnati, Sons of the Revolution, Daughters of Confederate Veterans, Sons of Union Veterans, etc.).

In conclusion, be certain to review your files for veterans' names, then gain their military and pension records. You and your readers will be glad you did.

Published Genealogies and Family Histories

As with all other categories of writings, few are the family researchers who do not know that published materials containing historical and genealogical materials and lineages vary vastly in accuracy, reliability, and quality. Most of us have encountered genealogies prepared with the utmost care and deliberation and other writings done so poorly as to require that all who read them speak out and give warning, lest fellow researchers be misled.

The tests applicable to other writings serve equally well with family histories and genealogies of others. While very few family history buffs are motivated to write other than the truth, whether or not they could have known that truth depends entirely upon whether the sources needed by them were available at the time, and if so, whether or not that writer was sufficiently diligent in his or her research within those sources. As an example, despite their training, diligence, and long, long efforts, early writers sometimes erred because, at the time of their writings, many records now commonly available—especially passenger lists and courthouse records—had not yet come to light or been abstracted. (And that fact should be a warning to all of us; many of our present-day beliefs will be considerably altered by discoveries and abstracts yet to be made.)

How can we know of the diligence (or lack of the same) by other writers, especially those of the distant past? Ask yourself, did the writer set forth his sources by way of foot- or endnotes? If so, you should spot-check them. If notes do appear, consider whether or not that writer used the most reliable sources available, e.g., were courts' records used or, instead, did the writer regularly use abstracts created by still other persons? If abstracts were used, were those abstractors known for their knowledge, diligence, and care? Did you find any glaring errors; errors that the previous writer should not have made even in light of the sources then available to him or her?

Think further: Where the author relied upon the memories of people unknown to you, were you, the reader, warned of the potential for error in such information? Does it appear that conclusions were drawn from bits of evidence that might have been equally interpreted otherwise or, instead, was the proof clear and convincing for you? Did the writer frequently presume the truth of writings that are now known to contain error, e.g., were records such as censuses used to establish spelling or precise ages?

In short, while remembering that we all have erred and, more than that, have unknowingly perpetuated errors made by others, read the writings of those others with great care. If mistakes appear there that you would not have made, be cautious; if one error was committed, it is likely that there were others. Once again, while their motives likely were quite proper, such earlier writers may not have had the opportunity to know the truth.

There is another factor to consider in utilizing materials of earlier researchers: Much more so than now, and very often due to the fact that few "genealogy books" then existed, many of the early writers wrote from tradition and lineages that had been set forth and passed on many years before their time. So it is that many "family trees" exist that are quite devoid of references and citations.

As an example, since the earliest times folks have been proud of their *Mayflower* ancestry, have perpetuated those tales and lineages in writing and otherwise, and have considered their ancestry so well established that it could (and should) not be questioned. So, what to do? Utilize those materials and quote them if necessary, however, if earlier conclusions may not now be independently proven, you should advise your readers of that lack of confirmability.

Genealogical Abstracts

As stated, the thousands of books and articles concerned with the many aspects of genealogical study vary in quality from dismal to brilliant, and it is of value to divide the many titles into categories. Those works called abstracts set out abbreviations of the original documents in the same order as were the original materials. Thus, an abstract of the deed records for a series of years may be expected to set forth deed information commencing with the first volume of that series to be abstracted and proceeding with the subsequent volumes in the order in which they were written. Such abstracts universally are indexed by the names of the parties mentioned in the documents, and often by subjects and places, as well.

Abstracts often are not detailed enough to provide you with that last bit of evidence that will conclude proof of some question; if all the details were rewritten in the abstract, it would not be an abstract anymore. Nevertheless, such works will direct you to the court record or sources, volumes, and pages where those scraps may be gleaned.

In gathering those last pieces, remember again that clerks, librarians, and registers of deeds and other records are not paid to do genealogical research. So, if the distance to the courthouse or archives is great and microfilm copies of the needed records are available through your inter-library loan system, LDS Family History Center, or a microfilm rental service, it is better to use those sources; that, even though some of the copies obtained there may not be of the quality obtainable from original records.

As do microfilm copies, properly done abstracts reveal the volumes and pages of the archives or courthouse records where writings, deeds, and other documents may be found, thus making it possible for the searcher to request copies of any writing by precise title, volume, and page. So, in letters to such sources, give the most complete names possible of all the parties, (grantors and grantees in deeds), the exact year and date (if known), and the name or title of the document (deed, lien, court order, etc.), and be sure to state the volume numbers and pages of the documents you want. In short, when seeking copies of anything from a library, courthouse, or archives, you must direct them to the source as precisely as you would in a footnote.

When seeking copies, always include a large self-addressed, stamped envelope—"SASE." It is a good idea to include $3.00 or $4.00 for each document with instructions that any refund due to you should be added to their coffee fund; they will appreciate it. Remember, if you do not send money, most clerks are required to take the time to write back and tell you how much the copies will cost, thus wasting your time and postage and theirs as well. Moreover, most will not write you a check for the small balance due you, and many will simply return your letter and original sum rather than fool with the small refund that might be due you. In short, be considerate with their time and display good genealogy manners.

Extracts and Summaries

You often will encounter books wherein specific passages having to do with certain subjects have been extracted from early documents, and the balance of the old writing has not been copied. As an example, Bruce revealed that in 1639 William Huntt and Edward Robins were commissioned to transport pork and grain from Virginia to New England.[7] Even though it was of little importance to that writer in his discussion, Huntt and Robins descendants would surely want to gain copies of that extracted commission, not knowing what other information may be found there.

Similarly, in his summary of another document, Bruce cited "Records of Lower Norfolk County, vol. 1686-1695, p. 204", and then continued as follows, "John Tucker, of Norfolk County, leased for a period of eight years a plantation to...Thomas Watkins...." [8] Surely, all serious students who descend from either of those men would want to seek out the record of the writing there summarized and glean such other evidence of the life of those people as might be found.

---

7. *Economic History, etc.*, vol. i, p. 330, citing "General Court Orders, Jan. 1639")
8. Ibid., p. 417.

Since those are just two of the thousands of such references, always be on the lookout for extracted or summarized information concerning any ancestors. Whenever found, go to the sources cited, and gain copies. Incredibly interesting facts and illustrations have been uncovered in that way.

As demonstrated, summaries and extracts often are found in works that are not genealogical in nature. The result is that the researcher and writer of family history also must be vigilant to notice entries in indexes to historical materials that reveal a discussion of some matter that likely affected an ancestor in their area. So, Bruce's several studies of seventeenth-century Virginia may be fertile ground in which to seek ancestors or knowledge of their environs during that period; studies having to do with commerce in North Carolina may well reveal activities in the neighborhood of your relatives; and works that consider the early Pennsylvania oil business may very much interest a writer whose family hailed from early Venango County; on and on.

Notice that what we have done is encourage you to think of your writing, not just as a study of individuals and families, but also in terms of the subjects—topics, events—to be encountered, and then upon your next library visit search the card catalog under those subject headings. If an ancestor lived in nineteenth-century Wyandot County, Ohio, it is certain that he or she knew of the *Old Mission Church* and of the burning of Col. Crawford, both of which add color and most interesting detail. If your great-great grandmother was born in old Blair, Huntingdon, or the neighboring counties or Pennsylvania, the history of the early canals at those places will provide interesting background material or even direct knowledge of that family. Somebody drove the mules that pulled such boats! Maybe it was one of your people.

Lists of Passengers, Servants, etc.

Before the year 1925, every single, solitary soul who migrated to this land came by ship; there simply was no other way to get here. That stark fact requires all of us who would investigate immigrations of ancestry before the early years of this century to delve into the lists of passengers and servants.

Passenger lists are myriad in number, as are the abstracts, transcripts, and commentaries that have grown out of those sources, and, particularly in England, hardly a year goes by without someone uncovering a "new" and previously undiscovered list of people transported to the colonies voluntarily or involuntarily. That state of affairs requires that as you write you also scan the library catalogs and published book lists, alert to any new or revised titles that might shed light on your own immigrant lineage.

Immigration, Generally

If you are to write effectively of the travels of your people, and recognize subtle bits of evidence concerning them, you must maintain an overall perspective concerning those who came, when they came, and what they found when they arrived. To that end, a few thoughts and facts concerning emigration from the old countries are appropriate, every one of which may be developed into backdrop and context for your work.

"Migration" maps, available from many genealogical bookstores or supply houses, are helpful in allowing the researcher to visualize likely routes of travel of their ancestors. One of the first waves of immigration occurred between about 1625 and 1665 when the Walloons settled in New Amsterdam, and the Dutch in what was known as New Netherlands and on the Delaware River. During the years 1635 until about

1655 the Swedes first came to the Delaware and 1682 witnessed the first Welsh settlements in and about Philadelphia. During 1683, 1684 and 1685 Rhinelanders and Palatines first came to what was to be eastern and Germantown, Pennsylvania. After 1685 the French Huguenots appeared in New Rochelle and New York City, New York, in and about Boston, Oxford, and Salem, Massachusetts, and in and about Charleston and environs, particularly along the Santee River.

Commencing in 1709 the Palatines came first to New York, then to the Schoharie and the Mohawk Valleys, particularly in and about Germantown and Bucks and Berks Counties, Pennsylvania. Thereupon (during the two decades following 1710) came a large number, if not the bulk, of the Scotch-Irish, first to western Pennsylvania, then down the Wagon Road to Virginia, the Carolinas, Georgia, and what would be Kentucky and Tennessee.

The half-century following 1725 brought heavy German migration, and during the middle years of that period came the Moravian settlements at Savannah, Georgia, Bethlehem, Pennsylvania, and in and about Winston-Salem, North Carolina. During the dozen years after 1825 the Irish immigration greatly increased (probably peaking about 1850), as did the flow of the German Jews. Between then and the last decade of the century, the Scandinavians came to western New York and Wisconsin, the Irish continued to arrive in great numbers, and an ever-increasing German population was found in and about Baltimore, Milwaukee, New York, and St. Louis. By the middle years of the century, at least 65,000 Chinese found their way to the employment offices of the western railroad builders.

During the closing years of the nineteenth century, the poor and disenchanted of Eastern Europe—Russia, Poland, Austria-Hungary, Greece, the Balkan states—as well as the first of the Italians came, and thereafter, during the first years of the twentieth century, in addition to those just named, great numbers again came from Germany, Great Britain, and Ireland. The peak of immigration was reached in the first years of World War I, with the bulk of those being from Eastern and Southern Europe and Italy.

Though a measure of improvement came as the seventeenth and eighteenth centuries passed, until the middle half of the nineteenth century, sea voyages were incredibly difficult. Those early journeys were agonizing to both soul and body, de-humanizing to the utmost, and while perhaps well known to you and other serious researchers, little understood to most who will read your words.

The early writings are filled with stories of storms, seasickness, diseases, and death. Most of your ancestors had never been on an oceangoing vessel (and until the 1880s almost all were sailing ships, of course), and not one in a million had made an ocean voyage. Your earliest ancestors first saw land after a month to six weeks of storms, seasickness, blistering sunburns, disease, rancid water, poor food, diarrhea, incredible filth and stench, and what we would view as no medical care at all.

If they came by the "southern route," the first landfall in the early days was in the Bermudan or Caribbean islands, particularly Barbados, and then ten days or so later they saw the coast of Georgia, Virginia, or Maryland. If they came by the northern passage, they first saw the shoreline of New England. Not until the middle half of the nineteenth century was there a continual stream of traffic directly to New Orleans, Mobile, Savannah, Philadelphia, and New York.

Even with the flowering of the Industrial Revolution and its wonderful inventions, sea voyages continued to be perhaps the most trying of all the experiences of the poor.

As it had been for the millennia past, it was the lot of the common man to be regarded as of little more worth than the cattle with which they often shared the voyages, and only as this twentieth century matured may it be said that their lives and comfort became of concern to the powers that were.

The textbooks tell us that most of our ancestors left the Old World by reason of 1) economic conditions, 2) religious discontent, 3) lack of opportunity for social mobility, and 4) personal problems. While such generalizations sometimes are helpful in maintaining perspective, you should remember (and tell your readers) that the reasons for the emigrations of most of your family lines are—and probably will remain—forever lost in the deep, soft black of the past.

Nor should you attribute or conjure up noble reasons for their decisions to undertake the long journey. You should cause your readers to understand that most of their ancestors were ordinary folks seeking to better themselves: usually economically, sometimes in their religions, and occasionally socially.

In researching those ordinary and frightened, yet willing passengers, remember that the lists of them found in our libraries are far from complete. In fact, the present lists contain only three million or so immigrants, yet more than twenty-one million came. So, as mentioned, as you write you will want to check newly published passenger lists whenever and wherever such become available.

Concerning Surnames and "Old Countries"

Tell your readers what their ancestral surnames mean. Not because they will learn much family history from those bits of information, but because names are interesting to us all. Those meanings are easy to come by, since most libraries have a copy of one or two of the many books that discuss and define such history and meaning.

Over and above their interesting meanings, names may become truly important in your search by reason of their origins. Indeed, when you reach that point in the past at which a family line disappears from our records, it may be that one of the few bits of remaining evidence you will have will be knowledge of where on the planet that name is most frequently found; an O'Connor points to Ireland, and Griffith to Wales, just as surely as a Koerner sends you to German records. And it is likely that you will find German and Scottish folks, as well as those who were Irish, Dutch, Italian, Scandinavian, and French; every nationality is somewhere represented in this great and proud nation.

So, if you have no details concerning your own ancestors' travels, tell of the plight of immigrants generally. And speak of names, and their meanings and origins. Your readers will enjoy knowing of such matters.

Gazetteers and Maps

Gazetteers and maps are of the greatest of importance to the writer of family history, just as are the general histories and the studies of particular aspects of life during the times of ancestors. Not only are valuable facts gained from such works, but they provide significant, enjoyable, and meaningful illustrations to accompany your narrative. You simply cannot do without them.

A gazetteer is a dictionary of places and points of interest in a specific geographical area. Many long-abandoned communities no longer appear on maps, even though they provided homes and addresses for our ancestors. Likewise, many rivers, streams, roads, cemeteries, and churches described in deeds and other old records are now renamed, moved or destroyed. Gazetteers often reveal such places. In addition, having learned the name of an abandoned community in which an ancestor lived, through use of a gazetteer one may learn of the county seat that served that ancestor, and thereby know where to go for further courthouse records. Then too, the genesis of counties is often set forth in gazetteers, without which one simply cannot do in-depth research.

Examples of the value of gazetteers and maps are everywhere; *Old Woman's Swamp* may be found in many early North Carolina land records, however it no longer appears on any modern map. Little wonder: the "swamp" is now called *Gillett's Creek*, is within the Camp Lejeune Marine base, and is shown only on local maps and in better gazetteers. No presently-published Marion County, Ohio, map reveals the community of *Lichens Chapel*, yet that place appears on many early Ohio maps and in historical gazetteers. Similarly, references to people living at *Cross Keys* in old Virginia are rendered less confusing by a gazetteer that reveals the whereabouts of at least three former and present-day communities known by that name.

At the time you are ready to select the illustrations to be used in your writings, you will require maps (both historical and current) that reveal the locations of farms, workplaces, and homes of ancestors. As to current maps, no better may be found than the U. S. Geological Survey Quadrangles, available on one scale or another for virtually every place in the United States. These are obtainable from the U. S. Geological Survey office in Washington, D.C., from any of the many Tennessee Valley Authority (T.V.A.) and other Department of the Interior offices across the country, and usually (as to their own area) from local chambers of commerce offices.

U.S.G.S. maps are contoured and done in great detail, they reveal all villages, towns, cities, roads (even old roads that now are jeep trails), rivers, streams, buildings, churches, visible cemeteries, monuments, battlefields, and historical sites, as well as many other places of interest to the traveler and researcher. Small portions of such maps, carefully and neatly marked, showing locations of happenings involving your family, are superb for inclusion as illustrations of your narrative.

The so-called "historical maps" that are copies of earlier maps also are desirable as illustrations. In addition to places, churches, cemeteries, streams, etc., these often name early landowners. Such maps often are available at very modest prices from the local historical society, the county surveyor or engineer, local surveyors, or may be gained by copying the same from early atlases to be found at local libraries. Be sure to inquire as to their availability. Not to be overlooked also are the many similar maps available for copy or purchase at the state libraries and archives, and at state historical and genealogical societies. But beware of copyright problems, and be sure always to obtain permission to use any outside source! (See Chapter VI for a consideration of copyright problems.)

An additional reason for using maps that reveal your ancestors' landholdings is that you will learn of their neighbors, thus facilitating identifications in censuses, and you also will gain knowledge of nearby churches, cemeteries, and sites of historical events that would have been observed by or in which your ancestors would have participated. While no longer appearing on any modern map, historic maps of old Bucks County, Pennsylvania, reveal the location of an "inn"—now long gone—on land that is known by their descendants to have belonged to the DeHaven and Kidder (In den Hoffen and Keiter) families. Thereby is revealed an activity of those families that otherwise would be difficult to uncover through ordinary genealogical sources.

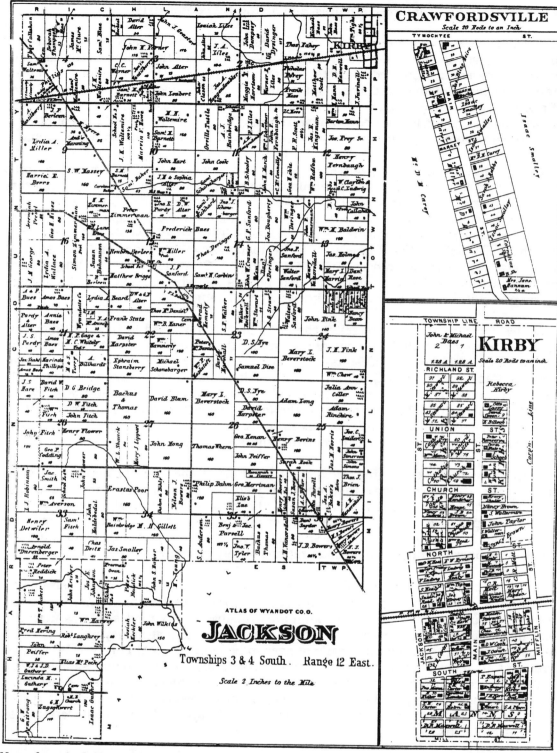

Here, from A. J. Hare, Atlas of Wyandot Co., Ohio, (Harrison and Hare, Phila., 1879) p. 51, is an extremely accurate map of Jackson Township of that county showing landowners as they appeared shortly before publication of that work. Notice that the insets of the villages of Crawfordsville and Kirby reveal even the configuration of buildings, and the map of the township reveals, again, the names of the owners, as well as cemeteries (NE1/4, Sec9, 4S and SE1/4, Sec. 14, 3S), schools (NW1/4, Sec., 11, 3S and SE1/4 Sec. 15, 3S), a blacksmith shop (SE1/4, Sec 10, 3S), and churches (SW1/4, Sec. 15, 3S, and in Kirby at the corner of Church and Main Streets). Not only are such properties of ancestors most interesting to visit, a photo of the land as it may have looked to them is of the greatest interest to your readers.

Almost any map is better than none. Even if what you have is nothing more than a recent county map, you will be able to tell of activities of ancestors in terms of the travel times and obstacles presented to early commerce and trade, and relate those activities to present day places and distances.

As further examples, if your ancestor fought with A. P. Hill's corps during the Civil War, a map illustrating the old "river road" from Harper's Ferry to Sharpsburg, renders the eighteen-mile forced march of those men to the battle of Antietam much more understandable and enjoyable. A map showing the positions of Washington's men at Yorktown makes an ancestor's participation in that battle and the surrender of Cornwallis seem much more real, and provides great pleasure when the reader visits that place. A present-day map showing a road named after one of your ancestral or collateral lines or a cemetery where some of those families are buried makes that area a *must-see* on the next trip to that area. So, whether for your own enjoyment or that of your readers, you must use maps!

Societies, Fraternities, and Sororities

Perhaps the most overlooked sources for genealogical data and family background are the records of societies, fraternities, and sororities. Such groups and organizations have existed since the earliest times, and whether still in existence or not, all have kept records, many of which are available to the researcher. The researcher should be aware however, that some of these groups are private and may not allow non-members access to their records.

The last half of the nineteenth century, especially during the decades following the Civil War, witnessed an enormous increase in interest and membership in such groups (more so in the North than in the old Confederacy, it must be admitted) because of the widespread prosperity that brought greater educational opportunities, a measure, albeit usually small, of leisure time, and, for most families, extra dollars. Then too, travel to and from meetings and conventions became easier, thanks to the illumination of streets, paving, and new sidewalks in many towns, the construction of wagon and buggy roads to everywhere, and the blossoming of train travel and communication.

The farmers too, having become small businessmen thanks to the Industrial Revolution, enjoyed their "granges," which provided increased bargaining power, control of markets, and camaraderie. And, not to be forgotten ever, the two-million-plus veterans, both Yankee and Rebel, by banding together through the U.C.V. (United Confederate Veterans) and the G.A.R. (Grand Army of the Republic), soon found that their power to affect government—their political influence—had been vastly increased.

Finally, societies and clubs were fun, and, after all, should not every gentleman of Victorian times have his "club" to which he went to exchange ideas, drink toasts, play billiards and cards, and do good works for the community? Should not their ladies also have a place to go where care of children, quilting, cooking, and good works were the business of the day?

So clubs there were, and they sprang to prominence by reason of their wide association and membership. Who does not know of the Orders of Odd Fellows and of The Cincinnati, the Colonial Dames, Sons Of The American Revolution, Daughters of The American Revolution, as said, the U.C.V. and the G.A.R. and the auxiliaries of their womenfolk, the U.D.C., Eagles, Elks, Lions, Masons, Shriners, Ladies Of The Maccabees, and Rebekah lodges and chapters, and of the Moose.

Here is a certificate of membership/insurance issued by "Woodmen of the World" in 1898 to A. I. Jones of Desota, Miss. Still a very active insurance company with assets in the hundreds of millions of dollars, "the Woodmen" was considered almost a fraternity or sorority by its insured members. Even today, they have meetings, elect as officers and representatives from among the insured, and have a news magazine or bulletin with anecdotes and photos of interesting events and ordinary "members."

As to their records, almost without exception, those organizations logged the names, ages, and residences of their members, usually gained facts concerning the spouses and children, and frequently kept data as to education, religious affiliation, military service, death, and burial. A vast quantity of that data still exists, and where it is yet extant, it is not difficult to locate.

But one example is necessary. At his death now nearly fifty years ago, Paul R. Drake, I, was a member of the *Eagles* lodge in Ohio. Not only do their records reveal his name, birth date, religion, place of employment, and military service, one may also learn from their records that they paid a $200.00 death benefit to his widow, whose name and address were recorded, that he once was an officer in that organization, and that he frequently donated time and labor to community causes sponsored by that lodge.

The first stop in your search for such data is the local telephone directory. Call those lodges, ask if they have records for the years during which you think you may find an ancestor, and if they have, make an appointment and go visit the lodge or clubrooms. As with churches, if they no longer have early records, ask where they might be found. As likely as not, the old records are at the state or national office of that group, or were sent to that state's archives. So call and ask; sometimes the results are spectacular.

City Directories

The publications that we refer to as city directories are a bit unique as genealogical sources. While published principally to make a profit, since directories do not induce repeat business if inaccurate, their creators have a greater motivation for accuracy than might be expected in other inexpensive publications of general interest.

Notice however, while occupations or callings were listed along with names, that information may not have enjoyed that same measure of accuracy, since in early days folks seldom told representatives of such publications that they were unemployed. Unemployment was often viewed, if not reprehensible, as at least undesirable.

Similarly, if a young man was working at being a house carpenter, or preacher, or cooper, or any of the many other trades that then were learned by doing rather than by formal training, even though he had but shortly before taken up that activity, he likely told the agent of the directory that such indeed was his work. If, however, he changed his mind, as often happened, and took up training in some other discipline during the following year, he then would appear engaged at that new calling. So, information as to trades and callings that appear in directories frequently are unreliable. Nevertheless, heads of households, addresses, names of persons at those addresses and within the families there are often stated very reliably. Finally, it is likely that some pretended to trades or callings as a matter of pride.

fine or popular enough, brick kilns should, at least, have more frequent and heavier draughts on them for our habitations, stores and warehouses.

TAVERNS.

As a distinct class of buildings, public houses, of different sorts, may claim our observance at this stage of our progress. By introducing them, however, persons and particulars, with which they are associated, ask for a like attention. That both may be connectedly presented, the succeeding method is adopted.

Such establishments were anciently called ordinaries and inns. Several requisitions were made of them by our early laws, of the ensuing tenor. They who kept them, were obliged to get licenses, and have "some inoffensive sign obvious for direction to strangers." They were not to suffer "any to be drunke," nor to tipple "after nine of the clock at night." They were required to clear their houses, "where week day lectures[1] are kept," of all persons able to attend meeting.

1633. "Noe person that keepes an ordinary shall take above 6ᵈ a meale for a person and not above 1ᵈ for an ale quart for beare out of meale time vnder

[1] In the first edition of this work, page 61, taverns are said to have been places for lectures in 1633. This is a mistake, occasioned as follows. The legislative records, in the State Library, speak of such services, as performed at "Ordinary Houses." This phrase could mean nothing else but taverns, in its most obvious sense, according to such authority, which was all the writer then had to consult. But the original records have the words, "att the ordinary howres," which evidently mean time and not houses. The last authority is decisive.

penalty of 10ˢ for eury such offence, either of dyet or beare."...

1637. John Holgrave, at the earnest request of the town, "hath vndertaken to keepe an ordinary for the entertaynment of strangers." Relative to persons of his calling, as well as others, the subsequent order was passed by the General Court. "No person shall sell any cakes or buns either in the markets or victualling houses or elsewhere vpon paine of 10ˢ fine, provided, that this order shall not extend to such cakes as shalbe made for any buriall or marriage, or such like speciall occasion."

1639. John Gedney succeeds Mr. Holgrave, but they reversed the change the next year.

1645. William Clarke is chosen for a similar employment. His widow, Catherine; with a family of children, takes his place the ensuing year. She was granted a license for £10 per annum, if "she provide a fitt man, that is godly, to manage the businesse."

1646. John Bourne is allowed to keep a cook shop. His petition craved to "sell such meate, as shall be by him provided and also beeare both in his own house and also abroade."

1648. As Mr. Downing's farm, on the road between Lynn and Ipswich and next to the Endicott farm, was convenient for an ordinary, a servant of the former was allowed to keep one there.

1651. The legislature forbid dancing at taverns.

1653. Elias Stileman had kept a house of entertainment in Salem, but, finding it unprofitable, he desired to sell wine.

1661. A house was erected for John Massey, which

Here, from a source not usually thought of as genealogical in nature—Felt, Annals of Salem (W.& S. B. Ives, Salem, Mass., 1849), Vol. I, pp. 416, 417—are accounts found in the town minutes of activities of ancestors that are incredibly interesting and valuable to the writer who descends from those named. It is interesting that in 1633 no innkeeper was to charge more than "6ᵈ" (6 pence, about $4.50 in 1996 dollars) for a meal, or "1ᵈ" (1 pence, about 75¢ now) for a quart of ale. Notice too that William Clarke died in 1645 and his widow, Catherine, was permitted to continue in the inn operation if she "provided a fitt man, that is godly, to manage the business." Lastly, notice that in 1639 "Mr. Holgrove" was mentioned, as was "Mr. Downing" in 1648, thereby revealing - as was typical in those times - that they were "gentlemen" and enjoyed a station in life above those of the other men whose names appear not preceded by "Mr."

FIRST SETTLERS.

Name		Year
Bownd, William	mr. g. l.	1636
Bownd, Anne	m. f.	1638
Brackenbury, Rich'd	mr. c. c.	1628
Brackenbury, Ellen		
Bright, Margery	mr. c. f.	1629
Conant, Roger	d. f.*	1636
Conant, Sarah	mr. c. f.	
Cotta, Joanne	m. f.	
Davenport, Richard	mr. c. c.	1628
Davenport, Elizabeth		
Dixy, William	c. f.	1629
Dixy, Anne		
Eborn, Thomas	m. f.	1634
Ellerd, Gertrude	m. f.	1634
Endicott, John	mr.	1628
Endicott, Elizabeth		
Felton, Ellen	g. l.	1637
Fogg, Ralph	m. f.	1634
Gardner, Thomas	mr. g. l.	1637
Gardner, Susannah		
Giles, Edward	d. f. c. f.	1629
Herrick, Henry	m. f.	1633
Herrick, Edith		
Holgrave, John	m. f.	1631
Holgrave, Elizabeth		
Horn, John	m. f.	1631
Horn, Ann		
Hutchinson, Alice		
Ingersoll, Anne	m. f.	1631
Johnson, Francis		
Johnson, Joanne		
Kendall, Presca		
King, William	mr. g. l.	1637
Laskin, Hugh	d. f. c. c.	1636
Lathrop, Thomas	m. f.	1634
Leach, Lawrence	d. f. c. f.	1629
Leach, Elizabeth		
Massey, Jeffrey	m. m.	1631
Maurie, Roger	m. f.	1631
Moore, Samuel	m. f.	1642
Moore, John	m. f.	1633
Moore, Hannah		
Norton, George†	d. f. c. c.	1634
Palfray, Peter	m. f.	1626
Palfray, Edith		
Pope, Joseph	m. f.	1637
Raynent, Richard	m. f.	1634
Raynent, Judith		
Reade, Thomas	mr. a.	1630
Roots, Richard	m. f.	1637
Saunders, John	m. f.	1637
Scruggs, Thomas	mr. c. c.	1638
Sharpe, Samuel	mr. c. f.	1629
Sharpe, Alice		
Sibly, John	mr. c. f.	1629
Skarlet, Anne (widow)	g. l.	1637
Stileman, Elias	mr. c. f.	1629
Trask, William	m. f.	1628
Veren, Philip	m. f.	1635
Veren, Dorcas		
Watson, Joanne		
Williams, George	c. f.	1629
Wolfe, Peter	m. f.	1634
Wolfe, Martha	m. f.	1634
Woodbury, John	d. f. c. c.	1628
Woodbury, Elizabeth		
Woodbury, Agnes		

1637.

Name		Year
Alderman, John	mr. g. l.	1637
Amyes, Joan*	g. l.	1637
Banks, Lydia †		
Bartholomew, Henry	mr. a.	1635
Brayne, Agnes (widow)		
Brown, John	m. f.	1633
Brown, Ales		
Browning, Tho's	m. f. g. l.	1637
Garford, Ann		
Gedney, John	m. f. g. l.	1638
Gedney, Mary		
Goldthwait, Thomas	m. f.	1634
Goodwyne, Susannah		
Goose, William	g. l.	1637
Hart, Mary		
Hathorn, William	mr. g. l.	1636
and wife.		
Holgrave, Joshua		
Holme, Deborah		
Humphrey, John ‡	mr. g. l.	1631
Joggles, Mary		
Lord, Abigail		
Marshall, Edmund	m. f. g. l.	1637
and wife.		
Marshall, Millesent		
Maverick, Moses	m. f.	1634
and wife.		
Moore, Ann (widow)		
Moulton, James	m. f.	1634

* R. Conant desired to be a freeman in 1630.

† Mr. Norton was to embark for Salem in 1629.

* In 1637, the General Court "gave £40 to Mrs. Ames, the widow of Doctor Ames, of famous memory."

† After being absent twenty-two years, she was dismissed, in 1664, to the church under the Rev. Mr. Nye, of London. In 1655, her land of 400 acres, called Plain Farm, was sold for £125.

‡ Mr. Humphrey was of Lynn in 1634.

FIRST SETTLERS.

Name		Year
Norman, Arabella		
Norton, Mary		
Peters, Hugh, Rev.	g. l.	1635
Ray, Bethiah		
Robinson, Anne (widow)		
Robinson, Isabella		
Skerry, Francis	mr. g. l.	1637
Turner, Elizabeth	m.	1636
Williams, Eleazer	m.	1635

1638.

Name		Year
Amyes, Ruth		
Avery, Thomas	m. f.	1643
Bachelder, Joseph	mr. g. l.	1637
Barney, Anna		
Blackleach, Elizabeth		
Burdsall, Henry		
Downing, Emanuel	m. f. g. l.	1638
Downing, Lucy		
Hart, John	g. l.	1637
Hindes, James	g. l.	1637
Jackson, John	mr. g. l.	1637
Jackson, Margaret		
Marrit, Triphene		
Moulton, Mary		
Nornan, Arabella		
Pickworth, Ann		
Robinson, Wm.	mr.	1637
Shafflin, Michel	mr.	1637
Skerry, Henry	mr. g. l.	1637
Spooner, Thomas	mr. g. l.	1637
Spooner, Amy		
Standish, Sarah		
Symonds, John	mr. g. l.	1637
Symonds, Mary		
Venner, Thomas*	mr. g. l.	1637

1639.

Name		Year
Antrum, Thomas	mr. g. l.	1637
Barnardistone, Catherine		
Batchelder, John	mr. g. l.	1639
and wife.		
Batchelder, Mary		
Beachamp, Edw'd	mr. g. l.	1637
Bishop, Richard	mr.	1635
Coucklin, Ananias	mr. g. l.	1638
Dixy, Catherine		
Dunlon, Elizabeth		
Edwards		
Fairfield, John	mr. g. l.	1639
Gardner, Tho's, Jr.	mr. g. l.	1637
Gardner, Margaret		
Garford, Jervas	mr. b.	1635
Gascoyne, Sarah		
Golt, William	g. l.	1638
Green, (widow)	g. l.	1638
Harbert, Mary		
Harnett, Sicilla		
Higginson, Francis	c. f.	1629
Holgrave, Lydia		
Holme, Obadiah	g. l.	1639
Holme, Catherine		
Kenestone, Dorothy, Mrs.	m.	1636
Kitcherill, Joseph	g. l.	1639
Lemon, Mary		
Lord, William		
Marsh, John	g. l.	1636
Moore, Thomas*	mr. g. l.	1637
and his wife Martha	r. i.	1636
Norris, Edward, Rev.	g. l.	1640
Osborn, William	mr. g. l.	1638
Page, Lucy		
Pease, (widow)		
Pickering, Elizabeth		
Porter, Mary		
Robinson, John	mr. g. l.	1639
Shafflin, Elizabeth		
Skarlet, Mary		
Southwick, Lawr'e	mr. g. l.	1639
and his wife Cassandra		
Standish, James	mr. g. l.	1637
Stephens, William	mr. m.	1636
Stileman, Elias, Jr.	m. f.	1642
Swan, Henry	mr. g. l.	1639
Swinnerton, Job	mr. g. l.	1637
Swinnerton, Edmund		
Tompson, Edmund	g. l.	1637
Trasler, Thomas	mr. g. l.	1638
Trasler, Eleanor		
Vermayes, Mark	mr.	1638
Ward, Miles	mr. g. l.	1640
Walker, Prescia		
Watson, Thomas	mr.	1637
Weeks, Alice		
Williams, Ann	mr. g. l.	1637
Woodbury, Wm.	mr. g. l.	1637

1640.

Barber, goodwife		
Barnett, Alice		

* Son of widow Moore.

* He was hung, drawn and quartered in London, 1661,—as a fifth monarchy man.

Here, and of value and interest to the family researcher (from Ibid., pp 172, 173), are abstracts from the records of old Salem, Mass., revealing newcomers and the year of their arrivals or first appearances in the town records. Perhaps no other readily available source would provide this data. Knowing of the arrival of a person or family helps by providing a likely period of departure from some other place. Notice again, some men are labeled "Mr." and others are not. Note too the last entry for 1638, where it is revealed that Thomas Venner was "hung, drawn and quartered"; that, perhaps the most gruesome of all punishments.

Family Bibles

While Bibles are books in every sense of the word, they differ from other published source materials in that our tests for accuracy, reliability, and evidentiary weight apply, not to the printed contents of the book, but rather to the entries made within it by people who often are long gone or unidentifiable by us. The measure of reliability we tend to accord such notations stems directly from where—in a Bible—such notations appear, and not necessarily from who wrote them.

Illustrating the point: if you were to encounter identical writings concerning names of family members, births, baptisms, deaths, and parentage in 1) a notebook found in a pile of other books and papers, 2) a cookbook kept by your grandmother in a kitchen drawer, and 3) a 150-year-old family Bible, few would disagree that, without further knowledge of the circumstances, we would presume the Bible notes to be most reliable, the cookbook next, and the notebook of the least evidentiary worth.

Why? We believe, whether always true or not, that ordinary God-fearing people try not to be deceptive when entering materials in the "Good Book;" the force of religion dictates that materials and notes placed there be truthful, even if not always complete or totally candid. Still though, even though the tests of honorable motive and honesty usually are met in matters of Bible entries, the researcher must examine each writing there with a view to whether or not the writer was in a position to know and understand the whole truth of the matter.

Sometimes reliability may be measured by circumstances over and above the fact that a Bible is the whereabouts of the information. Do you recognize the handwriting? Were the entries made by several different folks? What was the avenue by which the Bible came to you? In short, the reliability of Bible entries may be considered to be increased or reduced by the circumstances, however, when no other facts are present we must rely on the assumption that people were (and are) not intentionally deceptive when writing in Bibles.

While Bibles are books, we cite them in a quite different way. While interested in the year of publication, we are not concerned with the publisher or place of publication. So, a Bible entry revealing a baptism might be cited as follows:

> 26. T. R. Roberts family *Bible* (published 1854), at "Baptisms"; the same in possession (1993) of Ms. Diane Drake Haskins, Birmingham.

Personal Correspondence

Since time immemorial, letters and correspondence have been exchanged by friends, relatives, lovers, and otherwise. Then as now, such writings often reveal important details about the writer, the recipients, and the people within their circle of acquaintances. Notice though, just as in your own correspondence, while in some passages such sources reflect in-depth knowledge of the subject matter and a desire to precisely set forth facts, other phrases, sentences and paragraphs clearly may be exaggeration, jest, or idle conversation.

A letter written in 1916 by a devout young lady who was attempting to assist others in search of the descendants of Sir Francis Drake, stated in clear and precise terms that her "...father's grandfather was a brother to...." the old privateer (or pirate, as you will). No matter how much she hoped and intended to speak the truth and be of assistance there, since Francis Drake died a middle-aged man in 1596, it would have been impossible for her great-grandfather to have been his brother unless that brother and the succeeding three generations each had a child when at least one hundred years old.[9] So, while her letter met the tests of proper motive and honesty by reason of her religious upbringing and devout character, she simply could not have had access to the true facts, otherwise she would not have written those words.

So, as we did in the 1854 letter from Betsy of Nebraska to James concerning her father's death (Chapter III), one must test the reliability and weight to be given the contents of all letters by the standards that would be used with any other writing or memo.

As to citing these materials, if private letters or documents are in the possession of a museum or library, that institution almost always will have assigned a title and an *accession* or file number by which the same may be located, and by which you may cite the original:

> *Sainsbury Abstracts for 1625* (Virginia State Library); p. 142, or

> *McDonald Papers*, Virginia State Library, Accession #412, p. 38.

However, if such materials are yet in a private collection, there are no specific rules, except that, as always, you identify the source with detail sufficient to allow your reader to go to the document:

> *Letter of March 8, 1883*, Thomas B. Worrell to Dr. W. K. Drake. Unpub., orig. in the Allison Drake family collection, Marion, OH (1995); p. 3, or

> *Letter*, Thomas B. Worrell to Dr. W. K. Drake, dated March 8, 1883; Unpub. and presently (1995) in possession of M. Diane Drake, Columbia, SC.

Newspapers

In addition to courthouse and family records, the archives and libraries have materials that you should again review.

As we all know, newspapers are very powerful tools of family history. Very much like a photograph, they speak volumes about the life and activities of that moment at that place. Indeed, perhaps there is no better source for background materials that add color and drama to the naked facts and dates that you have gathered.

Such local "papers" may have notices of births, deaths, funerals, activities of courts, schools, fraternities, sororities and clubs, and may contain advertisements, obituaries, and information concerning the politics, morals, and attitudes of the community and its leaders, and tell of community functions and the participants, and of office seekers, appointees to offices, and election results. All are of immense value to you.

As with all sources, the evidence found in newspapers will vary greatly as to reliability and genealogical value, and the researcher must ever bear in mind and apply the tests set out above, particularly as to motive, incentive, and opportunity to know the truth. In that regard, notice that in many instances the publisher of a paper had little occasion to confirm the information given to him or her by others now unknown to you (and usually to the publishers, as well), and such contributors, as likely as not, were not family historians or genealogists.

---

9. The writer was Ida Drake Staley.

MARRIED.

In this city, 9th, by Rev Dr Ide, SAMUEL DAVISON and MARY ANN JEMISON.

At South Adams, 31st ult., DAMAS BENNETT and JULIA FORTIER.

At Holmes Hole (Martha's Vineyard), A. B. WHIPPLE, principal of the Pittsfield High School, and ESTHER DAVIS of the former place.

At Brattleboro, 2d, STEPHEN W. HOPKINS and ADALINE MARIA WALLEN.

At Baltimore, 19th ult., Rev JOHN T. PRYSE of that city, and HANNAH D BROWNE of Guilford, Vt.

At Bellmont, Alabama, 11th ult., Dr GEORGE D. HALL of Gaston, and SARAH E. PARKS, formerly of this city.

BORN.

In this city, 9th, a daughter to CLARK W. BRYAN.

In this city, 8th, JAMES ANTONIO, son to William Renney.

At Easthampton. 5th, a son to WILLIAM HAMILTON; 6 h, a son to H G. KNIGHT

At Southampton, 1st, a son to DAVID B. PHELPS.

At Hadley, 2d, a daughter to JOHN BURKE; 5th, a daughter to DANIEL COOK, and a daughter to JOHN A. MORTON

At Pittsfield, 28th ult., a son to HENRY BUTLER; 31st, a daughter to MILO ROBINSON, and a daughter to HENRY BOWER; 1st inst a son to EDWIN STODDARD of Rondeau, Canada; 3d, a daughter to GEORGE H. LAFLIN of Chicago

At Ashfield, 27th ult., a daughter to W. F. SHERWIN of Hudson, N. Y.

At Palmer, 22d ult., a son to SAMUEL PARSONS.

At Rowe, 3d, a son to JOHN BALLOU, and a daughter to M. C. GOODNOW.

At Deerfield, 25th ult., a daughter to ROBERT CHILDS; 4th inst, a son to B. ZEBINA STEBBINS

At North Leverett, 26th ult., a daughter to DIAH BALL; 29th, a daughter to EZEKIEL WALES, and a son to ALLEN GLAZIER.

At Buckland, 15th ult., a son to EDWIN BEMENT.

At Coleraine, 30th ult., a daughter to R. M. POWERS.

DIED.

In this city, on Saturday, Aug. 5th, after an illness of one week, FRANCIS SANFORD, eldest child of Abel D and Julia Irene Chapin, age 21 mos

In this city, 6th, after a severe illness of ten months, SMITH BARRETT, 41.

At Monson, 1st, ELIZABETH A., 23, wife of A. D. Tower.

At Brattleboro, 31st ult., ELLEN C., 18, daughter of Samuel Eason, formerly of Guilford, Vt.

At Bernardston, 4th, a child of S. S. Bellows, 10 months.

At Deerfield, 31st ult., Widow ANNA CHILDS, 80.

At Buckland, 26th ult., Miss ESTHER TAYLOR, 78.

At Brooklyn, N. Y., 3d, JULIET, 1 year. daughter of Henry W Warner late of Greenfield, Mass.

At Brattleboro, 30th ult., LEMUEL K. BEMIS, 63.

At Ware, June 16th, JERUSHA, 84, wife of Thomas Bacon; 1st inst, THOMAS BACON, 90.

At Somers, Ct., 6th, EDWIN S PEASE, 21.

At Pelham, 20th ult., of whooping cough, MAHLON, 7 weeks and 5 days—27th ult., CHILION, 8 weeks and 5 days. twin sons of Rev F. Fisk.

At Chicago, 7th ult., CARVER BUTTERFIELD, 42, formerly of Amherst, Mass.

At Warehouse Point, Ct., 27th, ult., E. HOADLEY EASTMAN, 27.

At Lanesboro, 6th, Miss RUTH COLLINS, 66.

At Pittsfield, 6th, Mrs MARIA MARSHALL, 48.

At North Adams, 2d, FRANKLIN, 3, son of Charles Baker.

At Southampton, 4th ult, LUCY P., 41, wife of Harris Nimocks.

At Chicago, Ill., of cholera, EZRA G. LEMON, 83, late of Hadley, Mass.

At Westfield 5th HANNAH DEWEY, 86; 6th, SQUIER LOOMIS of Russell, 73; 8th, a child of Alonzo Powers, 18 months; 9th, ALONZO POWERS, 28.

At Chesterfield, 6th, of small pox, BENJAMIN BRYANT, 57.

At Cummington, 21st ult, ELIZABETH, 45, daughter of Asa Porter; 1st inst., LEVI BATES, 83.

At Goshen, 25th ult., WILLIE, 2 year. 1 month; 31st, FRANK, 3 years 5 months; 1st inst., CHARLES L., 23; 5th, MARTHA, 5 years, children of Franklin Naramore; 6th, EDWARD W. NSLOW, 1 year 11 months, son of Caleb C. Dresser; 7th, a child of Willard M. Nichols, 3 years. All the above died of dysentery.

In this city, 9th, EDWIN, infant son of John Miller.

At Great Barrington, 3d, BENNETT PICKETT, 90. His remains were taken to his native place, Sherman, Ct., for interment.

At North Adams, 4th, AZUBA, 72, widow of David Estes, late of Bennington, Vt., whither her remains were taken for burial.

At South Adams, 27th ult., BENJAMIN BRACKETT, 63; 8th inst., STEPHEN TEMPLE, 91, a revolutionary pensioner.

At Centerville, 4th, NANCY, 42, wife of Albert Darling.

At Palatine, Ill, 29th ult., JANETTE KETCHUM, 21, formerly of Clarksburg, Mass.

At Pittsfield, 5th, CLARISSA, 25, wife of Thomas Villas.

At Saratoga Springs, 25th ult, SARAH PERRY, 61, wife of Samuel Gates, formerly of Richmond, Mass.

At Leicester, 24th ult., ESTHER G, 43, wife of Lorin Young.

At Keokuk, Iowa, 1st, WILLIAM P. CARTER, 39, formerly of Otis, Mass.

Here, from the Springfield Weekly Republican (Mass.) of August 12, 1854, we learn of the births, marriages, and deaths of citizens of that vicinity. Having learned from a Bible that an ancestor was born near that date, from a vital record that a couple was married about then and there, or from a headstone that she or he died then, as above here, you might here learn names of parents, as with the birth of James Antonio Renny; the maiden name of an ancestral woman, as in the marriage of Adeline Maria Wallen; or of a prior residence, such as that given in the obituary of Carver Butterfield, all of which might be invaluable in further research.

In addition—and properly so—newspapers and similar publications have profit as their objective. To increase profit, a maximum number of people must be pleased through a wide variety of interesting writings. Contributors of such general interest articles often lack the motive to be as accurate and precise as genealogists require; witness the "pulp" papers sold at the supermarket checkout line.

There is another problem with newspaper accounts of events. Most folks did (and do) enjoy recognition and appreciate seeing their names and relative accomplishments in print, and publishers of newspapers and other popular materials are aware of those human factors. So it is that writers and publishers of biographies and personal sketches often take liberties with the facts—"literary license," as it is called. Publishers sometimes are equally guilty of embellishing naked facts in order that the same be more interesting. As a result, the desire for accuracy and the requirement to check the information submitted are to a measure reduced by the desire to please and, so again, to increase sales at a profit.

Still though, by carrying lists of those delinquent in their taxes or the advertising of local businesses and services, and by relating such facts as the arrival at the early post offices of mail addressed to named persons (*mail lists*), the attendance of certain individuals at events within the area, or the engagement of named persons in certain occupations, newspapers provide powerful, sometimes even conclusive evidence that those people had been there. So, while a newspaper account relating the ancestry of some citizen might be suspect due to the editor's desire to please, or by reason of lack of motive and opportunity for accuracy, a statement that an ancestor was there at that time, or that he or she was engaged at some calling or office, may be valuable and reliable evidence as to the lives of those people.

Obituaries, especially in newspapers, require special attention, sometimes are tedious to sort out, and must be carefully examined concerning the facts found there that you intend to use as proof. In these writings, error is most often caused by loss of memory or inability to know of the real truth, especially where the deceased is an elderly widow or widower. The name of the dead person and the date of death likely are quite accurate, since surviving relatives usually are sure as to those matters. However, watch out for nicknames and middle names since often they are considered as not vital, and are erroneously given or left out by the relative who provided the facts for the column. As but one example, an 1892 obituary column for Mrs. Phoebe Jane Midlam gave her name as "Jennie Medlum"; the first name was actually her nickname, and her surname was not spelled as the family usually spelled it.

Then too, the date of the marriage of the deceased, if not given by the aggrieved husband or wife, may well be in error, especially as to the day and date. Notice though, as shown in our earlier Joseph Midlam example, that most children would be rather sure as to place and date of birth of that parent. Similarly, the place of burial is almost always precise, since it is likely that the mortician, family, and person reporting the death carefully ascertained that fact in order that mourners and preacher show up at the right time and place.

Finally, as with obituaries, newspaper reports of other events must be examined with an eye to whether or not the publisher was likely to have had accurate information as to that matter; that is, did the publisher or editor have the opportunity to know the truth? Again, notice that the publisher of the article likely did not personally make any lists of names of attendees or participants in events and, instead, probably relied on the memory and accuracy of someone else. Observe, too, that while a list of those in attendance at some funeral or other event may not have included an ancestor who in fact was there, if a person was said to have been present, he or she likely was, so you have a location for that ancestor, at least on the date of that event.

If you quote from a newspaper or similar publication, you should use one of the several accepted methods of citation. A popular method is to 1) name the paper, 2) name the city, area or discipline it serves, 3) give the volume and number of that issue, 4) state the date of the issue, and 5) give the page or pages upon which the information appeared:

> *The Evening Bulletin*, Providence, Rhode Island, Vol. 1, No. 275, Dec. 17, 1862, pp. 1 & 2.

or perhaps:

> *Evening Bulletin* (Providence, RI), Dec. 17, 1862, Vol. 1, #275, pp. 1, 2.

Magazines and Periodicals

While facts about particular families appearing even in genealogical publications should be checked for accuracy, articles in magazines or periodicals not considered scholarly or dedicated to history or genealogy are much more suspect, and must be examined in light of who and for what reason the publication included the information given. As examples, excellent as they may be for their purposes, magazines designed to serve employees or members of a union, alumni groups, and fraternal organizations usually are not known for in-depth studies or precision, likely contain a high percentage of accounts of happenings and upcoming events of interest to their members or associates, and have other purposes that are not conducive to accuracy, such as the solicitation of dues and donations.

Because of those motivations, literary license may be more tolerable to their readers than in other publications where a high level of accuracy is expected by subscribers. Accordingly, even when such periodicals include family history materials, the publishers often do not aspire to a high level of historical accuracy.

Still though, notice that the presence in such a publication of a short biography or obituary—even if exaggerated as to accomplishments—may very well be accurate and reliable as to where he or she worked, what their task or calling was, how long they had worked for or been a member of that organization, to whom they were married, perhaps how many children they had, and where they lived at the date of the publication. So, as to those matters, the source may be highly reliable, notwithstanding other shortcomings. As always, look down in the bottom of the basket; many of the eggs may be unbroken.

Magazines and periodicals are usually cited as follows: 1) name of author 2) title of the article in quotation marks, 3) name of periodical in italics, 4) volume and number, 5) date of issue, and 6) page:

> Bernard Bailyn, "Does A Freeborn Englishman Have A Right To Emigrate?" *American Heritage*, vol. 37, Feb./March, 1986, p. 27.

fore, the resident tax-payers of Antes,[1] and the kind and value of property owned by each, were as follows:

Ake, John, acres, 500; grist-mills, 1; saw-mills, 1; valuation, $2140.
Ale, Daniel, acres, 210; valuation, $570.
Allen, William, acres, 487; valuation, $507.
Aiken, Samuel, acres, 150; value, $105.
Bell, Edward, acres, 500; grist-mills, 1; distilleries, 1; value, $2665.
Bell, John, cattle, 1; value, $10; tax, 2 cents.
Bell, Thomas, acres, 200; value, $440.
Burdine, John, acres, 200; value, $240.
Boyle, Henry, cattle, 1; value, $10; tax, 2 cents.
Buttonberg, William, acres, 174; value, $254.
Bradley, Manasseh, acres, 200; value, $290.
Clark, William, acres, 100; value, $670.
Clark, John, acres, 250; value, $1060.
Crane, Abraham, acres, 200; value, $890.
Coventry, Jacob, acres, 100; value, $200.
Cherry, Nicholas, horses, 2; cattle, 1; value, $79.
Condron, James, acres, 280; value of property, $1760.
Ooyar, Mary, acres, 400; value of property, $210.
Domer, George, acres, 270; value of property, $360.
Deckert, Henry, acres, 100; value of property, $130.
Doyle, Dennis, acres, 100; value of property, $150.
Edington, Robert, horses, 2; cattle, 1; valuation, $70.
Edington, Samuel, acres, 117; valuation, $167.
Fetter, Jacob, acres, 250; value of property, $580.
Glasgow, Richard, acres, 300; value of property, $660.
Glasgow, John, Jr., acres, 200; value of property, $280.
Glasgow, John, acres, 383; value of property, $1689.
Gallagher, Thomas, horses, 1; value, $30.
Galbraith, Mary, acres, 230; value of property, $960.
Glasgow, William, cattle, 2; value, $20.
Gallagher, Charles, acres, 100; value of property, $450.
Hutchinson, William, acres, 243; value of property, $241.
Hunter, John, acres, 100; value of property, $150.
Harrier, John, acres, 100; value of property assessed, $110.
Hopkins, James, acres, 70; value of property, $370.
Hopkins, James, Jr., acres, 150; value, $250.
Hopkins, Jonathan and Benjamin, acres, 300; value of property, $680.
Harrier, George, acres, 200; value of property, $280.
Hunter, John, Sr., acres, 10; value of property, $30.
Hutchinson, John, acres, 100; value of property, $130.
Hutchinson, Joseph, acres, 317; valuation, $1268.
Igou, Joshua, acres, 300; value of property, $390.
Igou, James, acres, 200; valuation, $240.
Irwin, Jared, horses, 1; cattle, 1; valuation, $90.
Kelchaner, Michael, acres, 198; valuation, $278.
Kelso, Joseph, acres, 400; valuation of property, $480.
Kenney, Thomas, acres, 234; valuation, $244. He taught a school in the vicinity since known as Elizabeth Furnace as early as 1800.
Lock, William, acres, 200; value of property, $280.
Lock, Thomas, acres, 100; value of property, $140.
Lefavoir, John, acres, 200; value of property, $270.
Lock, Philip, acres, 200; value of property, $100.
Myers, Jacob, acres, 150; valuation, $660.
Matthews, Abraham, acres, 150; valuation, $500.
Meredith, William, acres, 143; value of property, $336.
McCauley, John, acres, 100; value of property, $140.
McClellan, John, horses, 1; cattle, 1; valuation, $240.
McFarland, Alexander, acres, 200; valuation of property, $1080.
Matthews, John, acres, 250; value of property, $790.
Neighbour, Nicholas, acres, 4; valuation, $34.
Oshel, George, acres, 250; value of property, $1040.
Oshel, John, acres, 287; valuation, $1148.
Patton, John, acres, 220; valuation, $880.
Priestley, Jonathan, acres, 200; valuation, $250.
Priestley, Shepley, acres, 50; distilleries, 1; value of property, $485.
Quigley, Thomas, acres, 450; value of property, $1420.
Root, Lemuel, acres, 250; value of property, $330.

Riggle, John, acres, 200; valuation, $100.
Roberts, Samuel, horses, 2; cattle, 2; value, $30.
Robinson, John, cattle, 3; value, $10.
Ricketts, Thomas, acres, 106; value of property, $610.
Ricketts, Richard, acres, 200; value of property, $260.
Swartz, Daniel, acres, 250; value of property, $530.
Swartz, John, acres, 500; value of property, $480.
Stephens, Giles, acres, 106; value of property, $716.
Slagel, Henry, acres, 215; value of property, $190.
Stephens, Thomas, acres, 152; value of property, $154.
Smith, John, acres, 341; value of property, $1063.
Snyder, Abraham (agent), acres, 100; valuation, $50.
Smith, Jacob, acres, 300; valuation, $390.
Stewart, Alexander, acres, 250; valuation, $1110.
Troxell, John, acres, 200; valuation, $650.
Trout, John, Jr., horses, 1; cattle, 2; valuation, $50.
Tipton, Jesse, acres, 150; valuation, $500.
Troxell, John, Jr., acres, 10; valuation, $40.
Tussey, John, acres, 200; value of property, $1240.
Taylor, James, acres, 134; value of property, $214.
Tipton, Caleb, acres, 200; value of property, $510.
Van Schoick, Timothy, acres, 100; value of property, $330.
Wallace, Michael, acres, 280; saw-mills, 1; value of property, $830.
Whitzel, Henry, acres, 300; value of property assessed, $330.
Wertz, Peter, acres, 100; valuation, $110.
Wyman, or Wymon, Felty, acres, 200; valuation, $200.
Yingling, Peter, acres, 200; value of property, $240.
Yingling, Frederick, acres, 200; value of property, $210.

At the same time the single freemen above the age of twenty-one years were Samuel Glasgow, John Kelchaner, Alexander Ale, Jonathan Hopkins, Benjamin Hopkins, James Hopkins, Jabez Stephens, John Myers, Richard Glasgow, Thomas Gallagher, Thomas Priestley, John Tyler, and James Taylor.

We thus find that the taxables in 1811 (other than single freemen) numbered but ninety-five, and that the manufactories consisted of grist- and saw-mills owned by John Ake, a grist-mill and distillery owned by Edward Bell, a distillery owned by Shepley Priestley, and a saw-mill owned by Michael Wallace.

Residents of 1820.—During the decade from 1810 to 1820 but a slight increase in population had been made, yet many changes had taken place among residents. Their names,[2] in the year last mentioned, were as follows:

Samuel Aiken, Alexander Ale,[3] John Ake, Sr., John Ake, Jr., William Ake, John Adams, Daniel Ale, Robert Allison,[4] Jacob Burley, Manasseh Bradley, John Boyers, John Boyle, William Buttonberg, Henry Boyle, Elizabeth Burdine, Edward Bell,[5] William Berry, Abraham Crane, Andrew Cherry,[6] John Crouse, Nicholas Cherry, William Carson, Israel Cryder, John Dodson, George Domer, Daniel Domer, Patrick Dougherty, Henry Deckert, Widow Edington, Jacob Fox, John Farnsworth,[7] John Glasgow, John Glasgow, Jr., Richard Glasgow, Lewis Given, Thomas Green, Benjamin Hopkins, Jacob Haines, John Hutchison, David G. Hunter, George Harrior, Barbara Hull, Joseph Holland, James Hopkins, John Harrison, James Harrison, John Hunter, Sr., John Homer, Henry Homer, Frederick Heffleman, Robert Hamilton, Peter Igou, Joshua Igou, James Igou, Jared Irwin, Thomas Johnston, Peter Kesler, Thomas Kenney, Samuel Kenney, Joseph Kelso, Thomas Lock, William Long, Matthew Low, Jacob Leamer, Garret McGuillen, Jacob Myers, John

---

[1] The reader will bear in mind that from 1810 until 1850, Antes included, besides its present territory, a considerable portion of Logan township, the latter division having been formed from Antes and Allegheny in 1850.

[2] In this, as well as in the preceding and subsequent lists, the assessor's mode of spelling names is followed.
[3] Owned a saw-mill.
[4] Owned an ore bank.
[5] Owned grist- and saw-mills, one distillery, and four hundred and seventy-seven acres land.
[6] Owned a saw-mill.
[7] Owned grist- and saw-mills.

From J. S. Africa, History of Huntingdon and Blair Counties, Pennsylvania (Louis H. Everts, Phila., 1883, Blair) p. 38, here is a list of resident taxables of Antes Township, Blair County (then Huntingdon County) in the year 1811. The page also contains a list of the "single freemen above the age of twenty-one years" for that same year, and a portion of the list of residents in 1820 (notice the women there, "Widow Edington" and "Barbara Hull"). This information, accessible by a simple search of the index to this county history, very likely is not available from any other single source.

County Histories

While quite like all other books and cited in the same way, we always should remain aware that the publishers of these sources usually were more concerned with profit than in genealogical accuracy, had no reason to develop a reputation for accuracy because the books were almost always one-time ventures, and accepted subscriptions and unverified information from nearly all who wished to be included in that volume. For these reasons, and the fact that the subscribers usually were not genealogists, all family information should be verified elsewhere.

Business Ledgers and Accounts

There was not a store on every corner in early times, and families often traded with the same merchants over many years. In addition, in all ages and places, business ledgers and transaction records have been kept, many of which have come down to us. Since, as now, merchants were called upon to be quite accurate at the risk of being cheated or being called a cheat, insofar as they bear on identification of persons and lineage by showing the whereabouts of families and the goods purchased by members of those families, these records usually are very accurate. Such ledgers also reveal much to the diligent researcher concerning the station in life and affluence (or lack of it) of a family.

If a family frequently bought luxury items such as expensive "stuff" (fabrics) like silk and casimeer (cashmere), rather than the coarse and inexpensive Virginia cloth and oznaburg,[10] or purchased Canary instead of ordinary rum, their relative wealth was revealed. Notice too, an absence in accounts of such luxury items as weskits, fancy shoe buckles, handkerchiefs, and silk hosiery reflects that the family seldom dressed in that style, and where common items—yarn, ordinary brandy, linsey-woolsy,[11] etc.,— are not shown, you have powerful evidence that the family produced those items at home.

Notice, though, that other information found in records of this sort, such as a payment of an account by a tobacco warehouse receipt,[12] may not reveal production of that commodity by the ancestor, since the family may well have traded (bartered) some other product made by them for those receipts, or may have received the receipts as payment or gifts from debtors or relatives.

So remember, unlike now and despite the complexities that arose through barter transactions and the use of documents such as warehouse receipts in place of currency, early merchants usually knew their customers and accounts very well and, by reason of the requirements of good business and the motivation to be accurate, they generally produced quite reliable records. In citing accounts or ledgers, no specific rules are applicable, except, as always with all sources, you must identify the source with detail sufficient to allow your reader to go directly to that same writing:

---

10. Coarse fabrics - "stuffs" - used for the clothes of slaves and work and play clothes for men and boys. See *What Did They Mean By That, A Dictionary*, etc., op. cit., pp. 155, 223.
11. Coarse linen and wool cloth spun and made into rough winter clothes for servants and working men.
12. Warehouse receipts were writings, not unlike checks, issued by warehouse owners, that stated how much tobacco, grain, or other commodity one had stored or given over for keeping by that warehouse. They were circulated widely across the colonies, and substituted for money of which the colonials had but little. Ibid, p. 225.

William K. Drake, *Daybook of Dr. William K. Drake, 1841-1856* (unpublished, orig. in possession of Bethany C. Drake, Columbia, SC): p. 9b.

or:

Account of G. Williams, *Connor and Bosca, Merchants, Marion, OH, Account Ledger #4, August-Dec., 1848,* (Accession #641, Tennessee State Library, Nashville): entry of Friday, Dec. 17, 1948.

Speaking of writing, it is time to begin.

Chapter V: Preparing For and Writing Narrative

"The manner of your speaking is full as important as the matter, as more people have ears to be tickled than understandings to judge."
Lord Chesterfield (1694-1773)

"Often a hen who has merely laid an egg cackles as though she had laid an asteroid."
Mark Twain

The creation of the narrative of your family history book involves more than picking up a pencil or pen, or pecking away at a keyboard. As with all works of size and complexity, literary and otherwise, there are matters and requirements that must be considered, remembered, and acted upon before the project can move forward.

First off, you must begin to think in terms of 1) *Theme*, 2) *Context (and Color)*, 3) *Flow*, 4) *Transition*, 5) *Equity of Treatment*, and 6) *Closure*. These six terms are but fancy ways of suggesting that you think of your story as a play, complete with characters, plot, action, and drama:

1) Select and then follow a broad story line. What is this play of yours going to be about? Will there be a common thread that may be traced through your work? What is your *theme?*

2) Provide ever present, yet always changing, backdrops—settings—for the ancestors that are the players in this drama of which you are about to write; such is *context*. Color is nothing more than a part of context, and is the tone or mood of the setting.

3) Be careful, gentle, and smooth in moving your readers from the actions and words of one actor or family to those of another, and do so even within each sentence, thereby providing *flow*.

4) Just as a playbill introduces each act, its setting, and its players, make introductions when moving from one chapter or major topic to the next. That is what *transition* is all about.

5) Treat your actors fairly. If worthy of being in your grand play, they deserve, if not equal time and space, at least an equitable division of the effort—*equity of treatment*—that you afford most others of their generation. Be prepared to make tough choices about what to relegate to an appendix, or omit entirely.

6) Do not forget your players. If you have brought them upon the scene, you must help them leave; *closure* is telling of their departures or disappearances from the records.

Selecting a Theme

If asked what you will write about, to answer "the family" is not good enough; everybody can say that, and your listener knows no more than before you said it.

Will you speak mostly of a single family line? Or instead, will you dedicate the effort to two, three, five or ten lines? Are the wartime activities of your families so vivid and recurring that they will be found throughout? Instead, will you dedicate your efforts to the daily lives of the many families? Or of a few? Will you concentrate on the mix of nationalities that are to be found in your ancestry? What of the efforts of immigrant ancestors to get here? Will your work speak largely of religious convictions and influences and church activities? Of westward movements? Of lives on frontiers? Of wealth, or the lack of it, across the generations?

Maybe you will speak mostly of professions, callings, and occupations. Will you, instead, spend your effort in revealing noteworthy accomplishments of several individuals? Will you speak of the landholdings of your many families? Of social stature? Appearances? Personalities? Of illnesses?

You can not tell of all of those aspects of life; life will not permit you the time. So then, which of these topics will most occupy your work? Will you speak of some of the above? Of none of these things? What, then?

Your first task is to make a statement concerning your intentions. Notice though, that statement is for you, and in all likelihood will never be read by any of your readers; its purpose is to serve as a constant reminder to you of what it is you are doing and how far afield you may go.

So, take pencil and paper, typewriter or keyboard and write, in one well constructed paragraph of two or three sentences, what you intend to talk about AND in what order you will do that. This chore will take time and will not be easy, however when you finish that paragraph you will have a firm basis and positive theme around which you can make future decisions concerning what to 1) discuss, 2) merely mention, or 3) set aside for future projects.

That paragraph might be as simple as:

"My theme will show that across now ten generations, we have consistently been honest, God-fearing, and patriotic Americans."

or it might be as elaborate as:

"I will write about ordinary activities—births, church affiliations, residences, occupations, marriages, military service, children, and deaths and burials—of ancestors known to me. I will start with our earliest known ancestor on mother's side, trace those families (including most collateral lines) forward to about 1950, then follow with the known lines on father's side, bringing them down to the same period. I will use my own experiences to demonstrate life and society in the twentieth century, and to make it more interesting, I will include general history, photos, clippings, maps, and other illustrations throughout."

or:

"I will write of the outstanding achievements and conduct of more than twenty family members, commencing with the banishment of Lawrence and Cassandra Southwick, continuing through the wounding of John Carner at Bunker Hill, including the heroism of Evan Haskins in the Chicago fire, and extending to the corporate success of P. R. Drake II in the 1980s. I will tell of the spouses and their families, and of the children and descendants of these principal characters, and will include timelines, photos, copies of documents, newspaper accounts, and obituaries."

or, finally:

"As I move through the generations, I will write of the residences and living conditions encountered by our people, commencing with myself and moving backwards in time. I will consider life in nineteenth-century Ohio and Nebraska, eigthteenth-century Pennsylvania, Virginia, and North Carolina, and conclude with what we know of the seventeenth-century Virginia homesites and lives of Owen and Mary Griffith and Adam and Sarah Thorowgood. I will include maps, floorplans and drawings of home styles, and photos of ruins of early ancestors' homes."

So, write that paragraph now, keep it always at hand, and whenever a new fact, record, memento, or illustration comes to you, ask yourself where, if at all, it will fit in the overall plan. Make that paragraph your guideline for the balance of your work.

Your plan and theme need not be carved in stone, never to be changed. As the writing progresses, you may begin to feel or even know that the theme, thrust, or aim of your work is moving in a slightly different direction than that originally intended. For example, even though you intended to show "average daily life" generation after generation, you may find that so many of your ancestors were caught up in the extraordinary demands of the frontier that the thrust of the early chapters of your book has become something more like "lifestyles required of frontier settlers."

Similarly, if your theme was "significant achievements," you may come to believe that the drudgery and never-ending physical labor of the ordinary housewife and mother in early Nebraska was equal to, if not greater than, anything any "hero" of the family ever did. Such a realization may require a new theme, through which comparisons are made between what should be viewed as noteworthy in early generations contrasted with what actions should be considered significant in more recent times.

If you do change your mind, STOP! Take the time to rewrite your theme paragraph, and use that new plan as the future guide. Any new theme almost surely will require that some changes be made or materials added to writing already done in order that, once again, the whole of the work may be on course. Make those changes, and then move on.

Keeping Your Personality and Views to Yourself

Writing family history is like being required to tell what is happening and what words and emotions are being expressed in a play you are watching through binoculars from a hill so far distant that not a whisper of sound can reach you. Just as there, where your feelings and attitudes are next to worthless in understanding the distant play, in telling of ancestors, while you can relate what you have seen of them, you can know almost nothing of their motivations and feelings.

In telling the stories of those distant players, always keep in mind one fundamental rule: responsible genealogists and historians—family and otherwise—never make judgments. No more than we would appreciate being judged by those who are alive two hundred years from now, no genealogist or historian worth his or her salt ever judges the conduct of those who lived two hundred years in the past.

Except as to events of last week or last month concerning laws, morals, attitudes, and beliefs today held necessary and proper by our contemporaries, we never use such words as good or evil, proper or improper, just or unjust, decent or indecent, moral or immoral, appropriate or inappropriate, or should have or should not have. The principles, morals, mores, and laws of our time have neither application to those who went before, nor to those who come after.

What was acceptable and proper to your ancestors may be quite unacceptable and improper now, and vice versa. Four-letter expletives (and far worse) were common among "refined" folks even down to the eighteenth-century. While now such conduct is intolerable, in the early days our ancestors almost never brushed their teeth or washed their hair, and there were no bathtubs or showers—not even in the White House—until the middle of the nineteenth-century. Seventeenth- and eighteenth-century American women usually could not own real estate, had almost no rights to gain a divorce or to avoid being whipped, and could not vote. On any given day in the early American colonies one might find slaves being bought, sold, or whipped, witches and dogs being dunked, pressed, or hung, corpses being 'stroked', 'idiots' being castrated, 'lunatics' being dipped in ice water, and petty criminals being sentenced to amputation of ears and to time in the stocks and pillories.

Our ancestors believed in demons and spirits, large doses of mercuric chloride were administered for syphilis, and leaves were burned on cold axes to alleviate earaches. Cup after cup of blood was taken from George Washington, in an effort to cure his death-dealing pneumonia. Even down to the middle of the twentieth century, many people put fence posts in the ground only during "the light of the moon," believing that they would not pull out or loosen as quickly.

No matter how foreign to our customs, beliefs, "common sense," or religions, such activities were not indecent, inappropriate, ignorant, dumb, stupid, or heathen; it simply was the way things were, and we do not judge such activities or even smile at them. Millions of our ancestors lived long, prosperous, and happy lives within those ideas and standards of conduct, and to now suggest, by reason of our background and what we egotistically view as an "advanced state and wisdom," that such conduct should not have taken place is pure nonsense, and very poor genealogy.

So, remember that we have not walked in the shoes of our progenitors, do not understand many (or most) of their ways, did not have to live on their frightening, harsh, and often dismal frontiers or under their kings, sheriffs, masters, husbands, and laws, and we simply can not now understand.

As someone said, "The past is like a foreign country; they do some things differently there." As good historians, we judge only ourselves, and we let our ancestors sleep on, proud as they were in their accomplishments, regretful as they may have been of their failings, and quite undisturbed by our self-proclaimed sophistication. So it is that, like on that distant hill, you must always stand very much outside and apart from your story, there to observe and study the characters, and then to tell—as best you can—of those lives and conduct, without weaving in any of your own beliefs, biases, and end-of-millennium "educated" attitudes.

Preparing for Disappointment

You must prepare now for what perhaps will be the most critical moment in your future writing career. That moment will come when, after writing the first page or two, you realize that the words do not come nearly as easily as you thought they might.

While you are quite able to think through person after person in family after family of generation after generation, all the while remembering myriad stories and details concerning each of them, you find that writing those words is hard; the verbs get lost, the sentences don't flow, and the urge to drift off into other subjects or persons is almost overwhelming. Do not despair! We all—every one of us—have had the same problems.

When that disappointing moment arrives, what you must do is to keep on writing, no matter how clumsy it all seems to you. No matter how unnerving the effort is or how poor the sentences are, continue until you have finished that complete thought, paragraph, or section. Then, still again, tedious though it may continue to seem, write an additional paragraph, and yet another. Write two or three or four pages. The chore of the moment is to get some of your thoughts on paper, and to cope with the disappointment that comes in knowing that the task is not an easy one.

The crudeness and problems you will encounter in that first writing effort are the stuff of redrafts. It is said that there are two kinds of work to be done after the actual composition and writing: 1) redrafting, where you adjust and rearrange thoughts, add ideas, context, and color, amend and delete this or that paragraph to gain equity, change direction or theme, and create flow and transition, and 2) editing, where you correct errors of grammar, punctuation, sentence structure and the like. The first, you do when you are of a mind to, and the second you save until you have finished a substantial portion or all of the book.

So, be forewarned; as were all of us, you will be disappointed in your first efforts. You will redraft that writing (and all the others that you do) either then or later, and sometimes several or even many times. (It is said that Michener rewrote some of the novel *Hawaii* no less than seventeen times.) Remember though, slow and aggravating as the first efforts may be, you will improve if you do not quit. You will—and soon—find that the words come easier and easier, and you will finish, first the sentence, then the paragraph, then the chapter, and one day, the book.

Leaving out Modern Views, Sentiments, and Guesses

Just as we do not judge those who went before, we should speak of their experiences in the same way that they did or would have. Try to imagine how an ancestor living at the time of an event would have spoken of it, and write in that tone.

As examples: since they realized that at least one of every five children born would probably die before adolescence, and so almost expected that to happen, so should you. The Southern view that "Sherman's March" was a violation of every principle of decency and honor known to man and, conversely, the Northern notion that war meant just that—total and complete war against all who in any way participated—both were legitimate views to be reported, yet not to be changed, approved, or censured by you. The attitudes reflecting the centuries-long conflicts with the American Indians (or "Native Americans," as you choose) were true feelings, legitimate to another time, and should be related without your views, whatever they may be, being plugged into the story. You are not writing a novel!

So write what you KNOW about them, but do not conjure up attitudes. It is safe and sincere to relate that as your ancestors of 1840 "...walked quietly away from a grave into which had been lowered the body of their beloved father, they probably wondered who would be next to go and what the future held," however to say that they cried or wept or wailed or probably fainted is something that you simply can not know, so do not write it. Here, as with all early events of which you have knowledge, you need but describe the scenes honestly and with sincerity, and your readers will supply any needed warmth and empathy.

Then too, let the events of the distant moment set the tone of your work. Where serious subjects are at hand, be exacting and to the point; war, for example, demands detail, sober thought, and careful reflection. Where the subject is light, so too address it; a tale of a sleigh ride calls up visions of cold nights, friendship, and fun, and a visit to a circus invites comments about children enjoying one of the greater pleasures of their time. And where the topic is factual in nature, be that way too; barn-raisings, teams of horses, telegraph offices, or cobbler's benches rarely were emotional experiences. They were everyday places of hard and demanding work. So, while a long ride to town in a spring wagon may seem romantic and bring feelings of nostalgia to you, remember that your 1875 ancestors likely would not have shared those feelings.

One final thought about writing your own views, character, and sentiments into the narrative: all of us have known people who are about as humorous as a train wreck, yet never cease in their attempts to be funny. And, who has not encountered the would-be intellectual who has something to say that is supposed to sound profound about everything under the sun, or the cocktail party boor, whose words are continuous and are really but "...great sound and fury signifying nothing...." Be not any of those people. Leave all pretensions in the other room, and write quietly, gently, and sincerely.

A summary is easy: You have undertaken to tell about ancestors, so do it as they would have. If, instead, you want to tell of yourself and your real or imaginary accomplishments, or describe your own or modern attitudes, feelings, and beliefs, do that in a different chapter or, better yet, in another book that has to do with you and your contemporaries, but do not mix the two.

Finding a Copy- and Proofreader

Most us need someone to read and critique our work. As to the proofreading—the punctuation and grammar part of that effort—if you are not confident in your ability to understand and abide by the established rules in such matters, then you will need someone to do it for you. As to the transformation of your thoughts into words, no matter how confident you are in your abilities, you should find another person—someone who understands transition, flow, context, etc.—to read your work and comment.

If the help sought is with your grammar or punctuation, compare your proofreader's comments with your own ideas and sources, decide which you prefer, and make the needed corrections. If, as do some of us, you punctuate so as to almost require your readers to read and inflect in a certain way (as did Mark Twain), tell your proofreader of that plan.

As stated, no matter how confident you are in your grammar, you surely will need help with the narrative—the text. The reasons are two-fold: As we compose, we often become so involved—enamored? enraptured?—with our thoughts, words, and phrases that we leap from thought to thought, supply the flow and transition only in our minds, and create something far less than that of which we really are capable. The other difficulty is that words and phrases which seem to us to clearly express deep feelings and sentiments often fall far short of that objective when read by others.

The ideal person to perform both tasks—check punctuation and grammar and edit the narrative in order that it be more than a series of disconnected, cold sentences—would be a close relative or friend, who would charge little or nothing, and who has a background in English and composition. Unfortunately, few of us have such a person among our acquaintances and kin.

So who, then? It is suggested that you contact a local college, there seeking a teacher or a student of advanced English, writing, or composition, or call the local high school for a teacher with similar background. Very often, such folks are happy to have an opportunity to earn extra money, and will work for modest sums. Having made such a contact, tell that person what it is that you need, and have him or her read a few of the more difficult or complex pages of your work. By so doing, both you and the contact will be able to agree on a price for the effort, which you surely should do before moving ahead with the project. In selecting a reader, choose one who will honestly analyze and critique your work, suggest additions and deletions, be critical where you have fallen short, and reassure you, where your work is deserving.

If your reader is a friend, he or she should be capable and willing to put aside that friendship during the course of this relationship. Why? Because you do not need compliments; when the work is completed, your family and friends will supply all of that you will be able to stand. For now, your requirement is critical help and suggestions, not flattery. And, do not be a prima donna; accept what your assistant says, make changes willingly, and do not cling to phrases simply because you think they seem neat or sound profound.

Most important of all, if your reader-helper says that she does not understand or comprehend this or that passage or paragraph, do not attempt to explain it to her, change it! If that reader—selected by you for willingness, ability, and knowledge—does not understand, neither will future readers. When you are not there, who will explain to that relative who bought your book?

In summary, you will need an assistant (to whom you will listen) with a background in English composition and writing, if not to correct your punctuation and grammar, surely to critically search your work for the basic elements of good narrative (equity of treatment, flow, closure, etc.).

Gaining and Regaining Data and Illustrations, and Writing

As we know, the stuff of sentences comes from the gathering of information, and as with all of us, you were not always careful with your collecting, recording and storing of such materials. Almost at once, you will find that some details are missing and that you have forgotten, lost, or misplaced some sources, records, and illustrations. Not to worry; while you can do nothing about such past errors, you can prevent them in the future, and at the same time learn or brush up on sentence structure and composition.

Similarly, upon retrieving old illustrations or finding new ones, you will make clear notes on the reverse concerning where you found it or who gave it to you and the person, family, or line with which it is concerned. An easy way to do that is to assign a letter or two and a number, those revealing the chapter and the illustration within that chapter. As an example, a map showing the farm of Daniel and Mary Martin Carner, that is—for now at least—the third illustration to appear in the chapter by that name, might be labeled "DM3," meaning Dan and Mary illustration #3. By so doing, you will not later have to reread the entire chapter in order to recall where you should place that illustration.

Back to the sentences to be constructed concerning new information gained: they are the backbones of future paragraphs and chapters. In writing them fully and completely, you will be considering the value of the new information, coming to decisions as to their relative importance, writing portions of future chapters, saving time, and practicing composition of sentences (and paragraphs), all at the same time.

If examples are needed, suppose you are writing about a different family line, and quite by accident you come upon the precise date of the death of triple-great grandmother, Martha Freeburn Midlam, which you did not previously know. Upon gaining that fact, rather than noting simply:

"Martha Midlam, 92, d. 2/28/1798, Williamstown, MA (source, M. Diane Drake, Columbia, Drake Bible)."

force yourself to write a full sentence, such as:

"The *Drake Bible*, now (1995) in the possession of Martha Diane Drake, of Columbia, South Carolina, reveals that Martha Freeburn Midlam, triple-great grandmother of the writer, died at Williamstown, MA, on February 28, 1798, at the age of ninety two years."

Another example— Rather than:

"Archives #S80961; Claudius Martin, 1 PA Rifles, enl. Reading, PA, 7/22/1777, disc. 10/28/1780"

you should write:

"Revolutionary soldier Claudius Martin was enlisted in the *First Pennsylvania Rifles* at Reading, Pennsylvania, on July 22, 1777. He was discharged on October 28, 1780. (citation: Claudius Martin, Rev. Vet. File #S80961, Natl. Archives)."

So, as you recover old facts and uncover new ones, if you consistently write them in complete sentence form, you will have both practiced composition and writing, and saved a great deal of time by commencing future paragraphs. As we learned, a family history is nothing more than a collection of such information and biographical data set forth, along with illustrations and other interesting historical facts, in a coherent and cohesive form.

Sorting Illustrations and Notes

Next, while it is perhaps the most enjoyable of your tasks, and at the same time the most time-consuming, you must—MUST—gather together all of the illustrations, citations, and notes that are in any way connected with any of your family. Those materials must be thoroughly sorted into the family lines, family units, and people of whom you intend to write.

We suggest that, as you sort, you place the illustrations and notes for each person, family, or line in separate old envelopes or used file folders, with the names of the lines or persons contained there clearly marked on the front of that envelope or folder. By so sorting and arranging your materials, you will have refreshed your memory as to what you know and have concerning that person or line, and also will have reminded yourself what you yet need to procure.

Even though you are eager commence, it is important that next, or at your earliest convenience, you commence the task of writing to those people or places who have additional materials to contribute, and also visit places where other maps, photos, deeds, etc., may be obtained. Then too, since colored photos are very expensive to reproduce in a book, it is suggested that this also is a good time to take negatives, colored photos and slides to your photographer for conversion into black and white "half-tones." If you have many such photos and negatives, the cost may be substantial, so take a few at a time, starting with those that are to be placed in the first chapter that you intend to write.

When to Write What

A few words should be said about *when* to do *what* writing. It is difficult enough to conceive and build sentences and paragraphs when you feel creative and do not have to force yourself, and almost impossible when you are not up to it; we all share that feeling. So, write whenever you feel like it, and do not write when you don't.

If you feel the urge to work on the project, yet find that you are not able then to think in sentences and paragraphs, turn to your illustrations and carefully write captions for them. By writing your captions on separate lined paper and numbering them just as you did the illustrations, you will have them ready when you are back at the writing of narrative, and in addition, that effort will keep fresh in your mind what illustrations you do and do not yet have. So, rather than delay your work, when you are not up to composing narrative, write captions. Finally, when you are doing or have done the captions, write more of the short letters seeking out the other illustrations that you do not yet have.

Preparing an Outline or Deciding Not to

An outline is not required, and as mentioned before, there are no old English teachers or genealogy policewomen who will come by to see if you have done one. One superb genealogist and writer has said that, when she was a senior in high school, she was required to create an outline, so she did two at the very same time; her first and her last!

So be it, however most of us find it easier to create at least a series of notes broken down in outline form, thus serving to organize our thoughts, refresh our memories, and assist us in forming the chapter sequence that will best serve our purposes. As an illustration, suppose you have a Haskins line, the earliest ancestors known in that line having been William Huntt and his wife, Judith, who lived in Virginia and owned land before 1675, and about whom you have a few additional facts. Those Huntts had a daughter, Mary, who in her turn married Owen Griffith, about whom you have a servitude anecdote and numerous other details. Owen and Mary had Anne, who, when she was eighteen, married Thomas Drake, a large landowner whose properties you have mapped. Thomas and Anne had Prudence Drake, who married a Connor, and Martha Diane Drake, who married Evan Haskins; he, your earliest known Haskins ancestor, and about whom you have many facts.

A rough and quickly made outline of what you could write about those folks above might read as follows:

Chapter 6; Earliest ancestors in the Haskins line
    The early Huntts; William and Judith _?_
        Their known landholdings in Virginia
        Their lives, deaths, and church attended
    The early Griffiths; Mary Huntt and Owen
        Their lives, including servitude, land, and deaths.
    The early Drakes; Thomas and Anne Griffith
        His lineage, landholdings, their church activities
        Their wills, deaths and places of burial
        Their daughters, Prudence (Connor) and Martha Diane, who
        married Evan Haskins
Chapter 7; Earliest known ancestors bearing the surname Haskins
    M. Diane Drake and Evan Haskins, church activities
        " " " " "   a study of their home
        " " " " "   issue and ages, 1740
        " " " " "   wills of
        " " " " "   deaths and graves

Even though you probably will later make changes in it, notice that by the simple act of writing this short outline you have again refreshed your recollections and brought a measure of organization to the subject of the Haskins family ancestors. So, if outlines serve you well, as they do most of us, write one; if not, don't bother.

The Writing of Narrative

As has been said, commence your book anywhere you choose. Suppose, for example, that in addition to the Haskins line, you have as ancestors, Daniel Carner and his spouse, Mary Martin Carner, and have very much enjoyed the research done and photos and anecdotes gained concerning them. Even though you may know and intend ultimately to write of, say, four generations previous to Dan and Mary and three generations after them, if you are most comfortable now with what you know of that marriage, that *family unit*, start there.

Having selected them as a beginning point, pull your file or envelope containing the illustrations, maps, and notes that have to do with that family, and have those materials before you as you commence writing. If those notes and illustrations are visible and at hand, they will serve as constant reminders of detail about which you might otherwise forget.

Unless you are using a word processor, by which corrections and interlineations may easily be made, you should always write in every other line. If you are using a typewriter, set the carriage return on the double-space mode. By so doing, it will be easy to insert citations, notes, and numbers assigned to illustrations, and later you will be able to add, delete, or correct text where needed.

Since, in this example, you have not chosen to start at either the earliest known or the most recent person known in the Carner line, you first should introduce your readers to Dan and Mary and their children. Even though you will not have yet written the chapters having to do with their ancestors, you soon will, and so you should start that chapter as though you had already written the preceding ones by telling the readers just where Dan and Mary fit in the complete Carner and Martin lines.

For example, you might commence the chapter with a short NGS or decimal numbered genealogy (see Chapter 2), a five-generation pedigree chart showing Daniel as #1, or you might start the chapter with a simple sentence, such as:

"Daniel Carner (1831-1908), the father of Maggie Belle (Midlam), Claude E., and Harry F. Carner, was the second son (third child) of Henry and Mary Bush Carner. Daniel's elder brother was Charles B. Carner, his elder sister was Elizabeth (d.s.p.), and his younger sisters, in order of their birth, were Mary Jane (Giesey) and Margaret (Roberts). Mary Bush Carner probably was a daughter of Charles and _?_ Bush."

Or you might use two of the three tools, say a pedigree chart and a numbered genealogy, or, for that matter, you could use all three, by following the pedigree chart with the short numbered chart, and then a summary of their positions in that portion of the Carner and Martin lines of which you intend to write. By this simple beginning, your reader is introduced, or re-introduced as the case may be, to the subjects of that chapter. So, whatever tools you choose to use, start your reader off with a very clear idea of the people of whom you are about to write.

Placing Illustrations and Notes

Following that short introduction section, it is time to write whatever you intend concerning those people, all the while remaining constantly aware of the illustrations you have pulled out. As you come to that place in the narrative where you think it appropriate to place an illustration, as said, make a note to that effect in the extra line below or in the margin of the text and, very importantly, also on the back of the illustration to be placed there.

Be sure to place photos and illustrations at that point in the narrative where their subject is being discussed. If you fail to do that, the effect is the same as changing the subject in the middle of a paragraph. If you have a photo of Dan Carner, place it within that portion of the narrative that speaks specifically of him. In short, look to your sentences; they will tell you what illustration belongs there or close by. Be aware though, there may be some restrictions involved in those placements, but your publisher or printer will be able to advise you.

When formulating, constructing, and writing citations of authority and notes (whether foot- or end-notes), it cannot be overemphasized or too strongly stated that, even though you may later choose to enter or move this or that illustration, you must not fail to enter the notes and citations where they belong AS YOU WRITE. If you do not do that, you will later find it necessary to go back through every sentence and then enter those matters, by which time your writing may be two or three hundred or more pages long and (though you may doubt it now) you will have forgotten the place and meaning of some of the citations now ready for inclusion.

In short, by not including notes as you go, you will have made your work exceedingly more difficult, if not almost impossible.

Construction

Your narrative—the most read and interesting portion of the total effort—is nothing more than 1) sentences substantiated by end- or footnotes, and often with illustrations, 2) paragraphs made up of one or more sentences, again, with illustrations that pertain to the subject of that paragraph, and 3) chapters made up of paragraphs, with illustrations that serve the whole chapter. The notes were discussed previously, but what of these other elements?

The Use of Words

Genealogists usually are not grammarians, as much as some of us might like to be. Most of us have spent a lifetime at other responsibilities, and time has often not been ours to dedicate to gaining in-depth understanding of diverse subjects. Then too, few of us have had the luxury even of courses in or study dedicated to the niceties and intricacies of language.

Be not ashamed of that; that your writing does not match that of Churchill or Morison is not to your discredit. You have gathered information and have knowledge that those who come after you will want, need, seek out, and enjoy, so do your best to convey it to them, and be proud, whatever and however you write. As with all of us, most of your critics will have written little or nothing of significance, anyway.

Concerning vocabulary, an old teacher of this author once said, "A capacity to use big words does not necessarily (or usually) reflect a capacity to think big thoughts." And, when a book reviewer of a well known genealogical journal recently wrote that somebook had caused many Virginians "to be redolent of their past," a daughter of the writer smiled and said, "Yes, and they were reminded of it too." As there, all too many writings, especially when done by amateurs like us, contain words and expressions that seem to be little more than the results of surfing a thesaurus.

The English language is a warm, expressive, and incredibly powerful tool, and it is not improved upon by seeking out big and seldom-used words and phrases. So, always avoid strained language, no matter how profound or scholarly it may seem at the moment. You are writing for others, so use words with which readers of any age or educational level will be comfortable.

The Nature of Sentences, Paragraphs, and Chapters

Even though the lexicographers and grammarians have struggled long and hard to define and explain the word *sentence*, we have chosen to use the words of ordinary family history buffs in attempting to bring a measure of understanding to this most basic element of any writing.

A sentence is a single thought, fact, or idea, and examples are helpful: "She had three children"; "He joined the Continental army," "She died of Bright's Disease"; "Three of their four children lived to maturity." Even though all of those examples are rife with inferences, those statements all relate one thought or fact: a number of children, an enlistment, a cause of death, and a mortality statistic.

While we might have added further description to each sentence, the central idea or thought must remain; "She had three children, all boys with red hair," "At Reading, Pennsylvania, on the 2nd of July, 1777, he joined the Continental army," "She died of

140

Bright's disease, having suffered terribly over many months," and "Three of their four children lived to maturity, one having died when but an infant."

Notice, as above, that two or more facts may be, and often are, an integral part of a single notion and sentence: "She demanded obedience, yet soon forgave those who disobeyed." There, while two separate facts are stated—1) she was unyielding, and 2) she was not long in forgiving—both are necessary parts of any description of that aspect of her personality.

Another sentence with two facts, one involving conduct, the other a probable attitude or conviction, both necessary to any portrayal of a man who placed duty ahead of preference, is found in the sentence, "He joined the army the day after the war began, even though he was not particularly patriotic." A similar example might be, "She took her children to church every single Sunday, even though she was not known as a God-fearing woman."

In short, whether one, two, or more facts or impressions are necessary to convey a thought, we speak in sentences that usually contain single ideas, concepts, thoughts, or descriptions, and so too should we write. We do not say "I am going hunting, and she will bake a cake," "He was over six feet tall, and her mother plays the organ," or "He wrote warmly of the death of his grandfather, who had always been a big eater of pork." Such sentences represent attempts to combine thoughts, ideas, or facts that are only distantly related, if at all; we sought to combine facts or ideas that in ordinary conversation do not belong together.

Think of how you would speak of certain facts, were you visiting with a friend or relative, then write them that way. Put yourself in the reader's place. Until more complicated sentences come to you naturally, maintain an intention to write in simple, straightforward ones. Just as you did not attempt to stand on the handlebars the first time you tried to ride a bicycle, you should not attempt complex and complicated sentences when first undertaking to write. So, keep it simple.

Ordering and Organizing Facts

Again consider the Dan and Mary Martin Carner family. They lived in the nineteenth and very early twentieth centuries. Mary Carner is buried in Ohio; died of blood poisoning in 1898; had three children who grew to adulthood; was short, stout, and quick of temper; married Dan in 1862; and had five sisters and three brothers. Daniel was short; of pleasant feature; died at the home of his unmarried sister (Libbie) in Altoona, Pennsylvania, on February 16, 1908; suffered from Bright's disease until it killed him; had several sisters (one of whom did not marry) and two brothers; was born in 1831; lived in Ohio until after his wife died, at which time he moved to Pennsylvania to reside with the unmarried sister; and at death was taken to Ohio for burial beside his wife, Mary.

What is wrong with the foregoing recitals of facts?? Just as your notes probably are now, those facts are quite out of order; they do not appear in the sequence that life dictates, the order in which genealogists think. As discussed briefly earlier, as writers of family history we think and speak of ancestors in the order of life itself; births, parents and siblings, then marriages and children, then, perhaps, physical appearances, occupations, and activities, then, maybe, illnesses, and finally the causes of deaths, the deaths, and the burial places. So, whether you do an outline or not,

141

before commencing to write, at least put your facts in the order in which they actually occurred.

By organizing the facts above in the order of their happening, it becomes easy to write the following sentence concerning the death of Daniel:

> "On February 16, 1908, in Altoona, Pennsylvania, Daniel Carner, then seventy-seven and in the care of his unmarried sister, Libbie, died of Bright's disease."

Within those words are at least nine (9) separate and distinct facts—you count them—concerning his death, and yet they are combined into a single, easily read sentence.

Notice, however, that such combinations of a considerable number of facts are not easy to construct, hence great care must be taken to make such a sentence easily understandable. If you find such construction difficult, as most of us do in the beginning, chances are your sentences should be shorter. Try it yourself.

Construction of Sentences and Paragraphs

So, if a sentence is a single thought, fact or idea, what then is a paragraph? As with sentences, we have chosen here not to use the precise definitions of the grammarians, even though it will be helpful for you to look up those words in a good dictionary.

Simply stated, unless the facts that are needed to convey an explanation or thought are so numerous or complicated that several paragraphs are necessary, a paragraph should contain a complete idea, description, explanation, concept, or complex thought. Said differently, it is usually a combination of two or more sentences that are closely related, and it sets out a complete thought, or adds to a prior paragraph where, by reason of complexity or detail, the thought or description was only partially spelled out.

Consider again our Dan and Mary Carner family. In telling of his death, we said:

> "On February 16, 1908, in Altoona, Pennsylvania, Daniel Carner, then seventy-seven and in the care of his unmarried sister, Libbie, died of Bright's disease."

We might have continued on to the construction of a paragraph by adding another sentence, as follows:

> "On February 16, 1908, in Altoona, Pennsylvania, Daniel Carner, then seventy-seven and in the care of his sister, Libbie, died of Bright's disease. Even though Bright's Disease was terribly painful and quite incurable then (or hardly even now), the fact that Libbie did not marry likely permitted her the time to administer the level of care needed to see Dan through to the end."

And we might have written even more, all the while still speaking of the single happening or event—Dan's death—by adding yet further detail:

> "On February 16, 1908, in Altoona, Pennsylvania, Daniel Carner, then seventy-seven and in the care of his sister, Libbie, died of Bright's disease. Even though Bright's Disease was terribly painful and quite incurable then (or hardly even now), the fact that Libbie did not marry likely permitted her the time to administer that level of care needed to see Dan through to the end. Immediately after death, Dan's remains were sent by train to Upper Sandusky, where he was interred in Old Mission Cemetery beside his wife, Mary Martin Carner."

That paragraph of three sentences was dedicated to Dan's passing. The first sentence revealed that subject by setting forth the precise date, cause, and whereabouts of death. After that first sentence, two additional rather complex sentences were added (and needed) to create a full paragraph that tells all we know concerning that demise. Notice, although we may have been supplied earlier with additional details describing the physical features of the husband and wife, telling of their siblings and Libbie, or, perhaps, speaking to the subject of their burials, we did not include these extra facts in our discussion of Dan's death.

Now, and significantly, consider the paragraph that you have just finished reading. By the time you reached the end of it, that long discussion of paragraphs through the use of examples about Dan Carner had grown to such complexity that, even though interesting, it became really tedious for you. You, the reader, needed a breather, and we did not provide it.

Even though they were necessary to your understanding, the facts and examples in that paragraph were too many and too much. It should have been broken in the middle, and another paragraph created to conclude the discussion.

So too should your writings help your readers. Remember to put yourself in the reader's place. When the explanation is tedious or the facts are numerous, give your readers a break—a respite—by dividing up long paragraphs into shorter ones (like this one and that just above).

Topic Sentences

Reread the preceding short paragraph. Notice that the first sentence there tells that your writings should help the readers. That is the *topic sentence*, and it reveals what that paragraph is all about. Now notice the other sentence in that paragraph. It addresses the issue set forth in the topic sentence. Most paragraphs are constructed in this way.

Refer again to the paragraph about Dan's passing. If we had attempted to complete that discussion by including the additional unrelated facts known to us, the paragraph would have become nonsensical; the topic sentence would have been ignored or disregarded, as follows:

> "On February 16, 1908, in Altoona, Pennsylvania, Daniel Carner, then eighty-seven and in the care of his sister, Libbie, died of Bright's disease. Even though Bright's Disease was terribly painful and quite incurable then (or hardly even now), the fact that Libbie was unmarried had made it possible for her to administer that level of care needed to see Dan through to the end. Immediately after death, Dan's remains were sent by train to Upper Sandusky, where he was interred in Old Mission Cemetery beside his wife, Mary Martin Carner. <u>Mary was short and stout and had five sisters.</u>"

By including that last sentence, we destroyed the sequence and logic of the whole paragraph; we changed the subject, such as to bring confusion to the reader. The facts as to Mary's stature and siblings, even though related to some broader discussion of her and Dan, and probably interesting to their descendants, have virtually nothing to do with his death and burial. By adding the sentence, we forced the paragraph to contain two separate and distinct thoughts, which were so far removed from each other that *flow* could not have been created.

In conclusion then, to construct easily read paragraphs is not difficult. Simply ask yourself exactly what it is that you want to talk about there, and state that as your first—the topic—sentence. If the topic is Dan's death, then write all you know about that subject, almost always in the order in which it happened. If you know so much about his death, and the details are so many that the paragraph becomes cumbersome or tedious, divide it into two or even more additional paragraphs.

If, instead, you want to write about Mary's physical appearance and her siblings, do so, but do not combine the two topics. Finish the death of Dan, create some transitional sentences, and then move into the subject of Mary and her appearance.

What Goes into a Chapter

If writing about Dan in a chapter entitled "Daniel and Mary Martin Carner," you might start with the earliest known facts concerning him, proceed to exhaust all the other facts and illustrations that you intend to include, and then conclude with his death, the transportation of his remains, and his burial. Following that effort, you might then start with Mary's birth, lead your reader through her life and their children with the corresponding details and illustrations, and, as with Dan, discuss her death and burial.

Notice though, since we were told that Mary died before Dan, it might be easier to write first of her life, their family, and her death and burial place, than of Dan's life; and conclude the chapter with a comment that his body was returned to rest forever at her side. Whether, in speaking of a family unit, you write first of the husband or first of his wife is a matter of preference, however it probably is easier for your readers if you are consistent; if you speak of a wife first in one chapter, give consideration to always doing that.

Closure: Whom and What Did You Forget?

Suppose that you write concerning the will of your fourth-great-grandfather, wherein he speaks of five grandchildren named Allison, Evan, Diane, Bethany, and Brittany. You also have written at length concerning those granddaughters, their lives and issue, however, since your research turned up nothing about the boy, Evan, you have closed the chapter, and moved on to another family line. Unless you explain, your readers can only wonder what happened to Evan, and by so breaking their chains of thought, you have distracted them, and made their reading effort even more difficult than it already is.

As with Evan, often you will know nothing of some of the children born to an ancestral marriage, of cousins who left town, or of brothers or sisters who went their separate ways after immigration; we all have folks who simply disappeared from the records. Then too, some lines are so remote that you will choose not to write of them. All those situations are excusable, IF you inform the reader of your reasons.

If, however, after once mentioning somebody, you fail to explain or account for him or her—provide *closure*—your readers are sure to suspect that 1) you forgot that person, 2) you considered him or her and his or her descendants to be unimportant, or 3) you were sloppy or neglectful. So, before ending each chapter, ask yourself, "Did I speak of or account for all persons I mentioned, or reveal to the reader why I did not do so? If you did not so account, you must do it.

Summary of Sentences, Paragraphs, and Chapters

In summary, each sentence should be written with an eye to the single idea or fact that you intend to there convey. Each paragraph or group of paragraphs should be concerned with some single subject or topic, and should identify and state those details directly having to do with that subject. Each chapter should use up all the needed facts and details, and fulfill all the expectations of the readers that you have aroused by your title to that chapter. If removed from your book, a chapter could stand alone.

Backwards or Forwards?

Before you have written much of the narrative, you must decide whether you want to work by moving backward through time, or instead, by commencing with the earliest known ancestor and moving forward. Either approach will work well, and as so often, the choice is yours.

If you decide to start with the earliest known ancestor of any of your lines, you will have chosen either a maternal or a paternal family as the first to be discussed. Your readers may not know the difference, however, especially if they are descended through some collateral line; what to you is a paternal line may be maternal to that reader. So it is that you must explain your choice.

As an example, if the title to your book is "The Haskins Family of Virginia," and your first chapter, as supposed in the earlier outline, is concerned with William and Judith Huntt and their daughter, Mary Huntt, who married Owen Griffith and had thereby Anne Griffith Drake, the mother of Martha Diane Drake (Haskins), your introduction might say something like:

> "We have commenced our story with what we know of William and Judith _?_ Huntt, the earliest known ancestors in any of our Haskins lines. William and Judith had, among others, Mary, who married Owen Griffith, and who, in her turn, had Anne Griffith who married Thomas Drake. Thomas and Anne Griffith Drake had, among others, Martha Diane Drake (Haskins)."

By that simple explanation, your readers will at once know who the Huntts, Griffiths and Drakes were, and how they figure into the story of the Haskins families of Virginia.

Illustrations and Notes Revisited

It is necessary that we return to illustrations and notes for a moment. If you are like most of us, you have many notes, photos, and mementoes that are concerned with more than one person or family line. A map showing the homesites of two separate families, or a photo showing two people, both of whom you intend to write about, are good examples.

As you work on the chapter or section that deals with the first of the two, make a mark or a notation on the illustration revealing what information or who you have there written about, and then place the used materials and notes in that file folder dedicated to the other person or subject also depicted or mentioned in that illustration. In that way, when you reach the discussion of the second person or matter, you will recall what portion of that illustration you have already used, where you used it, and who you have previously written about.

As an example, suppose you have a map that shows the early homesite of Evan Haskins and his family, which also reveals the lands of the widow, Allison Drake, and her family. If you now write of Evan and use that map as an illustration, when you later commence the narrative about Allison you should refer your readers back to the same map by giving its page number. Moreover, by noting on the back of the map that you used it in the Evan discussion and then placing it in the Allison file, you will be able to keep track of that prior use.

You likely will find that you have lost some of the citations needed. When that happens, simply enter what you do remember about that source on the blank lines below the narrative so that it too may be corrected or amended later. When you have the complete citation at hand, as said before, be sure to write it carefully, completely, and properly, so that you will not have to return to that note for still further work. (For their proper form, see Index at "citations of authority" and "notes.")

Flow and Transition

The term *flow* means simply that you have moved from one thought to the next with ease and logic. You have so created your sentences, paragraphs, and chapters that there is a smooth and logical progression from one subject into the next. Just as, when engaged in daily conversation, you should not change the subject abruptly and to the surprise of your listeners, so too in your writing.

To illustrate: Suppose, as in the earlier short outline, we have written the concluding paragraph about the death of Anne Griffith Drake, and the paragraph following opens our discussion of her children:

> "By reason of the modest wealth of the family, their larger than average landholdings, and her expensive headstone, we may guess that Anne spent her final years in comfort. Whatever the truth as to that may be, she died, at something over eighty years of age, on January 25, 1759, and was probably buried in the Nottoway Chapel churchyard. No will was recorded, hence she probably died intestate.
>
> John, Thomas, William, and Lazarus Drake were married and had issue before 1753, and Martha Diane Drake married Evan Haskins in June of 1755. To that union were born William, Thomas, Drury, and Henry Haskins."

That change of subject was too abrupt, too disarming for the reader; we moved from a statement about Anne having no will to facts concerning her sons, daughter and son-in-law. We provided no bridge over that intellectual gap. So, how do we make such changes of subject so that the narrative "flows"? How do we move smoothly from one topic to another? That task is not difficult.

We can create that flow by inserting any of a variety of simple sentences to the end of the first paragraph (where Anne was the topic). We might write there:

> "Anne left five grown children, four sons and one unmarried daughter," or

> "Left to mourn Anne were her five grown children," or

> "The next generation of Drakes following Thomas and Anne consisted of four grown men and one unmarried woman."

Notice, any of these three sentences bridge the gap between the paragraph about Anne and the new discussion of her children.

We could just as easily have created the needed flow by adding to the beginning of the next paragraph (having the children of Thomas and Anne, particularly Martha Diane, as its topic). We could there add,

"It was through the children of Anne that the Haskins line joined the Drakes," or

"Those who survived Anne and Thomas Drake were five in number," or

"It is at this point, through the marriage of Thomas and Anne's only daughter, Martha Diane, that we first view our Haskins families."

So, the addition to the second paragraph of any of those sentences would again bridge the intellectual break between the two separate and distinct complete thoughts. Flow has been accomplished, without which the reader would have been left to ponder and spend the time to deduce how Anne Drake became related to a line of Haskins families.

Though flow on an even broader scale is necessary between chapters, those words of *transition* need not be lengthy. Suppose you have concluded the chapters concerning your maternal line—all of it—down to the birth in 1940 of your mother, Diane Haskins. You now are about to write the first of the chapters that are concerned with the families of your father, and you intend to commence with his earliest known ancestor, George Davis, who lived in New Jersey in 1804. You have called that new chapter "Our Earliest Davis Ancestors."

Notice that the title—"Our Earliest Davis Ancestors"— will appear at the top of the first page of this new chapter; the reader thus knows that you have changed the subject. One more paragraph will complete that shift of gears. You might start the new chapter by writing,

"Jane Haskins (born 1940) married John Davis, born 1936, and thereby brought into existence the family unit to which this writer was born. As to John's ancestry and kin, we shall commence with his fourth-great-grandfather, George Davis, who is known to have lived in New Jersey in 1804."

That simple sentence not only ties you, the author, to the Davis line, but it also provides for the reader a smooth transition from the Haskins to the Davis stories.

Smooth movement—transition—between major subjects and chapters is absolutely necessary, and our failure to supply that component is caused by nothing more than lack of experience in writing. While we consistently supply transitional thoughts throughout daily conversation (lest we be accused of "changing the subject"), we simply forget to do so when writing. When writing, we seem to mistakenly presume that the reader knows what thought comes next.

So, heed this warning: Always presume that the reader knows absolutely nothing about your next subject (which usually is the way it really is), and must be moved—urged, led (pushed?)—gently into that new discussion. To fail to observe that simple rule is to arrive at the end of your work with little more than a series of disconnected paragraphs and isolated chapters full of details, many of which are boring enough standing alone, and rendered even more so when they do not flow together.

The Need to Create Interest

Let us be realistic; genealogical facts, as written by most amateurs, are colorless and unbelievably tedious to read, enjoy, or appreciate. That is not criticism of those diligent and fine folks, it is just plain fact.

Consider some of the usual reasons for reading historical and genealogical materials. They are, 1) to satisfy our curiosity, 2) to gain information or data, 3) to vicariously share in the activities, adventures, sensations, thoughts, and feelings of early people, 4) to make meaningful comparisons, 5) to assist us with further works, and 6) to pass leisure time.

While any of those reasons might cause some people to sample your work, there is more to it than that. After the sampling, they must read on, read on to the end, and come away entertained and informed, and they will not do that unless you add color and context, the "broad bursh of history," as we said. So, if you plan to set forth nothing more than a series of names, abbreviated events, and dates, without adding context and color, you should stop reading here and now, for we can help you no more.

Without context, your writings are nothing. Unless you always remember that your ancestors were living, breathing, loving, hating, short or tall, fat or skinny, handsome or homely people, who did things, had experiences, lived long or short lives, suffered illnesses, and died, just as you have and will, your work will not be interesting to anybody. If you do not again breathe life and experience into those folks, your efforts are destined to be relegated to some obscure shelf or closet, never more to be considered as other than a conversation piece.

Context (and Color)

At the beginning and throughout the writing of each and every chapter—indeed, every paragraph—ask yourself the simple question, "What do I need here to provide the reader with a mental picture of the people and the times?"

Using the Broad Brush of History

We know of a fine old gentleman who, when doing his first ever family research, said that he "...loved genealogy, but cared nothing for history." In but a few days or weeks, he came to realize, however (as we all have), that the only difference between the two lies in the scope, breadth, and focus of the studies involved.

The history you sought to understand (and sometimes hated) in high school almost always was a consideration of great names and characters of the past, vast movements of people that took place over long, long periods, and the impacts upon those millions of the streams of ideas and technology, all with dates and in chronological order. Genealogy or family history, on the other hand, may be described as a study of a relatively few people who usually were neither great nor well known, movements of those people and their immediate families to places where they hoped to better themselves or their lives in some usually small way, and the many effects that ideas, religion, occupation, and technology had upon their often harsh and almost always demanding daily lives.

Where a chapter in your old high school text might speak of Patrick Henry, General Lee, or World War II, your book may tell of an ancestor who, as a lowly private in the

Continental Line, was at Yorktown watching when Cornwallis surrendered the British army; while that schoolbook may speak of the influence of Catholicism in early Maryland, you might speak of the devotion to that church by some great grandmother whose school was taught by nuns; and where the broad brush of history might reveal the Industrial Revolution, you could tell of the 1875 coming of the railroad to the home town of some great-great grandparent.

So, as you write, consider the story of your family to be a play, and think of that broader history as the changing background and scenery—the setting—in front of which the play was acted out. When your great-great grandmother, who had twelve children between 1870 and 1895, comes upon the scene, tell of the coming of running water to their little town during those years. When you speak of the life of your Civil War triple-great grandfather, tell also of the early trains by which he went off to war, all the way from Columbus to Cincinnati! And, all will enjoy knowing that an ancestor lived near Boston in April of 1775 when Paul Revere rode through the countryside warning that the "Redcoats" were coming.

Subtleties that arise from the history of your family are equally important. While you may not have thought of it in that way, you might remember being told of your Johnson great grandparents, who came to Muncie from the mountains of eastern Tennessee and maintained much of their old Scotch-Irish attitudes and language— their *hill-billy accent*, as your mother called it. Then too, what of the other Johnson kin, whose name had been spelled "Johansson," and who migrated from Sweden to the cold timber country of Minnesota and from there to Oregon? And you have a photo of a 1910 baptism *by immersion* in a river in Indiana that included some of your ancestors, not to mention the 1890 newspaper clipping (which you also intend to include) that tells of the invention of the incredible electric light and the prospect of electricity being brought to Cass County some day.

By speaking of the coming of and wonder at those and myriad other events and inventions, you will provide your readers with marvelous opportunities to know of the pleasure or pain, awe or fear that your people felt.

Finding Context

The historical or genealogical society or a chamber of commerce near the residences of ancestors will be able to tell you of historical events that took place in the vicinity. For example, in the case of Dan and Mary Carner, it so happens that, not two miles from their graves, Col. William Crawford was burned at the stake by the Wyandot Indians. A mark on a map and two or so short paragraphs describing that most horrid event will be absolutely fascinating to your readers. You will have placed the Carners— common, poor, nearly illiterate farm people though they were—on the stage of the great play of American history.

Photos of local schools, churches, courthouses, jails, trains, horses and wagons, fairs, picnics, even old bridges, all add color and life to cold, barren names and dates. If, you are not able to travel to those places to obtain illustrations, you may write to the local historical or genealogical society,[1] and ask if someone there will help you gain such a map or photo. They almost always will do so, and will usually only charge you for copies of the photos themselves. Send those letters off as you proceed with your writing; you have plenty of time to receive answers before you finish your work.

---

1. Most historical and genealogical societies may be contacted by a letter asking for the street address to "Reference Desk, Public Library, __(name of county seat)__ and _zip code_ (of that town).

Through these simple methods, color will have been provided and context will have been shared with your readers.

After One Family Line, Then What?

One of the more tedious problems in writing family history is encountered at the end of your story of some entire family line. Suppose you have now finished with all you intend to write about your maternal Carner lines. Having started with the Dan and Mary Martin Carner chapter, you then spent two chapters dealing with four preceding generations in both the Martin and the Carner lines, back to the earliest known of those people (circa 1750), including the siblings and their families in each of those generations, following which, in two more chapters, you brought the known Carner and Martin lines to the twentieth century. In addition, you have put in place numerous illustrations and notes, and have woven in some broader history—context. You are ready to write about your other maternal line; that of the Snyders, of whom you have information back to about 1780. Now what?

If your readers are to have any big picture of it all, in addition to the transition paragraphs at the beginning, you must tell your Snyder story in such a fashion that they recognize who of the Snyder line lived or did something at about the same time as did people of the Carner-Martin line. For example, since you have already told that Dan and Mary Martin Carner were married in 1862, if you again mention that marriage year when you arrive at that same period in the narrative about the Snyders, the reader will be able to relate one family to another.

Such linkage is easy to accomplish, and the Snyder narrative might read, in part, as follows.

"It will be remembered from the earlier chapters that Dan and Mary Carner were married in 1862. It was at that very same period that George and Susan Snyder sold their farm, packed up their kids and belongings, and went off to old Ohio," or

"So, in 1862, the very same year that Dan and Mary Carner were married, George and Susan Snyder and the children arrived in Ohio, their son George, Jr., went off to the Civil War, and their eldest daughter, Betsy married John Moore."

Notice, by calling the Carner marriage year into the Snyder story, both are much more understandable and enjoyable. To fail to do that requires the reader to stop and recall (if he or she yet can) when the Carners were married, thereby entirely losing the flow and Snyder story line which you have tried so hard to create.

Finally, it is equally important occasionally—perhaps once in a chapter, and usually near the beginning—to create a paragraph that draws a number of family lines together at a certain time period, again to bring to the reader a realization of how it all fits in the broader perspective. Suppose that, having finished the Carner, Martin, and Snyder lines, we now are writing about the Drakes. Such a simple paragraph might read:

"During the years 1830 to 1860, Will Drake, his wife, and their growing family of five children were working and living on their farm in the north of Plumstead Township of Bucks County. At the same time, as we have seen, George and Susan Snyder and their young family were farming in Cumberland County, Dan Carner was working as a teamster on the new canal near Hollidaysburg, and young Mary

Martin was still at home with her parents in little Frankstown, all in central Pennsylvania."

At once, and without being required to make the effort necessary to again look up or recall those details, your reader is reminded of who was where during the years when Will Drake lived in Bucks County. So, be sure to occasionally tie several family lines together.

Equity of Treatment

You must treat your actors fairly; because they deserve it, and also because your work is not thorough and complete if you do not. If a person is included in your list of players, then he or she also is worthy of, if not equal time and space, at least an equitable division of the effort dedicated to most folks of that generation.

And, it makes no difference that such an ancestor was poor, common, illiterate, a criminal, a reprobate, or a deserter from the family or some army; just as you spoke of those of many accomplishments, so too must you speak of those whose credits were few. Speak of the well-known among them, but also speak, without judgment, of the lesser of them, and do so honestly and without embarrassment. Whether an ancestor was King Charlemagne, a prostitute, a drunken drayman, or a billionaire, you carry their genes, and they are a part of your story.

Those who were successful left many records, while the less fortunate left few. So be it. Yet even when you don't find much, and if the record that you find is "bad" in the eyes of your family, you have a duty to reveal it, and to do so honestly. Where there was no record found, reveal that too, and tell that you looked long and hard for what little you did relate.

In summary, speak equally, truthfully, and forthrightly of everybody of whom you learn; and where you found nothing, say so.

Using Yourself and Your Times to Close the Story

As you reach the end of the narrative, the question arises: Having brought the families of both my lines to recent date, what do I say, if anything, about my own lifetime and period of history? The answer probably is, "better less than more." Having dedicated years of research to the many lines and collateral lines that are the ancestry of thousands of people, including you and your known kin, and dozens of hours to the writing of their stories, you should conclude with a minimum of tales wherein you are the principal actor. You probably should not occupy a major position among the players.

That is not to say, however, that a history of your times will not be interesting to readers of the distant future. In fact, it will. The story of your life, however lacking or bubbling over in grandeur it may be, will be interesting if you tell, not of every one of your feelings and accomplishments, but rather of those that truly were noteworthy in the long run of life.

Your high school prom does not rank in that category, and your own marriage is of no more importance and future interest than was that of your great grandmother. Your baby picture, for example, if it is clear and reveals a dress, house design, furniture, or baby carriage, will be of interest far in the future, however a poor snapshot of you with a neighbor child and someone's dog will not. Likewise, a clear photo of your home, automobile, or boat, or a newspaper clipping telling of your sorority or political activities may be of lasting interest in the grand story of your families, while a picture of you, as a child, mowing the yard, playing in a wading pool, or sticking out your tongue surely will not.

When deciding what to show and tell about you, your immediate family, and your contemporary kin, ask yourself three questions, 1) Are these illustrations of sufficient quality to be included? 2) If I had the same illustrations concerning my great grandmother, would I include them? and 3) in 100 years will readers be interested in this? If the answer is no to any one of those questions, do not include those items or memories.

If you have decided to do a chapter about your times with you as the principal player, then think carefully back over your lifetime. What events did you witness that rank with the noteworthy events of the past?

If you were in the Korean War or a nurse in Vietnam, tell of your service, but do so in a minimum of space, unless you really did play a significant part or were wounded or captured. Were you an office holder? In the great scheme of things, short of being president, senator, governor, or justice, your tenure likely will be 'little noted nor long remembered', but it is important, so tell of it in that number of words that the title or position deserves, and no more. Were you present at a great event? Did you see a president or know a governor? Did you witness or find yourself in a calamity or disaster? Was a significant landmark opened or created in your time? Do you remember the landing on the moon? The end of the passenger train as a means of travel? Tell of such matters, but again, do so in a number of words that will not bore your reader.

Your illnesses and injuries, unless truly life-threatening or dreadfully serious are almost sure to bore your readers; would you be terribly interested in reading about your great-grandmother's strep throat? Her arthritis? Are you terribly sympathetic over an ancestor that had chicken pox or a hernia? Of course not, so then spare your readers from your similar experiences. Finally, do you care whether or not an ancestor fell out of a haymow or broke his toe? If not, do not tell of your own accidents of that nature.

So, readers of the distant future will be interested in your wars, religion, transportation, housing, entertainment, occupation or profession, work hours and requirements, the fact that you lived at the advent of the computer, space flight, and advanced medical technology, and will find it curious that you had no television, enjoyed hunting—the "blood sports"—and used a typewriter with carbon paper or a telegraph "key." So, tell, not of a word processor, but how you struggled without it; not of a mammogram, but how helpless and frightened you and your kind were until such came upon the scene; not of your long trips to the homes of friends, but of the difficulty and time consumed before interstate highways could take you there; and not of the many grouse and deer you killed, but how the pioneer hunter mind-set lasted until even after the end of the twentieth century.

Further examples are so many that to continue is unnecessary. Ask yourself, what did I do and see that my ancestors did not and my descendants will not? What became useless or ended during my lifetime? And what came upon the scene that I found truly remarkable, enjoyable, or time or life saving? It is those matters that your descendants will want to know about.

Just as you do, your readers will appreciate sincere feelings, if you are brief and not maudlin about it. A favorite uncle, or friend with whom you fished, reminiscing with a grandmother on a spring evening, a day of hunting in a Vermont woods, a flower kept and a good-bye at the deathbed of an aunt, all are worthy of telling. So, in the chapter concerning you and your times, write about such human feelings, but do not—please do not—tell about climbing trees, graduating from catechism class, having a part in some high school play, or of falling off your bicycle on the way to Aunt Jane's.

Addressing Ancestors

Just as we do not impose upon our ancestors our ideas of what is proper and improper, we also do not refer to them with other than their given names, unless we are positive that their contemporaries did so. Names, then and now, were sources of pride, and customs prevailed that are foreign to our society, a few of which are here mentioned.[2]

Briefly, unless you find evidence that an ancestor was spoken of as "Mr." or "Mrs.", you should not use those terms. In the English-speaking world of the seventeenth, eighteenth, and nineteenth centuries, those titles were carefully reserved to only those of very high station in the community. Similarly, the term gentleman and lady were used to refer only to those who, through birth or wealth, had earned or come to claim those recognitions of social position. Interestingly, since in early Virginia to be addressed as "Mister" was more desired than being known as a physician or "chirurgeon" (surgeon), "Dr." Richard Parker and "Dr." Nathaniel Knight, among others, probably abandoned the latter titles in favor of the former.[3]

English men, both here and in the mother land were ranked in descending order; noblemen, gentlemen, and yeomen. Those educated in the "arts and mysteries" of the more complex trades —pewterer, joiner, cabinetmaker, glassman, etc.—were written of with those callings following their name, e.g., "Claudius Martin, Stonemason" or "James Shaeffer, Silversmith." Their wives were often referred to as "goodwife," especially in early New England, New York, New Jersey, and Pennsylvania; Claudius' wife likely was "Goodwife Martin" or "Goodwife Hannah Martin."

The term planter had meanings, from lessee, to large farmer, to gentleman, depending upon the period, and if a man owned even a small tract of land, he often was called "Yeoman." So, given a bill of sale for a horse from "John Carner, Husbandman" to "Daniel Martin, Yeoman," you may presume that John was a farmer and Daniel owned land. Where an individual had no title or higher calling, he was referred to by such words as "laborer," "teamster," or "hired hand," and where he had no training or position, he often was referred to as "common" or a "commoner," particularly in the South; both, terms almost of derision for the lowest classes in the society of that day.

In summary, refer to your ancestors by their names without titles, unless the records reveal that those who knew them did otherwise. Unless they really were, it is pure pretension to speak of an ancestor as "Lady," "Gentleman,"or "Plantation owner."

Having finished the near-final draft of your work, what further matters need to be considered?

---

2. For an excellent discussion of titles and manners of referring to each other, see P. A. Bruce, *Social Life Of Virginia In The Seventeenth Century* (Whittet & Shepperson, 1907), pp. 115-117, and see Chapter VII, generally
3. See *Now In Our Fourth Century*, etc., op. cit., pp. 28 & 30

Chapter VI: Copyright Considerations, Publishing, and Marketing

"You can only sell so many Fuller Brushes to your grandmother."

An unknown sage

If we could dash off to the past whenever we took a notion, spend a few minutes watching and asking questions of this or that ancestor, and take pictures of their homes and activities, our problems of proof and worry over using the works of others would be all but gone; we would simply quote what we heard, cite our own experiences, and gain *copyright* protection for the finished product. Since we can't do any of those things, we are called upon to search existing records, to cite and quote others who have done the same, and then, if we have created anything new, seek protection for it.

Just as we may gain a degree of protection in the form of copyrights for the writings we do, other folks can and have done likewise. So it is that whether we write in narrative, or create an abstract, extract, compilation, or some combination of all of those, we must be ever mindful that the rights of others may come into play.

For our purposes, copyright problems are broken down into two categories; a) unpublished works of others, and b) published works of others. As to the former, very little use is ever permitted. As to the latter, the general rule is that before we may copy such works to any substantial degree we must either gain "license"—permission—or use those writings in a fashion that falls within the *Fair Use* provisions of Title 17, United States Code.

So, ideas reduced to writing may be protected, and that is especially true if those writings, as in a), have not yet been published. The courts long ago declared that the privacy and exclusivity of unpublished writings should be preserved, and that protection continues, even though the author may have declared that he or she has no interest in the publication of the writings, now or in the future.[1] Thus, just as you may not take up and use the furniture of another without permission, a writer may not commandeer the unpublished materials and writings of another writer for any purpose.[2]

For how long does the protection continue for writings that have neither been "published" or copyrighted? The statute is clear: If such writings were created before 1 January, 1978, the duration of the protection is for the life of the author plus fifty years, provided however, that no matter how long ago the writing may have been done, that protection will not end before December 31, 2002.[3] For those writings done after 1 January, 1978, the protection extends through the same time period of years, i.e., the life of the author plus fifty years.[4]

---

1. *Salinger v. Random House, Inc.* (1987, CA2 NY) 811 F.2nd 90, 99; 13 Media Law Review 1954; 1 U.S.P.Q.2 1673; cert. den'd, etc., 108 S. Ct. 213. The court also there reminded the litigants that Title 17, Section 301 (a), U.S.C., recognized in the copyright owner "...a right of first publication...." Ibid., p. 94.
2. *New Era Publications, etc. v. Carol Publishing, etc.*, (1990, CA2 NY); 904 F.2d 152, generally; 17 Media Law Reports 1913. As to unpublished writings, it was thought that the court therein might expand the *Fair Use* doctrine; apparently not. (see infra) Also see *Salinger v. Random House*, op. cit., p. 100. That an author has a common-law right to unpublished writings was clearly recognized as early as 1872. *Parton v. Prang* (1872, CC Mass.) F. Case No. 10784, and see *Cantor v. Mankiewicz* (1960 Sup) 203 NYS2d. 626, 125 U.S.P.Q. 598
3. 17 U.S.C., Sections 301, and notes accompanying
4. 17 U.S.C, Section 302

So, unless a writer or his or her heirs choose to grant permission to use or "publish" the work, that author (or his heirs) is entitled to retain his peculiar rendering of thoughts to the exclusion of the world for a very long period indeed.[5] That exclusivity afforded unpublished writings continues, even though a proposed use might otherwise be quite *fair* under the law; fairness does not provide an excuse for a use of unpublished works.[6]

As stated, the other category with which we must concern ourselves is that of "published" works. While the word published usually refers to writings that have been printed and sold, the word may be applied to actions that are not so clear cut.

While myriad definitions of the word "publish" are at hand (and the courts long ago recognized that the definition varies with the facts in every case[7]), this word generally means that an author has consciously caused or permitted his or her words, whether printed and bound into books or not, to become open to the scrutiny of the intellectual community; he or she has introduced the writing materials into the "public domain;" has freely set those thoughts and words adrift in the ocean of writings. Notice too, it makes little difference whether or not such writings and ideas were formally written, had merit, or even whether the public had any interest.[8]

So, if you type your work, make a handful of copies down at the local print shop, give one to the library and the rest to the historical society and your family, you almost surely have "published" that work, whether you intended to or not. If so, and if you gained no protection in the course of that little distribution, in all likelihood your words and expressions may be used by anyone for any purpose. Similarly, even if you only made one copy, gained no measure of protection and gave it to the state archives (or maybe even a local library) without instructions that it be held private and out of circulation, you have probably "published." So be careful; if you do not intend to publish, do not place your writings in a position where others unknown to you may see and read them.

To understand how copyrights and the *Fair Use* doctrine apply to published writings (both our own and those of others), we must know and remember a little something about the law and its application. We protect words and manners of expression with *copyrights*, and within that word itself is a measure of definition; "copyright" means "a right to control copies."[9] That right is as old as the Constitution itself; Article I, Section 8, paragraph 8, declares that our government has a duty "...to promote the progress of...useful arts, by securing for limited times to authors...the exclusive right to their respective writings and discoveries." Said another way, products of our intellect are protectable by law, just as are any other of our belongings.

As discussed in Chapter 1, it is necessary that in all copies and printings of your work, including the very first, you make your copyright assertion on the page

---

5. For overall perspective in the matter of Fair Use, the reader is advised to examine Justice O'Connor's opinion in *Harper and Row, etc. v. Nation Enterprises* (1985) 471 U.S. 539, 563; 85 L. Ed. 2nd 588; 105 S. Ct. 2218

6. *New Era Publications, etc. v. Carol Publishing, etc.*, op. cit.

7. *Marx v. U.S.* (1938, CA9 CA) 96 F.2d 204; 37 U.S.P.Q. 380; where, in published works, the definition is said to vary from those cases in which the effort was not for sale. Also see *American Visuals, etc. v. Holland* (1956, CA2 NY) 239 F.2d 740; 111 U.S.P.Q. 288; wherein the definition turned on whether the complainant contended he had not published, or that he had and sought protection under the rather narrow definition of the statute.

8. See generally *Ladd v. Oxnard* (1896, CC MA) 75 F. 703

9. "...(T)he sole right of multiplying copies...." said *Jewelers Circular, etc. v. Keystone Publishing etc.*; (CA2 NY) 81 F. 83, 94.

immediately after (usually on the reverse of) the title page. Thereupon, application should be made to the copyright office for the necessary forms and instructions, the same to be filled out and returned, with the required fee and copies of your work.

Thus, whether it be through the use of computer memory, recorder, movie camera or, as is usually the case with the family historian, the written word, authors have rights to and may gain protection for their manners of expression—their words. Notice, however, that ideas, conceptions, plans, and good intentions concerning a writing that may be done in the future have no protection; we can protect our writings, but not our intentions and plans to write.[10]

So, then, how do we use words of others that have been protected? The law recognizes that concept which scholars have understood for centuries: all knowledge is cumulative, and if mankind is to relay the notions, ideas, and findings of others, demonstrate errors there made or confirm or distinguish truths, earlier works by other authors must be quoted and pondered.[11]

While courts have recognized that intellectual need, and are prone to be much, much more liberal in permitting uses of published expressions of underlying ideas than they are with unpublished materials, even with published works there remain strict limitations upon such uses.[12] As said, those limitations are the stuff of the Fair Use doctrine.

The courts have said generally that the term Fair Use "...relates to the extent to which copyrightable materials may be used without express license...." or permission.[13] Here too, just as did the word copyright, the expression itself provides a measure of meaning: Use of the published words of another will be permitted if, in the eyes of the law, that use is "fair" to the author; that is, use will be allowed if the original writer is not thereby unreasonably deprived of an economic or intellectual advantage that might result from his or her exertions (notice the word "might"). Another writer has said that the Fair Use doctrine recognizes "...a privilege in others to use copyrighted material in a reasonable manner without consent."[14]

Recognizing the need for further delineation, and at the same time voicing its intention that "good faith and fair dealing" are to be considered as basic precepts in every use,[15] Congress has set forth, not a true definition, but rather, guidelines for use by all in planning conduct.

Still though, and to our distinct disadvantage, there is a "catch" in the legislative pronouncement. An examination of the words of the statute reveals that—unlike most "laws" that order or restrict conduct—this provision contains no prohibitions; we look

---

10. *Mazer v. Stein*, (1954) 347 U.S. 201, 217; 98 L. Ed. 630; 74 S. Ct. 460, reh. den'd, etc., 347 U.S. 949. Also see *Christianson v. West Publishing*, etc., (1945, CA9, CA) 149 F.2nd 202, 202; 65 U.S.P.Q. 263

11. *Henry Holt & Co. v. Liggett & Myers*, etc. (1938 DC PA) 23 F. Supp. 302, 304; 37 U.S.P.Q. 449; wherein consent to a *Fair Use* was implied as to those working for the "advancement" of the arts. Also note that within the field of arts and science "broad scope" is given to *Fair Use. Loews Inc. v. Columbia*, (1955 DC CA) 131 F. Supp. 165, 175; 105 U.S.P.Q. 302; aff'd, etc., p. 175

12. Provided, however, that such commentary may not be done to promote sales of such writings. *Amana*, etc. *v. Consumers Union* etc. (1977, ND Iowa) 431 F. Supp. 324, 326-327; 195 U.S.P.Q. 56. Indeed, commercial motives are a strong factor in determining infringement. *Financial Information, Inc. v. Moody's Investors Service, Inc.* (1984, CA2 NY) 751 F.2d 501, 508; 231 U.S.P.Q. 632; aff'd, cert. den'd, etc., 108 S. Ct. 79

13. *Loews Inc. v. Columbia*, etc. op. cit., 356 U.S. 934, generally

14. H. Ball, *Law of Copyrights and Literary Property* (1944); p. 260

15. *Time, Inc. v. Bernard Geis*, etc. (1986, DC NY) 293 F. Supp. 130, 146; 159 U.S.P.Q. 663

here in vain for hard rules by which to abide or activities to avoid. Indeed, upon close scrutiny it becomes apparent that the sentences provide nothing more than the barest parameters to be used by all—courts and word peddlers alike—in determining what is "fair." The net result is that we act and interpret the congressional guidelines at our own risk, and further, we do so with the full knowledge that some court, at some later day, may decide that we erred and punish us.

The Fair Use provisions read, in part:

> "Notwithstanding...(the prohibitions herein)...the fair use of a copyrighted work, including such use by reproduction in copies...for purposes such as criticism, comment,...teaching (including multiple copies for classroom use), scholarship, or research, is not an infringement of copyright. In determining whether the use made of a work in any particular case is a fair use the factors to be considered shall include-
>
> (1) the purpose and character of the use, including whether such use is of a commercial nature or is for non-profit educational purposes;
> (2) the nature of the copyrighted work;
> (3) the amount and substantiality of the portion used in relation to the copyrighted work as a whole; and
> (4) the effect of the use upon the potential market for or value of the copyrighted work."[16]

Of great importance to amateurs like us, notice that the words nowhere require or even speak of any *intention* to do harm. Indeed, malicious intent is conspicuous by its absence; criminal intent of the infringer is not even discussed; culpability is not required; we need find no 'bad guys'.

Said still differently, unlike in nearly all areas of the law where restriction, punishment, or fines result from breach, in the Fair Use provisions Congress did not see fit to require that an infringer *willfully* undertake to break the law—to steal the expressions of others. It is enough simply that he or she did so; it is sufficient to show that the infringer, whether knowingly or not, undertook conduct which, through the use of the work product of somebody else, might bring profit in any form, or that he or she undertook to assume even a small portion of some potential market of the person whose words were stolen.[17]

So, the rules of Fair Use are simple enough to state, or so it would seem; if, as contemplated in *subsection 1*, we are teaching, comparing or being critical of, or confirming what another writer has said, we may use expressions of that other person. However, if the purpose and character of our use of another's words, rather than being of an intellectual nature, is to gain a measure of profit (directly or indirectly) then we must leave the expressions of those others alone. We may not lay back while another labors, and then seek to profit through the utilization of the time, labor, verbiage,

---

16. Title 17, U.S.C., Section 107, as amended.
17. The commercial motives and intentions of the infringer were considered in *Financial Information, Inc. v. Moody's Investors Services, Inc.*, op. cit., 751 F.2d 501, 508; Here again, see *Loew's, Inc. v. Columbia Broadcasting, etc.*, op. cit.

sentence structure, or the articulation of thoughts of that other writer, all the while pretending the product to be ours.[18]

Subsection 2 of the statute requires a consideration of the nature—perhaps of even the subject—of the original work. Presumably, our collective need for the intellectual community to examine, study, and compare scientific and factual works of others is greater than our needs where, for example, the writings concern genealogy, the arts, or history. Said another way, a greater use will be considered fair and permitted in scientific investigations than where the writings are of other disciplines.[19]

Of the statute, sub-sections, numbers 3 and 4 have the greatest impact on genealogical and historical writings; the works that we usually undertake. *Subsection 3* directs that courts look to the *amount and substantiality* of the portion used in relation to the copyrighted work as a whole, and *Subsection 4* requires that consideration be given to the *effect of the use* by another upon the potential market for or the value of the copyrighted work to the author.

As to those two required considerations, several examples are necessary:

First, suppose a writer has copied verbatim previously unpublished tax records of a Pennsylvania county and, in addition, has prepared a unique index for that work, showing both the townships or residence and the names of the taxable persons, as well as a narrative preface and introduction to the work. Is the effort copyrightable?

Yes, however the protection afforded by the copyright will extend only to the index, the preface and the introduction. Concerning those sections of the work, by the use of "skill, labor and judgment" there has been created something of worth both to the writer and to the marketplace for such information; something that is recognizably a work product of that author, and for which a market may exist.[20] Importantly, here note that the transcription of the tax records is not protectable—not copyrightable—no matter how new, unique, well done, or complete. Such records are "public" and free to all; they are within the public domain.[21] Likewise with any other naked facts, historical, scientific, or otherwise.[22] So, we would be free to use this author's copied tax records, no matter how much time and effort went into their production.

Another example: let us presume that our imaginary author uses the same index, narrative preface, and introduction, however, by reason of the absence in the records of any punctuation and the difficulty of interpreting the old handwriting and spelling found there, she creates a restatement of those records that is more readable and understandable than were the lists themselves. Even though she used the same non-copyrightable tax records, by doing more than merely copying them she created a writing—a *compilation*—that is copyrightable.[23] The desirability of protecting efforts

---

18. In *Maxtone-Graham v. Burtchael* (1986, SD NY) 631 F. Supp. 1432, 1437; 299 U.S.P.Q. 538; aff'd, cert. den'd, etc., 107 S. Ct. 2201, whether or not the intention was to save effort through the use of the work of another was considered, and a determination that the plagiarizer "...did not seek to save effort or make profit...." was made.
19. *Harper and Row, etc. v. Nation Enterprises*, op cit., 563
20. *Doran v. Sunset House, etc.* (1961, DC CA) 197 F. Supp. 940, 944; 131 U.S.P.Q. 94; aff'd, etc.
21. Even the earliest decisions recognized that records such as courts' orders and decisions were *public* and not subject to copyright protection. *Little v Hall* (1856) 59 U.S. 165, 15 L. Ed. 328.
22. *Financial Information, etc. v. Moody, etc.*, op. cit., p. 505
23. Note, however that changes and edits must be more than trivial. *United States v. Hamilton* (1978, CA9 Idaho) 583 F.2nd 448, 451; 200 U.S.P.Q. 14. What constitutes a compilation was considered in 88 A.L.R. Fed 151.

such as this that involve unique background, training, and expertise was early recognized.[24]

So, this new writing is protectable. But notice, such a work is not afforded that protection because of the idea of doing it, or by reason of the underlying tax records which were interpreted and set forth, or as a reward for the writer's diligent efforts. The recognition is granted by reason of the discretion, "selection" and "editorial judgment" required of, and exercised by, our writer in restating the old tax records in a more intelligible form.[25] Interestingly, one court has observed that in a compilation such as this, by reason of the selection and judgment exercised "the whole is greater than the sum of its parts...."[26] As to this work product, only if they were to be used minimally, or were to be legitimately critiqued, commented upon, differentiated from, or used for classroom study could these words be taken by others without risk of punishment.

Let us here define "abstracts" and "extracts," both of which are found frequently in genealogical writing. An abstract is a summary of information, usually presented in a shortened form, and so probably eligible for protection, while an extract is an excerpt or selection still in the original wording, and therefore likely not eligible.

Where profit is the only discernible motive for the use of words by an infringer, it should be apparent that, even if that infringer steals but a single word from such a protected work, the taking is not permissible. However, such a use would be of so little consequence that the courts should not and will not be bothered, even though, as said, in theory an infringement has taken place.[27]

When, then, is a taking such that the law should intervene; when is the use *substantial*, and how do we measure the *character* of the use? Suppose the infringer were to copy thirty pages of the forty-page work on Pennsylvania tax records mentioned above, add one sentence at the end which says "I disagree with the author's interpretations," and then market that writing through the *Genealogical Helper*. Fair Use as criticism, critique and comment? Of course not. On its face, the character and substantiality of the use, and obvious purpose to profit, are displayed; the second writer set out to capitalize upon the labor of another and added nothing unique, new or intellectually innovative; his work only "mirrored" the first.[28]

Next, with the same basic facts, suppose the infringing writer undertakes to market the tax records of the first author in order to raise funds for a non-profit historical foundation of which he is the salaried president. Is it Fair Use because of the non-profit aspect of the sales? Almost surely not—and not by reason of his office, even though that fact surely gives color to the overall picture—but rather because the true effect of such sales of that portion of the first author's works would be to seize and diminish a finite market as contemplated by Subsection 4, which market was

---

24. *Hanson v. Jaccard Jewelry Co.* (1887 CC MO) 32 F. 202, 203.
25. The "editorial judgment"aspect is implicit and expressed within the wording of the code section at 17 U.S.C. 101: "A compilation is a work formed by the collection and assembling of preexisting materials...that are <u>selected, coordinated or arranged</u> in such a way that the resulting work constitutes an original work of authorship."
26. *Financial Information, etc. v. Moody's Investors, etc.*, op. cit., p. 505.
27. Concerning the legal disdain for and unwillingness to consider plagiarization of but tiny portions of writings (the so-called *de minimus* rule), *see Toulmin v. Rike-Kumler, Inc.* (DC OH) 137 U.S.P.Q., aff'd (CA6 OH), 316 F.2d 232, 137 U.S.P.Q. 499, 500; cert. den'd., etc.
28. *Holdridge v. Knight Publishing Corp.* (1963, DC Cal) 214 F. Supp. 921, 924; 136 U.S.P.Q. 615

exclusively that of the first author by reason of his or her effort.[29] So, the statute does not provide exemption for charitable or non-profit uses.

Concerning the importance to be accorded the limited nature of the market for literary products, it has been said (and most significantly for the genealogist) that "...the effect of an illegal use upon the potential market for or the value of a copyrighted work is the single most important element in any consideration of whether or not an activity should be looked upon as a 'fair use';...the original writer...needs only to show that if the challenged use should become widespread, it would adversely affect the potential market for the copyrighted work...(and the investigation by the court)...must take account not only of harm to the market for the original writing, but also of any harm which might come to the market for derivative works."[30]

With market in mind, return to the example: presume that the infringer sells the same writings (thirty of the forty pages, with the barest comment that he disagrees with the conclusions) to the local historical society which has but twenty-five members. By reason of that limited exposure, even though the taking surely was substantial, one might say that he has only marginally affected the market, if at all. So, infringement? Most likely still, yes; the second writer has continued to use a substantial portion of the work product of the first. His effort still is not legitimate criticism, and no matter how small the market portion taken or assumed, he entered it with the words and efforts of the first author as his stock in trade. In this example, it is sufficient to say that, should this particular sales scheme become widespread, there would be an adverse effect upon the market; the sales need not have actually done so.[31]

Fairness is very hard to establish where any sales actually were made, no matter how few dollars were gained by the infringer. As the court has said, while the definition of Fair Use within intellectual activities is broad indeed, it narrows greatly as we move into the commercial arena.[32] Indeed, "Every commercial use is presumed unfair."[33] So, evidence of any sale or intent to sell quite usually precludes Fair Use.

What if the same infringer, using the same thirty or forty pages, prefaced his work with the words: "For the most part, this writing was done for classroom study and through the verbatim use of the materials of the former author, for which we sincerely thank her." Infringement? Almost surely, yes. The substantial portion taken and the sales effort and manifest profit motive revealed belie scholarly intention, no matter how extensive the acknowledgment and gratitude expressed. The statute provides no exemptions for acknowledgments and credit given to others.[34] So, "thanks" is not a substitute for permission.

Suppose next that instead of thirty pages, the infringer used but one page of the writings of the first, added other pages of the same tax records copied verbatim, did his own introduction and preface, and then marketed the work. Infringement? Likely not, since the use of the first author's work was minimal and the second writer did not "mirror" the first effort.

---

29. Whether of not the economic value was unfairly diminished was considered in *Fisher v. Dees* (1986, CA9 CA) 794 F.2d 432, 437; 13 Media L R 1167, 230 U.S.P.Q. 646

30. See *Harper and Row, etc. vs. Nation Enterprises, etc.*, op. cit., p. 568; Justice O'Connor there citing *Sony, etc. v. Universal Studios, etc.*, 474 U.S. 451, 484; 8 L. Ed. 2d 574; 104 S. Ct. 774

31. Ibid.

32. *Loews Inc. v. Columbia, etc.*, op. cit., p. 175

33. *Sony v. Universal Studios, etc.*, op cit.

34. *Toksvig v. Bruce Publishing Co., Inc.*, (1950, CA7 WI) 181 F.2d 664, 666; 85 U.S.P.Q. 339

However, suppose that the first writer, while searching the Pennsylvania tax records, had uncovered an entry revealing that General Lee once had owned land at Gettysburg, a fact never before known to any historian. If that was the one page taken by the infringer, that taking might well preempt a most valuable market; a market that the first writer earned and deserves by reason of his or her extraordinary effort. Here, the words taken by the infringer had that great "substantiality" contemplated by Subsection 3.[35] The use—while very small in numbers of words and percentage of the whole first writing—was a substantial taking. So, an infringement upon the work of another is not excused merely because it is small compared to the total work, if that quantity was of great interest and novelty.[36]

Mere numbers of words or pages taken usually have not been determinative, one way or the other. Where numbers or pages were argued to be appropriate as bases of decision, the courts usually have looked for and found additional reasons for concluding infringement or absence of the same. As examples, ninety-two percent was considered excessive, where a court also found that the infringer preempted the only market for the writing.[37] Conversely, a use of 4.3% was acceptable as a Fair Use, where the court found the infringer's effort to be legitimate critique,[38] and where the "public good" was said to be served, a use of 8% to 15% was permitted.[39]

However, a use of 10% of 42 letters and 33⅓% of 17 other letters (unpublished) of a "famous" author was held excessive, where other redeeming factors were not found.[40] The use of but a few minutes of several movies was held "unfair," where those few minutes were "substantial in quality" and were the "best scenes";[41] and, finally, a use of but "four bars" of a musical composition was an infringement where those four bars were the "central theme" of the music.[42]

So, while the numbers of pages or words copied are given weight and considered in determining infringement, standing alone, except in extreme cases, a mere count or percentage of expression or words taken is not conclusive.[43] Still though, as said, even in those cases where the quantitative aspect was considered significant, courts have looked beyond the numbers and found infringement.

Then too, admitting of the fact that the use of a large portion of the writing of another might be permissible under different circumstances, it has been said that a "...use is not fair where the article is not only based in large part on the book but also mirrors the manner and style in which the copyright owner set down factual and historical material....(and expressed that author's)...thoughts and conclusions."[44] So, just as in good genealogical research, in determining whether or not to rule that a

---

35. *Harper and Row, etc. vs. Nation Enterprises*, op. cit., pp. 564, 565, and generally, and see *Harris v Miller* (DC NY) 50 U.S.P.Q. 306

36. *Harper and Row v. Nation*, etc., Ibid, and see *Sheldon v. Metro-Goldwyn Pictures, etc.*, (1936, CA2 NY) 81 F.2d 49, 56; 28 U.S.P.Q. 330, cert. den'd, etc., where it was said that the "...plagiarist cannot excuse the wrong by showing how much of the work he did not quote."

37. *Quinto v. Legal Times of Washington* (1981, DC Dist. of Col.) 505 F. Supp. 554, 7 Media L. R. 1057, later proceeding etc., 214 U.S.P.Q. 668

38. *Maxtone-Graham v. Burtchaell*, op. cit., 1438

39. *New York Times v. Roxbury etc.* (1977 DC NJ) 434 F. Supp. 217, 2 Media L. R. 2209, 194 U.S.P.Q. 371

40. *Salinger v. Random House* , op cit., 811 F2d 90, 98. Note here the weight given the unpublished aspect of the writings.

41. *Roy Export, etc. v. Columbia Broadcasting, etc.* (1980 SD NY) 503 F. Supp. 1137, 208 U.S.P.Q. 580, aff'd, etc., cert. den'd, etc.

42. *Robertson v. Batten, et. al.* (1956, DC CA) 146 F. Supp. 795, 111 U.S.P.Q. 251

43. *Quinto v. Legal Times of Washington*, op. cit., and see *Maxtone-Graham v. Burtchaell*, op cit., at p. 1436

44. *Holdridge v. Knight Publishing Corp.*, op. cit.

taking was an infringment, all facts must be considered and accorded appropriate weight.

It generally makes no difference that a plagiarizer changes the arrangement of words of another; rewriting text is not sufficient to avoid the label of infringer. Indeed, in one instance, even though the accuracy of the material copied was checked extensively by the infringer and numerous changes made, the court found a violation, stating "...it was the starting material...(which was)...the key to determining infringement."[45] So, the making of changes to an original effort is not sufficient to divest the author of protection. Moreover, even extensive paraphrasing will not accomplish that end, since "...it makes no difference that the Defendant has done considerable work in the nature of corrections and additions...."[46] Finally, one court stated flatly that, in the absence of justifying circumstances, an act of paraphrasing in and of itself is infringement.[47]

Significantly, and in keeping with the absence in the statute of any requirement of criminal intent, even if a use of the words and expressions of another is wholly honest, unintentional or subconscious, still it is prohibited.[48] As to what has been written by another, neither forgetfulness nor ignorance provide excuse or justify forgiveness; "Unconscious plagiarism is actionable quite as deliberate."[49] Note though that the measure of damages awarded the second author—the punishment of the infringer— well might be less where there was a showing of honesty and a true lack of intent to plagiarize.[50]

In conclusion: The genealogist should be constantly aware a) that unpublished works of others probably may not be used for any purpose, and b) where a use of the published words of another is truly for instruction or intellectual investigation and exchange (and most of our work is not), the Fair Use doctrine usually will protect the activity. On the other hand, c) where the motive for the use of the words of another in any way appears to be profit (remote, financial or otherwise, and ours quite usually is) such use, even if limited in quantity, will find scant protection under the present law. Finally, d) where the materials of another are to be copied or used, even if the user considers the use 'fair' he or she surely is advised to gain written permission from the author.

So, be careful. While you may cite others as authority almost at will and without concern that you may be in violation of the law, to copy their words, style, even nuances, without permission quite likely brings the risk of punishment. Enough of copyrights.

Publication of Your Writings

There are two principal reasons—two purposes—for writing family history. They are 1) to preserve for future generations what you have gathered together and learned, and 2) to make available what you know to as many interested people as possible.

---

45. *U. of Minn v. Applied Innovations, Inc.* (1987, DC Minn) 05 U.S.P.Q. 2nd 1689
46. *Ladd v. Oxnard*, op. cit., p. 704. Also see *Landsberg v. Scrabble*, etc. (1979, CD Cal) 212 U.S.P.Q. 155, etc., cert. den'd, etc., 469 U.S. 1037
47. *Holdridge v. Knight*, op. cit., p. 924
48. *ABKCO v. Harrisongs Music*, etc. (1983 CA2 NY) 722 F.2d 988, 998; 221 U.S.P.Q. 490, etc.
49. *Sheldon v. Metro-Goldwyn Pictures Corp.*, 81 F.2d 49, 54; also see *De Acosta v. Brown* (1944, CA2 NY) 146 F.2d 408, 410-411; 63 U.S.P.Q. 311, cert. den'd, etc.
50. Ibid., *Sheldon v. Metro-Goldwyn*, etc., pp. 410-411

When you finish the writing, you will have accomplished that first purpose; disorganized though they were, you will have gathered together and written about all of those memories, records, and mementos that you could in the time you had. The second purpose is quite different; you must now decide to what extent (and expense) you will go to see to it that folks other than your immediate family have access to what you have written.

Even though the word has other meanings (see copyrights discussion above), for our purposes now, publication means simply that you have made your writing available to others. You can do that in a number of ways:

1) by typing (or computer printing) your book, paying a nearby printer or copy shop to make that number of copies that are needed for your immediate family and interested relatives, put those copies in a 3 ring or spiral binder of some sort with a label on the front, distribute those copies for pay or not, as you see fit, and call it done;

2) by engaging a local printer (or copy shop) to make an attractive, heavy paper cover for, copy the pages of, and bind your writings, notify all known relatives of your completed effort and the price (that is, do the marketing yourself), wait for some money to come in from those sales, and hope you make enough to offset your costs (which you may, if you mention enough people in the book and send enough notices of your publication). This is probably the most used of the methods;

3) by contracting with one of the many large publishing houses, such as Heritage Books, Inc.,[51] to print, publish, and sell your book through their advertising and marketing departments. In this type of relationship, you will a) provide the publishing house with camera-ready copy, illustrations, and cover art, b) pay them for such additional services as they may render at your request (proof reading and editorial work, illustration placement, etc.), and c) receive a percentage of the total sales in the form of a royalty payment. In an arrangement of this sort, except for your costs and expenses in preparation of the camera-ready copy and the costs of any extra services that you may need and for which you pay the publisher, the costs are borne by that publisher.

4) entering into a relationship with a publisher, by the terms of which you will supply a final draft, or a computer disc, of your work, following which the publishing house will do the formatting, editing, proof reading, placement of illustrations supplied by you, cover art, printing, and—most important of all—the marketing. In a contract of this type, you write the book and supply the illustrations, and they do the rest.

Notice: while the last option (#4) is best for the writer, it usually is the least desirable for the publishing house. While you have to complete the long effort and do it in a clear, concise, and very professional way, the publisher has to bear the whole of the expense and risk of editing, printing, advertising, and sales. Then, should your work not sell as expected, they lose much more here than where they merely spent administrative and advertising time, as in #3.

That economic risk for the publisher results from the simple fact that family history narratives do not sell well. No matter how beautifully and properly done, the audience—market—for such works is limited to a) those archives, libraries and institutions that maintain a collection of family histories, b) those few libraries that

---

51. 1540-E Pointer Ridge Pl., Bowie, MD, 20716-1859, the publisher of this book.

continually add to their collections of writings concerned with local families, c) those private citizen researchers, who, though unknown to you, share family lines with you, and d) your immediate family and close kin, who buy your book (whether they care about genealogy or not) because they are curious, you are their friend and relative, or because they feel like they should have one "for the grandchildren someday."

The advantages to you of choices #3 and #4 are significant. While you now have probably one hundred or so potential purchasers, once you have asked all of those folks to buy, short of a diligent and on-going effort, you will have few further new buyers to solicit. Then too, while as you grow older your zeal and enthusiasm will wane as a result of which your sales will fall to almost nothing, a publishing house has a continually changing audience and increasing list of prospective buyers. Said another way: you will quit selling when you are tired, your publisher probably will not.

It is sometimes said that options (#3 and #4) are disadvantageous because they cost the writer some measure of "editorial control." For the reasons that publishing houses, much more so than genealogists, are familiar with how and what to sell and how a book should be constructed and organized, we think that loss of control—if indeed there really is any—is of almost no consequence. To paraphrase Socrates: if you want to build a bridge, you better find yourself a bridge builder.

In summary, despite what is best from your standpoint, a publishing house will but very rarely undertake such expenses and risk as would be incurred in #4, and will enter into an arrangement such as #3 only when your work is professionally and well done and involves many families traced to the early years. As to #1 and #2 above, they are easy to accomplish, and your choice depends entirely upon how much money you have or choose to spend on the project and how much effort you will dedicate to future sales.

Marketing: Developing Your Own List of Prospects

A few words need to be said concerning your own efforts to market. Whether you intend to do your own selling, or have entered into some relationship with a publisher, your knowledge of prospective buyers is very important. Of all the people on the planet, you best know who might first be interested. So start now to develop that list.

When you do not feel up to composition and are not in a mood to write captions or select illustrations, work on your list of prospective buyers. That list will consist of a) close relatives and friends, b) distant relatives and correspondents of whom you have learned in your research, c) libraries, museums, archives, and professional genealogists in your immediate area, and d) large genealogical libraries, museums, collections, and states' archives.

As to close relatives and friends, tell them that your work is underway, that they will appear there (if you intend to include them), and ask for their assistance with photographs and mementos. You will gain valuable illustrations, and they will be complimented and begin to think about buying the finished product.

Incidentally, you will find that some folks—even close relatives—are reluctant to loan such photos and items. When that is the situation, examine the items carefully, pick those few that you will be sure to use, then ask if they will have them copied, for which you will pay.

As to distant relatives and correspondents who might be buyers of your book, go through your files of letters, list the names and addresses of every person who is a known relative (especially those who have helped you with research or are active genealogists), and constantly update that list whenever you learn of kin of whom you did not know before. When you are near the end of your writing it will be helpful to write a note or postcard to each of those persons, tell them of your progress with the book, ask for suggestions and photos (again, offering to pay for such), and tell them when you think you will have completed the work. (Don't forget that those folks—relatives or otherwise—who help should be considered for mention in your acknowledgments.)

As to libraries, archives, and genealogists, add these to your list of buyers whenever you come upon them. You will be writing to these people and institutions and informing them of the book when it is finished and available for sale. When you write these letters, be sure to list all the surnames that you have researched (without detail as to individuals), and state the areas—towns, counties, regions—that you studied and discussed in the book. Remember, local libraries, museums, archives, and genealogists have a purpose that is somewhat different than yours. They seek to provide a wide range of information and, as often as not, have no personal interest in your family stories and tales. A letter to such a person or institution might read:

Dear Sir (or Madam, etc.):

I have recently completed a study of several family lines common to your area, particularly those of Alexander, Bater, Beaty, Cody, Haskins, Johnson, Kitchen, Taylor, Thompson, and Wright. In addition, I have written concerning Cumberland and Fentress counties and the area generally.

The book is soft bound, 8.5" x 11", illustrated, 340 pages, with a full-name index of 960 entries, and is priced at $30.00, including postage, delivery to be expected in July. If you have any questions, I would be pleased to answer the same. I have taken the liberty of enclosing a form for ordering.

Hoping to gain your response or further inquiry, I am

Very truly yours

Notice that the letter names the family lines in alphabetical order, just as you would look for them in an index, names the counties discussed, and fully describes the book and the price. In short, the letter supplies all the information (and the order form) needed for the busy institution or genealogist to make a decision to purchase.

As to all large libraries, museums, state's archives, and major collections, the letter might read:

To The Book Purchasing Department:

Dear Sir or Madam:

I have recently completed a study of some family lines common to the state of Ohio, especially the central counties of Delaware, Hancock, Harden, Marion, and Morrow. Those family lines are Alexander, Bater, Beaty, Cody, Drake, Haskins, Johnson, Kitchen, Taylor, Thompson, and Wright. An additional twenty associated lines have been discussed and indexed.

The book is soft bound, 8.5" x 11", 340 pages, illustrated, with a full-name index of 960 entries, and is priced at $30.00, including postage, delivery to be expected in July. Payment by purchase order is welcome. If you have any questions, I would be pleased to answer the same. I have taken the liberty of enclosing a form for ordering.

Hoping to gain your response or further inquiry, I am

Very truly yours

Unless the recipient of your letter is a friend or close relative, it is likely that they have little time for (nor interest in) extended correspondence. Accordingly, your purpose should be to provide all information needed in a single letter. So, let your promotional letters be to the point and complete, and always honest.

Pricing Your Book

The price of your finished work is determined mostly by its size and number of pages and illustrations, and that decision is almost entirely yours, unless you have contracted with a publishing house.

In determining price, first look in any genealogical book catalog and find out how a comparable book, equally bound, is priced. Then ask yourself these two questions: 1) what will the printer charge me per copy delivered to me? (your time and hours spent don't count; you could never charge enough to pay those costs), and 2) how much will the packaging envelope and postage be for me to mail the book to the purchasers? Add those two amounts together, add 15% to 30%, and compare that sum to the book catalog price.

If your price is higher than the price in the catalog for a similar book, you probably should lower it to near that price; most of your buyers know what books should sell for. If your price is lower, you should consider raising your price to a level just below that for similar books, again for the reason that buyers expect to pay similar prices for similar works.

Perhaps the most important rule of all is, charge everyone in the same category the same price. If you have chosen to discount the price to relatives, do so, but charge them all equally. If you charge one cousin less than another, no matter how justified or noble the reason, the word will leak out. By differentiating between kin, you can only make enemies. Moreover, if your book is worth $30.00 to one cousin, it is worth that to all others.

Finally, you may find that some libraries, societies and professional genealogists are accustomed to being granted a discount on all books they buy, and some may even have a policy of not buying unless there is such a discount. When that situation arises, simply ask what discount they require, and then offer whatever you are able. However, as with kin, if you discount your work to one institution, do it for all that ask; if they do not ask for a discount—and some won't—maintain the price at retail.

Advertising Your Work

In the event you have contracted with a publisher, one of whose services is marketing, it is likely that you will do no formal advertising. However, even when such is the case, remember that you have many names of potential purchasers that they do not have.

So it is that, even where the marketing is not your responsibility, you should obtain copies of the "blurb" (the summary of the book written by the publisher for advertising purposes) from the publisher, and send one to each of your interested relatives and those local libraries that might have a particular interest in your study of the people of their area. In both cases, include instructions that the buyers should order directly from the publisher.

Notice though, before sending blurbs you should inform your publisher of your plans, and gain their approval for your activities. During that discussion, be sure to learn to what institutions, if any, they grant discounts, in order that you may mention that fact where necessary in your own sales efforts. Note too, they may not want you to make contact with any institutions, and if that is their approach, abide by their wishes.

Finally, even though you may be permitted to purchase books from your publisher at a discount, that is not a license for you to go into business as their competitor. If you want to sell your own books to people who might otherwise have been customers of your publisher, discuss the matter with the publisher and gain permission. In short, be as honest in your dealings as you are in your writings; if a publisher has confidence enough in you to undertake to print and sell your works, you should be grateful enough to act only as an assistant to them, if that is their desire.

Conclusion

As said at the outset, you will not here learn to write genealogical narrative, no matter how many times you read these pages. Practice is the only avenue to that knowledge. What have here been presented instead, we believe, are some basics of that art.

We first reviewed the *basic elements and order of a book*, and how to construct those elements in a fashion that would be most helpful to your readers. Next we moved through a number of suggestions for use in *planning the format* of your book, including some ideas for the use of the many tools devised long ago by other writers. Following that, and before you could commence the review and organization of the results of your years of research, we considered *evidence and proof*, what those are, and how they are used and demonstrated in good genealogical narrative.

From there, we considered some advanced research techniques, in order that your review of your findings might be made more effective and perhaps a bit easier. In that regard, we discussed *gleaning* in libraries, archives, courthouses, cemeteries, churches, and private sources. In order that you *prepare for and commence writing narrative*, it next was appropriate to consider those principles of genealogical writing that would cause your work to be somewhere inside the bounds of the rules of good grammar and something more than an unorganized and boring litany of dates and names.

In drawing to the close of this work, and in order that you be more able to gain the many advantages that the law and marketplace provide, we wrote of *copyright considerations, publishing, and marketing*. And, in *conclusion*—here—we undertook to provide something of a review of the order and sense of it all.

Finally, it is said that conclusions should set forth a challenge; here, it is that you pay your debts to those many, often unknown, fine folks who went before you.

Just as a musician feels great joy and a deep sense of accomplishment upon the performance of his or her work, albeit upon instruments made by others quite unknown to him or her; and a builder, having met the obligations owing to those who worked and to those many who supplied the lumber and brick and mortar, is proud beyond measure and entitled to great credit when a beautiful structure is completed, so too the family historian when at last the pencil is laid down and the book completed.

It is then, when the last word of the last paragraph on the last page is written—and not before—that you too may say that your debts have been paid, and it is time to be proud. Only at that time will you no longer owe for the rich heritage passed to you by those who have disappeared into the soft, deep black of the past, and not again will you have to say, "You know, someday, in return for what those incredibly decent, hard working people did for me, I'm gonna write all that down."

Good luck in your efforts.

Paul Drake, 1996

APPENDIX

The four National Archives order forms on the following pages are <u>samples</u>, intended only for informative purposes. Real forms have several duplicate pages, and some other pages which are not relevant for inclusion here. You may request these order forms, free of charge, from:

> National Archives and Records Administration
> 7th and Pennsylvania Ave NW
> Washington DC 20408

To assist you in your research, you might want to photocopy the 1850, 1880, and 1910 census forms. For inclusion in this book the original forms had to be reduced, so when you make copies you might want to enlarge them again (approximately 110-115%) to improve readablilty and ease of use.

NATIONAL ARCHIVES ORDER FOR COPIES OF VETERANS RECORDS

Dear Researcher,

Before completing the form, please read both sides of this page for ordering instructions and general information about the types of records that can be ordered with this form. Mail order photocopying service by using this form is available ONLY from *General Reference Branch (NNRG-P), National Archives and Records Administration, 7th and Pennsylvania Avenue NW., Washington, DC 20408.* For more information, please write to us at the address above.

IMPORTANT INFORMATION ABOUT YOUR ORDER

The success of our search depends on the completeness and accuracy of the information you provide in blocks 3-18 on this form. Please note that each NATF Form 80 is handled separately. When you send more than one form at a time, you may not receive all of your replies at the same time.

Military service records rarely contain family information. Pension application files generally are most useful to those who are doing genealogical research and contain the most complete information regarding a man's military career. We suggest that you first request copies of a man's pension file. You should request copies of a bounty-land warrant file or a military record only when no pension file exists. If the veteran's service was during the Revolutionary War, bounty-land warrant applications have been consolidated with pension application papers. You can obtain both files by requesting the pension file only.

We will copy complete compiled military service and bounty-land application files. When we are unable to provide copies of all pension documents because of the size of a pension application file, we will send copies of the documents we think will be most useful to you for genealogical purposes. Many of the documents in these files are repetitive or administrative in nature. You may order copies of all remaining documents in a file by making a specific request. We will notify you of the cost of the additional copies.

Do NOT use this form to request photocopies of records relating to service in World War I or II, or subsequent service. Write to: *National Personnel Records Center (Military Records), NARA, 9700 Page Boulevard, St. Louis, MO 63132.*

INSTRUCTIONS FOR COMPLETING THIS FORM

Use a separate NATF Form 80 for each file that you request. Remove this instruction sheet. You must complete blocks 3-7 or we cannot search for the file. Print your name (last, first, middle) and address in the block provided at the bottom of the form, which is your mailing label. The information must be legible on all copies. Keep the PINK copy of the form for your records. Mail the remaining three pages of the form to: *General Reference Branch (NNRG-P), National Archives and Records Administration, 7th and Pennsylvania Avenue NW., Washington, DC 20408.* DO NOT SEND PAYMENT WITH THIS FORM. When we search your order, we will make photocopies of records that relate to your request. For credit card orders, we will mail the copies immediately. For other types of orders, we will invoice you for the cost of these copies and hold them until we receive your payment.

SEE THE REVERSE OF THIS PAGE FOR DESCRIPTIONS OF THE TYPES OF RECORDS THAT CAN BE ORDERED WITH THIS FORM.

NATIONAL ARCHIVES TRUST FUND BOARD

INSTRUCTIONS

NATF Form 80 (rev. 10-93)

Information and instructions for completing NATF-80

NATIONAL ARCHIVES
ORDER FOR COPIES OF VETERANS RECORDS
(See Instructions page before completing this form)

DATE RECEIVED IN NNRG

INDICATE BELOW THE TYPE OF FILE DESIRED AND THE METHOD OF PAYMENT PREFERRED.

1. FILE TO BE SEARCHED
(Check one box only)

☐ PENSION

☐ BOUNTY-LAND WARRANT APPLICATION
(Service before 1856 only)

☐ MILITARY

2. PAYMENT METHOD *(Check one box only)*

☐ CREDIT CARD (VISA or MasterCard) for IMMEDIATE SHIPMENT of copies

Account Number: Exp. Date:

Signature: Daytime Phone:

☐
BILL ME
(No Credit Card)

REQUIRED MINIMUM IDENTIFICATION OF VETERAN - MUST BE COMPLETED OR YOUR ORDER CANNOT BE SERVICED

3. VETERAN *(Give last, first, and middle names)*

4. BRANCH OF SERVICE IN WHICH HE SERVED
☐ ARMY   ☐ NAVY   ☐ MARINE CORPS

5. STATE FROM WHICH HE SERVED

6. WAR IN WHICH, OR DATES BETWEEN WHICH, HE SERVED

7. IF SERVICE WAS CIVIL WAR,
☐ UNION   ☐ CONFEDERATE

PLEASE PROVIDE THE FOLLOWING ADDITIONAL INFORMATION, IF KNOWN

8. UNIT IN WHICH HE SERVED *(Name of regiment or number, company, etc, name of ship)*

9. IF SERVICE WAS ARMY, ARM IN WHICH HE SERVED
☐ INFANTRY   ☐ CAVALRY   ☐ ARTILLERY

If other, specify:

Rank
☐ OFFICER   ☐ ENLISTED

10. KIND OF SERVICE
☐ VOLUNTEERS   ☐ REGULARS

11. PENSION/BOUNTY-LAND FILE NO.

12. IF VETERAN LIVED IN A HOME FOR SOLDIERS, *GIVE LOCATION (City and State)*

13. PLACE(S) VETERAN LIVED AFTER SERVICE

14. DATE OF BIRTH

15. PLACE OF BIRTH *(City, County, State, etc.)*

18. NAME OF WIDOW OR OTHER CLAIMANT

16. DATE OF DEATH

17. PLACE OF DEATH *(City, County, State, etc.)*

NATIONAL ARCHIVES TRUST FUND BOARD   NATF Form 80 (rev. 10-93)

DO NOT WRITE BELOW - SPACE IS FOR OUR REPLY TO YOU

☐ **NO—We were unable to locate the file you requested above. No payment is required.**

DATE SEARCHED	SEARCHER

☐ REQUIRED MINIMUM IDENTIFICATION OF VETERAN WAS NOT PROVIDED. Please complete blocks 3 (give full name), 4, 5, 6, and 7 and resubmit your order.

☐ A SEARCH WAS MADE BUT THE FILE YOU REQUESTED ABOVE WAS NOT FOUND. When we do not find a record for a veteran, this does not mean that he did not serve. You may be able to obtain information about him from the archives of the State from which he served.

☐ See attached forms, leaflets, or information sheets.

☐ **YES--We located the file you requested above. We have made copies from the file for you. The cost for these copies is $10.**

DATE SEARCHED	SEARCHER
FILE DESIGNATION	

Make your check or money order payable to NATIONAL ARCHIVES TRUST FUND. Do not send cash. Return this form and your payment in the enclosed envelope to:

NATIONAL ARCHIVES TRUST FUND
P.O. BOX 100221
ATLANTA, GA 30384-0221

PLEASE NOTE: We will hold these copies awaiting receipt of payment for only 45 days from the date completed, which is stamped below. After that time, you must submit another form to obtain photocopies of the file.

Here is an example of National Archives *Form NATF-80*, the same discussed in Chapter IV, Part 2 p. 104. Only through its use may one gain whatever information the National Archives has concerning a veteran or widow or dependent of a veteran of any of our wars. Notice that items #1 through #7 <u>must</u> be completed, while items #8 through #18 are requested but not required, and also observe that in question #1, you must select the category of records you need.

We can only search for a record based on the information you provided in blocks 3-18. The success and accuracy of our search is determined by the information you provide. Often there are many files for veterans of the same or nearly the same name. If there are five or fewer files for men with the same name as the individual in whom you are interested, we will examine all the relevant files and compare their contents with the information that you have provided us. If the veteran's identity seems obvious, we will furnish you a copy of the file we think is the correct one.

If there are more than five files, we will not make a file-by-file check to see if the information in the numerous files matches that provided for the veteran in whom you are interested. In such cases, we suggest that you visit the National Archives and examine the various files, or hire a professional researcher to examine the files for you. We do not maintain a list of persons who do research for a fee; however, many researchers advertise their services in genealogical periodicals, usually available in libraries.

PLEASE NOTE: This mail order photocopying service is available ONLY from *General Reference Branch (NNRG-P)* at the address below. Please address all inquiries about your order to the General Reference Branch at this address or call us at 202-501-5170. When you send more than one form at a time, each form is handled separately. Therefore, you may not receive all of your replies at the same time. Allow a minimum of 8 to 10 weeks for processing your order. More information about the availability of records pertaining to military service or family histories may be found in our free genealogical information leaflets and forms. You may request these, as well as order additional copies of this form, by writing to:

> General Reference Branch (NNRG)
> National Archives and Records Administration
> 7th and Pennsylvania Avenue NW.
> Washington, DC 20408

Further information accompanying NATF-80

TYPES OF RECORDS THAT CAN BE ORDERED WITH THIS FORM

PENSION APPLICATION FILES

Pension application files, based on Federal (not State) service before World War I, usually include an official statement of the veteran's military service, as well as information of a personal nature. Pensions based on military service for the Confederate States of America were authorized by some Southern States but not by the Federal Government until 1959. Inquiries about State pensions should be addressed to the State archives or equivalent agency at the capital of the veteran's State of residence after the war.

BOUNTY-LAND WARRANT APPLICATION FILES

Bounty-land warrant application files are based on Federal (not State) service before 1856. Documents in a bounty-land warrant application file are similar to those in a pension application file. In addition, these files usually give the veteran's age and place of residence at the time the application was made.

MILITARY SERVICE RECORDS

Military service records are based on service in the UNITED STATES ARMY (officers who served before June 30, 1917, and enlisted men who served before October 31, 1912); NAVY (officers who served before 1903 and enlisted men who served before 1886); MARINE CORPS (officers who served before 1896 and enlisted men who served before 1905); and CONFEDERATE ARMED FORCES (officers and enlisted men, 1861-65). In addition to persons who served in regular forces raised by the Federal Government, volunteers fought in various wars chiefly in the Federal Government's interest from the Revolutionary War through the Philippine Insurrection, 1775-1902.

Compilations of information concerning most military service performed by individuals in volunteer organizations during the 19th and early 20th centuries are available, but such records were not compiled for Regular Army officers who served before 1863 and for Regular Army enlisted men and Navy and Marine Corps personnel who served during most of the 19th century. Records pertaining to such service are scattered among many files and generally contain few details concerning a man's service. We cannot undertake the research necessary to locate all such documents. If you request a military service record, we will copy the documents that best summarize the veteran's service.

The record of an individual's service in any one organization is entirely separate from his record of service in another organization. We are unable to establish accurately the identity of individuals of the same name who served in different organizations. If you know that an individual served in more than one organization and you desire copies of all of the military service records, submit a separate form for the service record in each organization.

Discharge certificates are not usually included as a part of a compiled military service record. Before 1944, Army regulations allowed the preparation of an original discharge certificate only, which was given to the soldier. Confederate soldiers in service at the time of surrender did not receive discharge certificates. They were given paroles, and these paroles became the property of the soldier.

ORDER FOR COPIES OF SHIP PASSENGER ARRIVAL RECORDS

Dear Researcher,

Before completing the form, please read this page for ordering instructions and general information about the records that can be ordered with this form. Mail order photocopying service using this form is available **ONLY** from *General Reference Branch (NNRG), National Archives and Records Administration, 7th and Pennsylvania Avenue NW., Washington, DC 20408.* For more information, please write to us at the address above.

IMPORTANT INFORMATION

WHAT WE HAVE: The National Archives has inbound Federal ship passenger arrival records dating back to 1820 for most east coast and gulf coast ports and a few lists dating back to 1800 for Philadelphia. Ship passenger lists in our custody are not complete. Fire, dampness, or other causes destroyed many records in the 19th century before the creating agencies transferred them to the National Archives. During the 19th century, no law required passenger arrival records to be kept for persons entering the United States by land from Canada or Mexico. No law required the keeping of outbound passenger lists.

WHAT WE CAN SEARCH: *Passenger Indexes:* We can search indexes if you supply the following information: full name of the passenger, port of entry, and approximate date of arrival. The following major indexes exist: Baltimore (1820-1952), Boston (1848-91 and 1902-20), New Orleans (1853-1952), New York (1820-46 and 1897-1948), Philadelphia (1800-1948), and minor ports (1820-74 and 1890-1924). *Unindexed Passenger Lists:* We cannot search these lists without more specific information than we require for index searches. To search unindexed passenger lists through 1892, you must supply port of entry, name of the vessel, approximate date of arrival, and the full name of the passenger. For those lists, we can also make a search with port of embarkation, exact date of arrival, port of entry, and the full name of the passenger. To search unindexed lists after 1892, we need the port of entry, the name of the vessel, the exact date of arrival, the full name of the passenger, and the names and ages of accompanying passengers, if any. *PLEASE NOTE: There is no index for New York for the period 1847 through 1896 or for the period 1949 through the present.*

ADDITIONAL INFORMATION: You may order copies of an entire passenger list by making a specific request. Write to the General Reference Branch at the address above. We will notify you of the cost. In addition, you or your representatives may search records that are too voluminous for the National Archives staff to search. We do not maintain a list of persons who do research for a fee. However, many researchers advertise their services in genealogical periodicals, usually available in libraries. *Naturalization (Citizenship) Records:* Naturalization records are separate from passenger arrival lists. The National Archives has copies of naturalization papers (1798-1906) for Massachusetts, New Hampshire, Rhode Island, and Maine and original records (1802-1926) for the District of Columbia. For information about citizenship granted elsewhere through September 26, 1906, write to the Federal, State, or municipal court that issued the naturalization. The Immigration and Naturalization Service, Washington, DC 20536 can furnish information on naturalizations that occurred after September 26, 1906.

INSTRUCTIONS FOR COMPLETING THIS FORM

Use a separate NATF Form 81 for each passenger arrival record. Remove this instruction sheet. Print your name (last, first, middle) and address in the block provided at the bottom of the form, which is your mailing label. The information must be legible on all copies. Keep the PINK copy of the form for your records. Mail the remaining three pages of the form to: *General Reference Branch (NNRG), National Archives and Records Administration, 7th and Pennsylvania Avenue NW., Washington, DC 20408.* Please allow 8 to 10 weeks for processing your order. **DO NOT SEND PAYMENT WITH THIS FORM.** When we search your order, we will make photocopies of records that relate to your request. For credit card orders, we will mail the copies immediately. For other type of orders, we will invoice you for the cost of these copies and hold them up to 45 days pending receipt of your payment.

Information and instructions for completing NATF-81

ORDER FOR COPIES OF
SHIP PASSENGER ARRIVAL RECORDS
(See Instructions page before completing this form)

DATE RECEIVED *(NNRG)*

INDICATE BELOW THE METHOD OF PAYMENT PREFERRED.

☐ **CREDIT CARD** *(VISA or MasterCard)* for IMMEDIATE SHIPMENT of copies

Account Number:

Exp. Date:

Signature

Daytime Phone:

☐ **BILL ME** *(No credit card)*

IDENTIFICATION OF ENTRY		
DATE OF ARRIVAL	FULL NAME OF PASSENGER *(Give last, first, and middle names)*	AGE / SEX
PORT OF ENTRY	NAMES OF MEMBERS OF IMMIGRANT FAMILY	
WHERE NATURALIZED *(if known)*		
SHIP NAME *(or Carrier Line)*		
PASSENGER'S COUNTRY OF ORIGIN		

NATIONAL ARCHIVES TRUST FUND BOARD   NATF Form 81 (rev. 4-92)

DO NOT WRITE BELOW - SPACE IS FOR OUR REPLY TO YOU

☐ **NO--We were unable to locate the record you requested above. No payment is required.**

MICROFILM PUBLICATION	ROLL	PAGE
RECORDS SEARCHED		SEARCHER
		DATE SEARCHED

☐ A SEARCH WAS NOT MADE because the records you requested are not documented in our ship passenger arrival list records. Please see the reverse of this form. Also, please see the enclosed pamphlet for further information about our holdings.

☐ A SEARCH WAS NOT MADE because insufficient information was supplied. Please see the reverse of this form.

☐ A SEARCH WAS MADE BUT THE RECORD YOU REQUESTED ABOVE WAS NOT FOUND. Please see the reverse of this form.

☐ A SEARCH WAS MADE BUT THE EXACT RECORD YOU REQUESTED ABOVE WAS NOT FOUND. We found a record that may be the one you seek. Please see the reverse of this form.

☐ **YES--We located the record you requested above. We have made copies from the record for you. The cost for these copies is $10.**

MICROFILM PUBLICATION	ROLL	PAGE
SEARCHER		DATE SEARCHED
ARRIVAL DATE		
PORT		
SHIP		

Make your check or money order payable to NATIONAL ARCHIVES TRUST FUND. Do not send cash. Return this form and your payment in the enclosed envelope to:

NATIONAL ARCHIVES TRUST FUND
P.O. BOX 100221
ATLANTA, GA 30384-0221

PLEASE NOTE: We will hold these copies awaiting receipt of payment for only 45 days from the date completed, which is stamped below. After that time, you must submit another form to obtain photocopies of the record.

Here is an example of National Archives *Form NATF-81*, the same discussed in Chapter IV, Part 2, p. 110. Only through its use may one gain what information the National Archives has concerning immigrants who came by ship. Even though you may not have all the details, you must complete as much as you can in the section labeled "IDENTIFICATION OF ENTRY." You may not write in explanations or details; they will not be read.

WE WERE UNABLE TO COMPLETE YOUR ORDER FOR THE REASON INDICATED BELOW:

1. ☐ We found several entries for persons of the same name arriving at the same port during the same period. Additional information, such as age, occupation, etc., will help in resolving this problem.

2. ☐ We found the requested information on the passenger index, but we regret that the corresponding passenger list is missing. A copy of the index card is enclosed.

3 ☐ We are unable to locate the passenger list for the ship listed and have found no entry on the passenger index for the requested party at that port.

4. ☐ We examined the passenger list for the requested ship and were unable to find an entry for the requested passenger.

5. ☐ The register of ship arrivals did not show any entry for the ship named.

6. ☐ Our only passenger lists for the cited port do not cover the date that you have requested, and we were unable to find any entry on the index to the lists we have.

7. ☐ Because of the poor quality of microfilm, the enclosed copy is the best we could obtain with our equipment.

8. ☐ We are unable to fill your request because the appropriate microfilmed indexes are illegible. If you can supply additional information -- including either the precise date (month/day/year) of arrival or the name of the ship and the approximate date of arrival (approximate month/exact year) -- we will undertake another search.

9. ☐ Passenger arrival records in our custody are not complete. Fire, dampness, and other causes destroyed many records in the 19th century before the creating agencies transferred the records to the National Archives.

10. ☐ Our index to New York passenger arrivals covers the period 1820-46 and 1897-1943. We regret that we cannot undertake a page-by-page search of the lists for the period 1847-96, inclusive.

11. ☐ Masters of vessels departing the United States were not required to list the names of passengers.

12. ☐ Overland arrivals into the United States from Mexico and Canada are not documented in passenger list records.

13. ☐ PARTIAL MATCH TO THE INFORMATION YOU SUPPLIED: We found a record that may be the one you seek. Differences from the information you supplied are explained below. If you wish to order this record, please complete a new form, attach this page, and resubmit.

_____

_____

_____

14. ☐ OTHER:

_____

_____

_____

NATIONAL ARCHIVES TRUST FUND BOARD   NATF Form 81 BACK (rev. 4-92)

Further information accompanying NATF-81

ORDER FOR COPIES OF CENSUS RECORDS

Dear Researcher,

Before completing the form, please read this page for ordering instructions and general information about the types of records that can be ordered with this form. For more information, please write to: *General Reference Branch (NNRG), National Archives and Records Administration, 7th and Pennsylvania Avenue NW., Washington, DC 20408.*

IMPORTANT INFORMATION ABOUT YOUR ORDER

What We Can Provide: The National Archives can provide copies of specifically identified pages of Federal population census schedules, ordered by mail. To receive this photocopying service, you must provide the name of the individual listed, page number, census year, State, and county; for the 1880 through 1920 censuses, also include the enumeration district. Frequently it is possible to use a census index to locate this information. In recent years, many private firms have produced statewide indexes to census records for specific years. These are available throughout the country in libraries that have genealogical collections. In addition to the printed indexes, there are microfilm indexes to the 1900 and 1920 censuses and partial indexes to the 1880 and 1910 censuses. From these printed and microfilm indexes, you can determine the exact page on which a family was enumerated and then place your order.

The National Archives does not search census indexes, nor do we provide census research service by mail.

Alternative Approaches: Federal population census records, 1790-1920, are available to you for research at the National Archives Building in Washington, DC, and in regional archives located in various parts of the United States (see the back of this page for addresses). Furthermore, many public and private libraries and other research institutions have purchased microfilm copies of Federal censuses. Your local library, genealogical, or other research institution may be able to advise you about the availability of census records in your area.

Microfilm copies of Federal censuses, 1790-1920, and indexes to the 1880 and 1900-1920 censuses can be rented through a program operating in local libraries and historical or genealogical societies. This is a program established by the National Archives with a private contractor. For more information, please contact your local library.

Microfilm copies of census records are available for purchase. An entire county or enumeration district for a given State or census year may be on one or more rolls of microfilm. For information about the cost of microfilm, write to: *Publication Services Staff (NEPS), National Archives and Records Administration, 7th and Pennsylvania Avenue NW., Washington, DC 20408.* Include in your inquiry the census year, the State, and the county or enumeration district.

INSTRUCTIONS FOR COMPLETING THIS FORM

Use a separate NATF Form 82 for each file that you request. Remove this instruction sheet. You must complete blocks 1-6 (and 7, when applicable) or we cannot search for the file. Print your name (last, first, middle) and address in the box provided at the bottom of the form, which is your mailing label. The information must be legible on all copies. Keep the PINK copy of the form for your records. Mail the remaining three pages of the form to: *General Reference Branch (NNRG), National Archives and Records Administration, 7th and Pennsylvania Avenue NW., Washington, DC 20408.* Please allow 8 to 10 weeks for processing your order. **DO NOT SEND PAYMENT WITH YOUR INITIAL REQUEST.** When we search your order, we will make photocopies of records that relate to your request. For credit card orders, we will mail the copies immediately. For other types of orders, we will invoice you for the cost of these copies and hold them up to 45 days pending receipt of your payment.

Information and instructions for completing NATF-82

ORDER FOR COPIES OF CENSUS RECORDS

(See Instructions page before completing this form)

DATE RECEIVED IN NNRG

INDICATE BELOW THE METHOD OF PAYMENT PREFERRED.

☐ **CREDIT CARD** *(VISA or MasterCard) for IMMEDIATE SHIPMENT of copies*

Account Number: Exp. Date: Signature   Daytime Phone:

☐ **BILL ME** *(No credit card)*

REQUIRED MINIMUM IDENTIFICATION OF ENTRY - MUST BE COMPLETED OR YOUR ORDER CANNOT BE SERVICED

1. CENSUS YEAR	2. STATE OR TERRITORY	3. COUNTY
4. TOWNSHIP OR OTHER SUBDIVISION	5. NAME OF HEAD OF HOUSEHOLD	6. PAGE NO. 7. ENUMERATION DISTRICT *(for 1880, 1900, 1910, and 1920 only)*

PLEASE PROVIDE THE FOLLOWING ADDITIONAL INFORMATION, IF KNOWN

	NAME	AGE	SEX	NAME	AGE	SEX
8. MEMBERS OF HOUSEHOLD						

NATIONAL ARCHIVES TRUST FUND BOARD   NATF Form 82 (rev. 4-92)

DO NOT WRITE BELOW - SPACE IS FOR OUR REPLY TO YOU

☐ **NO--We were unable to locate the entry you requested above. No payment is required.**

SEARCHER	DATE SEARCHED

☐ REQUIRED MINIMUM IDENTIFICATION OF ENTRY WAS NOT PROVIDED. Please complete blocks 1, 2, 3, 4, 5, 6, and 7 and resubmit your order.

☐ Due to the poor quality of the microfilm, the pages you requested cannot be reproduced clearly on our equipment.

☐ The microfilm roll for the State and county for which you requested copies is missing and will take 1 to 2 months to replace.

☐ OTHER:

_____

_____

_____

_____

☐ **YES--We located the entry you requested above. We have made copies of the entry for you. The cost for these copies is $6.**

CENSUS YEAR	STATE OR TERRITORY
COUNTY	
MICROFILM PUBLICATION ROLL	PAGE NO.
SEARCHER	DATE SEARCHED

Make your check or money order payable to NATIONAL ARCHIVES TRUST FUND. Do not send cash. Return this form and your payment in the enclosed envelope to:

NATIONAL ARCHIVES TRUST FUND
P.O. BOX 100221
ATLANTA, GA 30384-0221

PLEASE NOTE: We will hold these copies awaiting receipt of payment for only 45 days from the date completed, which is stamped below. After that time, you must submit another form to obtain photocopies of the record.

Here is an example of National Archives *Form NATF-82*, the same discussed in Chapter IV, Part 2, p. 90. Only through its use may one gain copies of censuses stored at the National Archives. Notice that items #1 through #7 must be completed, any further information you have should be provided under #8.

THE NATIONAL ARCHIVES REGIONAL ARCHIVES SYSTEM

You may visit one of the regional archives listed below to research Federal population census records, 1790-1920. We suggest that you call for current hours of operation. Please note: The mail order photocopying service by using this form is available **ONLY** from **General Reference Branch (NNRG), National Archives and Records Administration, 7th and Pennsylvania Avenue NW., Washington, DC 20408.**

National Archives - New England Region
380 Trapelo Road
Waltham, MA 02154
Phone: 617-647-8100
Areas served: Connecticut, Maine, Massachusetts, New Hampshire, Rhode Island, and Vermont

National Archives - Mid-Atlantic Region
9th & Market Streets, Room 1350
Philadelphia, PA 19107
Phone: 215-597-3000
Areas served: Delaware, Pennsylvania, Maryland, Virginia, and West Virginia

National Archives - Great Lakes Region
7358 South Pulaski Road
Chicago, IL 60629
Phone: 312-581-7816
Areas served: Illinois, Indiana, Michigan, Minnesota, Ohio, and Wisconsin

National Archives - Southwest Region
501 West Felix Street
Fort Worth, TX 76115
Phone: 817-334-5525
Areas served: Arkansas, Louisiana, New Mexico, Oklahoma, and Texas

National Archives - Pacific Southwest Region
24000 Avila Road
Laguna Niguel, CA 92656
Phone: 714-643-4241
Areas served: Arizona; southern California counties of Imperial, Inyo, Kern, Los Angeles, Orange, Riverside, San Bernardino, San Diego, San Luis Obispo, Santa Barbara, and Ventura; and Clark County, Nevada

National Archives - Pacific Northwest Region
6125 Sand Point Way
Seattle, WA 98115
Phone: 206-526-6507
Areas served: Idaho, Oregon, and Washington

National Archives - Northeast Region
201 Varick Street
New York, NY 10014
Phone: 212-337-1300
Areas served: New Jersey, New York, Puerto Rico, and the Virgin Islands

National Archives - Southeast Region
1557 St. Joseph Avenue
East Point, GA 30344
Phone: 404-763-7477
Areas served: Alabama, Georgia, Florida, Kentucky, Mississippi, North Carolina, South Carolina, and Tennessee

National Archives - Central Plains Region
2312 East Bannister Road
Kansas City, MO 64131
Phone: 816-926-6272
Areas served: Iowa, Kansas, Missouri, and Nebraska

National Archives - Rocky Mountain Region
Building 48, Denver Federal Center
Denver, CO 80225
Phone: 303-236-0817
Areas served: Colorado, Montana, North Dakota, South Dakota, Utah, and Wyoming

National Archives - Pacific Sierra Region
1000 Commodore Drive
San Bruno, CA 94066
Phone: 415-876-9009
Areas served: Northern California, Hawaii, Nevada (except Clark County), and the Pacific Ocean area

National Archives - Alaska Region
654 West 3rd Avenue
Anchorage, AK 99501
Phone: 907-271-2441
Area served: Alaska

NATIONAL ARCHIVES TRUST FUND BOARD

NATF Form 82 (rev. 4-92)

Further information accompanying NATF-82

ORDER FOR COPIES OF EASTERN CHEROKEE APPLICATIONS

Dear Researcher,

Before completing the form, please read this page for ordering instructions and general information about the types of records that can be ordered with this form. Mail order photocopying service by using this form is available **ONLY** from *General Reference Branch (NNRG), National Archives and Records Administration, 7th and Pennsylvania Avenue NW., Washington, DC 20408.* For more information, please write to us at the address above.

IMPORTANT INFORMATION ABOUT YOUR ORDER

What We Have: The Eastern Cherokee Applications of the U.S. Court of Claims, 1906-09 (M1104), contain sworn evidences of identity. The application required each claimant to state fully his or her English and Indian names, residence, age, place of birth, name of husband or wife, name of tribe, and names of children. It further required the English and Indian names of the claimant's parents and grandparents, place of their birth, place of their residence in 1851 if they were living at the time, dates of their death, and a statement as to whether any of them had ever before been enrolled as Indians for annuities or other benefits and, if so, with what tribe. Each claimant was also to furnish the names of all brothers and sisters, with their ages and residences, and the names and residences of all uncles and aunts. Applications were required to be made under oath and to be supported by affidavits of two witnesses who were well acquainted with the applicant. With each application is a card showing final action taken and the reasons therefore. Filed with many of the applications are inquiries concerning the status of the cases, requests for further evidence, protests about unfavorable actions, form letters that had been sent by the special commissioner to the applicants as notices of rejection of their applications and returned by the Post Office Department as unclaimed, affidavits and statements of witnesses, powers of attorney, and last wills and testaments. The applications are arranged by the number assigned at the time the application was received. There are some gaps in the application numbers; these are explained on insert sheets at the appropriate places on the film. The indexes are arranged alphabetically by name (either English or Indian) of claimant.

What We Can Search: Limitations of staff time prevent the National Archives from making comprehensive searches of Eastern Cherokee applications or indexes. We can search indexes if you can supply the following information: (1) full name, both English and Indian, of the applicant and (2) Eastern Cherokee application claim number.

INSTRUCTIONS FOR COMPLETING THIS FORM

Use a separate NATF Form 83 for each file that you request. Remove this instruction sheet. You must complete blocks 1-3 or we cannot search for the file. Print your name (last, first, middle) and address in the box provided at the bottom of the form, which is your mailing label. The information must be legible on all copies. Keep the PINK copy of the form for your records. Mail the remaining three pages of the form to: *General Reference Branch (NNRG), National Archives and Records Administration, 7th and Pennsylvania Avenue NW., Washington, DC 20408.* **DO NOT SEND PAYMENT WITH THIS FORM.** When we search your order, we will make photocopies of records that relate to your request. For credit card orders, we will mail your copies immediately. For other types of orders, we will invoice you for the cost of these copies and hold them up to 45 day pending receipt of your payment.

NATIONAL ARCHIVES TRUST FUND BOARD   **INSTRUCTIONS**   NATF Form 83 (rev. 4-92)

Information and instructions for completing NATF-83

ORDER FOR COPIES OF
EASTERN CHEROKEE APPLICATIONS

DATE RECEIVED IN NNRG

INDICATE BELOW THE METHOD OF PAYMENT PREFERRED.

☐ **CREDIT CARD** *(VISA or MasterCard) for IMMEDIATE SHIPMENT of copies*

Account Number: Exp. Date: Signature   Daytime Phone:

☐ **BILL ME** *(No credit card)*

REQUIRED IDENTIFICATION OF ENTRY - MUST BE COMPLETED OR YOUR ORDER CANNOT BE SERVICED

1. ENGLISH NAME	2. INDIAN NAME	3. EASTERN CHEROKEE APPLICATION NUMBER

NATIONAL ARCHIVES TRUST FUND BOARD   NATF Form 83 (rev. 4-92)

DO NOT WRITE BELOW - SPACE IS FOR OUR REPLY TO YOU

☐ **NO--We were unable to locate the file you requested above. No payment is required.**

SEARCHER	DATE SEARCHED

☐ **REQUIRED MINIMUM IDENTIFICATION OF ENTRY WAS NOT PROVIDED.** Please complete items 1, 2, and 3 and resubmit your order.

☐ **A SEARCH WAS NOT MADE** because the records you requested are not among the Eastern Cherokee Applications. The names and application number you submitted do not appear to match any Eastern Cherokee Application file. Your information may relate to an Indian census or to an earlier claim file.

☐ We cannot copy the file you requested because there are numerous files for Cherokees with the same or nearly the same surname. We suggest that you visit the National Archives or hire a professional researcher to examine the files for you.

☐ The names you provided above are listed under a different application number, _____. If you wish to order this record, complete a new form, attach this page, and resubmit.

☐ We do not have a name similar to the ones you have listed on this form. The application number you provided is for the names listed here. If you wish to order this record, complete a new form, attach this page, and resubmit.

ENGLISH NAME
INDIAN NAME

☐ OTHER: _____

_____

☐ **YES--We located the file you requested. We have made copies from the file for you. The cost for these copies is $10.**

MICROFILM PUBLICATION	ROLL NUMBER
SEARCHER	DATE SEARCHED
PAGE NUMBERS	
APPLICATION NUMBER	

Make your check or money order payable to NATIONAL ARCHIVES TRUST FUND. Do not send cash. Return this form and your payment in the enclosed envelope to:

NATIONAL ARCHIVES TRUST FUND
P.O. BOX 100221
ATLANTA, GA 30384-0221

PLEASE NOTE: We will hold these copies awaiting receipt of payment for only 45 days from the date completed, which is stamped below. After that time, you must submit another form to obtain photocopies of the record.

Here is an example of National Archives *Form NATF-83*, the same vital research having to do with Native Americans. Only through its use may one gain what information the National Archives has concerning those with Cherokee ancestry who applied for benefits when the U.S. Court of Claims entertained such applications during the years 1906-1909 (microfilm M1104).

1850 CENSUS   UNITED STATES

State _____ County _____ Township _____ Town _____ Call No. _____

Page	Dwelling Number	Family Number	Names	Age	Sex	Color	Occupation, etc.	Value - Real Estate	Birthplace	Married within year	School within year	Cannot read or write	Enumeration Date	Remarks

Here is a typical form designed to preserve the information provided in *the Decennial Census of 1850*, the first census to state and give the ages of all members of every household. As suggested on page 95, in addition to that most valuable data, the diligent researcher will also carefully consider the wealth of other information found there.

1880 CENSUS – UNITED STATES

State _____ County _____ Township _____ Town _____ Call No. _____

Page	Dwelling No.	Family No.	Names	Color	Sex	Age prior to June 1st	Month of birth if born in census yr.	Relationship to head of house	Single	Married	Widowed	Divorced	Married in census year	Occupation	Miscellaneous Information	Cannot read or write	Place of birth	Place of birth of father	Place of birth of mother	Enumeration Date

Here is a typical form designed to capture the information provided in the *Decennial Census of 1880*. In addition to being the first census to precisely establish the ages of those names, it also expanded on many other aspects of the lives of our citizens. Along with those for 1850 and 1910, the census of 1880 is considered by most genealogists to be one of the most important of those censuses yet opened to the public.

1910 Census – United States

State _____ County _____ Township or other Division of County _____
Enumeration Date _____ Roll _____ Sheet _____ Dist. _____

LOCATION
- House number
- Number of dwelling house in the order of visitation
- Number of family in the order of visitation

NAME
of each person living in this family on April 15, 1910
(Include every person living on April 15, 1910. Omit children born since April 15, 1910)

RELATION
Relationship of the person to the head of the family

PERSONAL DESCRIPTION
- Sex
- Color or race
- Age at last birthday.
- Single, married, widowed, or divorced
- Number of yrs. present marr.
- Mother of how many children: Number born / Number Now living

BIRTHPLACE
- Place of birth of this person.
- Place of birth of father of this person.
- Place of birth of mother of this person.

CITIZENSHIP
- Year of immigration to U.S.
- Naturalized or Alien

OCCUPATION
- Trade or profession or particular kind of work done by person, as spinner, salesman, laborer, etc.
- General nature of industry, business, or establishment in which person works, as cotton mill, dry goods store, farm, etc.
- Whether an employer, employee, or working on own account.
- Out of work on April 15, 1910 if employee
- Weeks out of work during year 1909

Speak English; or, if not, language spoken.

EDUCATION
- Able to read?
- Able to write?
- Attended school any time since Sept. 1, 1909

OWNERSHIP OF HOME
- Owned or rented
- Owned free or mortgaged
- Farm or house
- Number of farm schedule
- Whether survivor Union, Confederate Army or Navy
- Whether blind (both eyes)
- Whether deaf and dumb

REMARKS

Line 1 2 3 4 5 6 7 8

Remove from book to make copies

Here is a typical form designed to capture the wealth of information provided by the *Decennial Census of 1910*, much of which was not gained in previous censuses. In addition to providing in-depth data concerning ages and marriages, this census also identified those citizens then living who had served in the Civil War. Along with those for 1850 and 1880, the census for 1910 is considered by most genealogists to be very important.

STATE ARCHIVES REFERRAL LIST

☐ Alabama Department of Archives & History, 624 Washington Avenue, Montgomery, AL 36130

☐ Alaska State Archives, 141 Willoughby Avenue, Pouch C, Juneau, AK 99811

☐ Arizona State Library, Department of Library, Archives & Public Records, State Capitol, 1700 West Washington, Phoenix, AZ 85007

☐ Arkansas History Commission, One Capitol Mall, Little Rock, AR 72201

☐ California Office of the Secretary of State, California State Archives, 1020 O Street, Room 138, Sacramento, CA 95814

☐ Colorado Department of Administration, Division of State Archives & Public Records, 1313 Sherman Street, 1-B20, Denver, CO 80203

☐ Connecticut State Library, Archives, History & Genealogy Unit, 231 Capitol Avenue, Hartford, CT 06106

☐ Delaware Division of Historical & Cultural Affairs. Bureau of Archives & Records Management, Hall of Records, Dover, DE 19901

☐ Florida State Archives, R. A. Gray Building, 500 South Bronough Street, Tallahassee, FL 32399-0250

☐ Georgia Department of Archives & History, 330 Capitol Avenue, SE, Altanta, GA 30334

☐ Hawaii Department of Accounting & General Services, Archives Division, Iolani Palace Grounds, Honolulu, HI 96813

☐ Idaho State Historical Society, Division of Manuscripts & Idaho State Archives, 610 North Julia Davis Drive, Boise, ID 83702

☐ Illinois Office of the Secretary of State, Archives Division, Archives Building, Springfield, IL 62756

☐ Indiana State Library, Archives Division, 100 North Senate Avenue, Indianapolis, IN 46204

☐ State Historical Society of Iowa, State Archives, Capitol Complex, Des Moines, IA 50319

☐ Kansas State Historical Society, 120 West Tenth Street, Topeka, KS 66612

☐ Kentucky Public Records Division, Archives Research Room, P.O. Box 537, Frankfort, KY 40602-0537

☐ Louisiana Secretary of State, Archives & Records Division, P.O. Box 94125, Baton Rouge, LA 70804

☐ Maine State Archives, State House-Station 84, Augusta, ME 04333

☐ Maryland State Archives, 350 Rowe Boulevard, Annapolis, MD 21401

☐ Massachusetts State Archives — Columbia Point, 220 Morrisey Boulevard, Boston, MA 02125

☐ Michigan Department of State, Michigan History Division, State Archives Unit, 717 West Allegan, Lansing, MI 48918

☐ Minnesota Historical Society, Division of Archives & Manuscripts, 1500 Mississippi Street, St. Paul, MN 55101

☐ Mississippi Department of Archives & History, 100 South State Street, P.O. Box 571, Jackson, MS 39205

☐ Director Records Management & Archives Service, Secretary of State's Office, P.O. Box 778, 1001 Industrial Drive, Jefferson City, MO 65102

NOTE: It should be noted that some soldiers served in State militia units which were never mustered into the service of the Continental, Federal, or Confederate Governments. Records of such State service, if available, are in State custody. You may be able to obtain information about the soldier in whom you are interested by writing to the address checked above.

STATE ARCHIVES REFERRAL LIST

☐ Montana Historical Society, Division of Archives & Manuscripts, 225 North Roberts Street, Helena, MT 59601

☐ Nebraska State Historical Society, State Archives Division, 1500 R Street, Lincoln, NE 68508

☐ Nevada State Library & Archives, Division of Archives & Records, 101 South Fall Street, Carson City, NV 89710

☐ New Hampshire Records & Archives, 71 South Fruit Street, Concord, NH 03301

☐ New Jersey State Archives, Bureau of Archives & Records Preservation, CN-307, 185 West State Street, Trenton, NJ 08625

☐ New Mexico State Records Center & Archives, Historical Services Division, 404 Montezuma, Santa Fe, NM 87503

☐ New York State Archives, 11D40 Cultural Education Center, Albany, NY 12230

☐ North Carolina State Archives, 109 East Jones Street, Raleigh, NC 27611

☐ State Archives and Historical Research Library, North Dakota Heritage Center, Bismarck, ND 58505

☐ The Ohio Historical Society, Archives-Manuscripts Division, 1985 Velma Avenue, Columbus, OH 43211

☐ Oklahoma Department of Libraries, Archives & Records Division, 200 Northeast 18th Street, Oklahoma City, OK 73105

☐ Oregon Secretary of State, Archives Division, Oregon State Archives & Records Center, 1005 Broadway, N.E., Salem, OR 97310

☐ Pennsylvania State Archives, P.O. Box 1026, Harrisburg, PA 17108-1026

☐ Rhode Island Secretary of State, Archives Division, Room 43, State House, Smith Street, Providence, RI 02903

☐ South Carolina Department of Archives & History, P.O. Box 11669, Capitol Station, Columbia, SC 29211

☐ South Dakota Department of Education & Cultural Affairs, South Dakota State Archives, State Library Building, 800 Governors Drive, Pierre, SD 57501-2294

☐ Tennessee State Library and Archives, 403 7th Avenue North, Nashville, TN 37219

☐ Texas State Library, Archives Division, P.O. Box 12927, Austin, TX 78711

☐ Utah State Archives & Records Service, State Capitol, Room B-4, Salt Lake City, UT 84114

☐ Vermont Agency of Administration, Public Records Division, 6 Baldwin Street, Montpelier, VT 05602

☐ Virginia State Library and Archives Division, 11th Street at Capitol Square, Richmond, VA 23219

☐ Office of the Secretary of State, Division of Archives and Records Management, P.O. Box 9000, Olympia, WA 98504-9000

☐ West Virginia Department of Culture and History, Archives and History Division, Science and Cultural Center, Capitol Complex, Charleston, WV 25305

☐ State Historical Society of Wisconsin, Archives Division, 816 State Street, Madison, WI 53706

☐ Wyoming Archives, Museum, and Historical Department, Archives and Records Management Division, Barrett Building, Cheyenne, WY 82002

NOTE: It should be noted that some soldiers served in State militia units which were never mustered into the service of the Continental, Federal, or Confederate Governments. Records of such State service, if available, are in State custody. You may be able to obtain information about the soldier in whom you are interested by writing to the address checked above.

NA 14031 BACK (3-88)

INDEX

INDEX